HERB GARDEN DESIGN

HERB GARDEN DESIGN

Faith H. Swanson and Virginia B. Rady

 UNIVERSITY PRESS OF NEW ENGLAND
Hanover and London, 1984

Copyright 1984 by Trustees of Dartmouth College

Printed in the United States of America

Library of Congress Cataloging in Publication Data

Swanson, Faith H., 1914–
    Herb garden design.

    Bibliography: p. 133
    Includes indexes.
    1. Herb gardens—Designs and plans.
2. Gardens—Design.   I. Rady, Virginia B., 1922–
II. Title.
SB351.H5S92   1984   635′.7   83-40556
ISBN 0-87451-296-4
ISBN 0-87451-297-2 (pbk.)

To

Noreen Sheridan Capen (d. 1971),
who was awarded The Herb Society of America's Medal of Honor
and who initiated the idea of a publication of herb garden designs;

to

those members of the society who generously permitted
the use of their herb garden designs;

to

The Herb Society of America, which sponsored this book.

CONTENTS

FOREWORD

This book did not begin as a book. Over the years of its early hopeful beginnings it was little more than a mishmash of barely related, formless attempts at jotting down what herb gardens are. The idea of a collection of herb garden designs originated in the Herb Society of America many years ago; several committees were formed and subsequently unformed, without resulting in a book or even in publishable articles. Then, seven years ago, Faith Swanson and Ginny Rady decided, with sparkling enthusiasm, to take on what they thought would be the easy and comfortable revision of what had been done so far. This was not to be.

Faith had had architectural training and could draft the designs, but she had not worked professionally nor on anything of this magnitude. Ginny had done some writing, especially poetry, but had not tried her hand at descriptive horticultural prose.

Neither knew what it meant to make a book.

I was publications chairman of the Herb Society of America and had long been a book editor. Their energy and charm caught me up, and I have had the pleasure of advising, wheedling, pushing, punching, and pleading to get the two would-be authors to become in-truth authors. And in the end they became not just authors but the creators of this excellent book—the first of its kind, for they had no model and no guide.

With false starts and honest stops, learning to ignore the conflicting and unknowledgeable advice too often given them, Faith and Ginny revised and reviewed and struggled, finally discovering within themselves the genuine herb garden design book. The turning point came when, bereft of hope, they asked themselves whether the manuscript would ever be of use, whether all their labor was to no avail.

For an answer they decided to design an herb garden from scratch, build it, and record every detail—all of the failures, alterations, successes. This they did, and the experience provided the final section of the book, tying together all the previous thoughts and proving the validity of their approach. Again they revised, and the publisher, carefully chosen, responded with delight.

The designs are taken more from the eastern than from the western United States for the reason that herb gardens have a longer tradition in the east and south; more of them exist to serve as examples. But geographic considerations matter only in relation to the plant material used and not to the design structures except as these are modified by the plantings.

For everyone this is a definitive as well as a beautiful book of herb garden designs. It needs no sequel.

Susan Frugé

PREFACE

This book of herb garden designs has been prepared with the uninitiated planner in mind. It is a marked departure from existing works that deal only in part with herb gardens and their design. While it has been our aim to be fundamental so that those who are approaching this project for the first time will find it a pleasure to proceed, we have also provided material that will prove interesting and valuable to the experienced planner.

Part I is devoted to the basics of herb garden design—considerations that are essential when plotting an herb garden. The text is an outgrowth of the authors' many years of experience in experimenting with growing herbs and their seven years of working with herb garden designs. The reader is led step by step through the mechanics of creating a drawing and is given instructions for proceeding with the preliminary work.

Part II presents plans for a variety of herb gardens. Some of these were created by landscape architects, while others were prepared by landscape designers, by their owners, or by contributors. Each plan was redrafted especially for use in this book. For unity and clarity all plans were made consistent in style and symbols. Then the redrafted plans were reduced as individually required to maintain readability of the planting plans and relevant information. Each plan has a commentary to point out design elements and a plant list with botanical and common names. The designs are grouped according to levels of difficulty, specialty, degree of maintenance required, historical interest, and educational purpose.

Part III is the documentation of a "trial garden." Believing it to be one thing to instruct others how to create an herb garden design and quite another thing to carry it out, we completed a test garden, carefully noting all the procedures and providing drawings to demonstrate the elements in Part I.

The more than fifty designs used in this book were selected from those submitted by members of The Herb Society of America in the United States and Canada. The herb garden designs alone, without accompanying commentary, would not have served the purpose of enabling a planner to create a design for an herb garden of lasting quality. To achieve this, the garden must be viewed as a source of pleasure and utility. A range of essential factors is considered herein, but of course not every aspect of herbs could be treated in great depth in this one volume.

As an aid in establishing acceptable practices of nomenclature, we have used *Hortus Third* as our primary reference for botanical names of plants and their common-name counterparts when they exist. *The International Code of Botanical Nomenclature of Cultivated Plants*, 1969 and 1980, governed the style of our lists of botanical names. Generic names are capitalized and specific epithets are lowercased, as in *Rosmarinus officinalis*. As is stated in the introduction of *Hortus Third*: "It is now recommended that all specific epithets commence with a lowercase letter, but the practice of capitalizing the first letter of epithets derived from persons, former generic names, and common (non-Latin) names is still permitted and is followed in *Hortus Third* as a guide to those who wish to continue the practice." We have departed from their practice and complied with the recommendation, because it simplifies considerably the listing of specific names. The lowercase is used for all common names except when proper nouns and adjectives are used with their original reference, and these are capitalized—for example, English thyme. Italics are always used for botanical names.

A glossary of terms has been included for ease in using this book. Likewise, lists of both botanical and common names were compiled with the expectation that this would eliminate much of the confusion the herb grower encounters when purchasing plants and seeds. The common name index includes names that have come to our attention as being in general use; although countless common names exist, they are too numerous for all to be listed in this volume.

Not all herbs are included in this herb garden design book; rather, these plans incorporate those generally in cultivation. Only a selection of the countless fancy name cultivars available has been used. Not all plants used are herbs, but each serves a purpose that justifies its inclusion.

We, the authors, hope that all users of this book will find it not only helpful but also a source of inspiration that will lead others to expand on the ideas presented herein. It is further hoped that this volume will provide many hours of pleasure as the user plans and executes a satisfying, functional herb garden that will reflect his or her interests and desires and become a joy for many years.

ACKNOWLEDGMENTS

No matter how dedicated we as authors may be, an undertaking of this magnitude requires different kinds and degrees of aid. We are grateful to many. Susan Frugé, former editor of University of California Press at Berkeley, and August Frugé, former director of same, were most helpful with their keen perception of a publisher's needs and their evaluations of our work that were always professionally rendered and with complete honesty. We could not have persevered and completed this project without such support. Lucile Teeter Kissack was our landscape-architect consultant throughout with the invaluable advice and help essential in a volume of this nature. The late Raymond C. Kissack gave us his estimate of the readability of the text in its early stages. A lecturer on herbs, Jo Lohmolder, has given us valuable information, letting us know what questions people have asked with regard to herb gardens. She has served, too, as expediter and typist, always encouraging us to stay with our project. Of the staff at The Garden Center of Greater Cleveland, Richard T. Isaacson, librarian, who compiled the three-volume *Flowering Plant Index of Illustration and Information*, has been especially helpful over the years. His assistant, Lee Buss, and the horticulturist, Alexander Apanius, have also been of assistance. Special thanks are due James C. Keebler and the late Everest P. Derthick, former managing editors, for their counsel in the earliest stages of this book. For assistance in a variety of ways we are grateful to Virginia B. Weatherhead, M.D., Trudi Bela, Alice Skelsey, Nell Neff, and Rexford Talbert. Wanda Ritchie, Genevieve Jyurovat, Betty Rea, Eleanor Gambee, and Joanna Reed, past presidents, and Elizabeth Bryce, president, of the Herb Society of America are to be thanked for the support they gave us. We are particularly appreciative of our husbands, Herbert J. Swanson and Robert B. Rady, for their patience and encouragement during the years required by this undertaking. Recognition is due Robert B. Rady for his efforts in constructing the test garden, which made possible the completion of our text. Finally, the congenial cooperation and consideration afforded us by the staff members of this publisher have made the final phase of our work a most enjoyable one.

Faith H. Swanson
Virginia B. Rady
December 1983

PART I HERB GARDEN DESIGN BASICS

"A garden is the mirror of a mind," wrote Henry Beston in his classic *Herbs and the Earth*. "Not difficult to plan, not at all difficult to maintain, a garden of herbs gives more months of garden pleasure and more kinds of pleasure than any other. Its interest is independent of flowers, its fragrances are given from the first leaf to the last, its uses make it a part of the amenities of the whole year, and its history and traditions touch all nations and all times."

Beston's last phrase can be affirmed by even the most superficial peek into the histories of gardens and garden designs. Records of herb gardens affiliated with schools of herbal medicine, temples of worship, or botanical gardens at universities span centuries in both the Old World and the New—and in both Eastern and Western traditions. But to consider a designed garden of herbs as "not difficult to plan, not at all difficult to maintain" is to be a romantic. The realist will accept the numerous demands both in planning and in maintaining an herb garden. Amateur planners definitely can use help in creating a functional as well as an enjoyable herb garden, and the more experienced gardeners constantly seek new modes of expression, new plants, new ways of seeing.

Why a "designed" herb garden rather than a random placement around the curves of the terrace or in straight rows alongside the vegetable plantings? Those who have grown herbs in such fashion are usually dissatisfied. They may be unaware that gardens dedicated to herbs alone exist and of the recurring beauty that such gardens can provide.

An herb garden presents an opportunity to enhance the home grounds, to increase the value of the property, and to have easy access to frequently used herbs. In order to create a fine garden design, it is necessary to gain familiarity with the individual characteristics of the herbs. A well-designed garden is easier to maintain; a well-maintained garden keeps its good design. As one constantly reinforces the other, the result is more pleasure and more utility year round. Perennial herbs, some of which are evergreen, have foliage that changes color with the seasons. The gentle quiet of fall and winter is followed in early spring by a heightening of the mauves and bronzes of thymes, which complete their metamorphosis in early summer, changing to subtle grays and greens topped with dainty blooms. Designing an herb garden provides a rare opportunity for creative expression similar to that of the artist when he or she paints a picture. As Henry Beston reflects, "A garden is the mirror of a mind."

A good design does not "happen." Fundamental questions must be answered in proper sequence, and decisions must not be left to chance. Where should the garden go? To simplify this decision, lay out a plan of the property, even though it may seem that there is no alternative to the spot you have in mind. Possibilities undreamed of may become apparent; what seemed a certainty may prove to be neither necessary nor even desirable. Consider the sheltered corner that catches the sun and avoids destructive winds, a front dooryard, a no-longer-used driveway turnaround with a stone base, or an abandoned, partially excavated area.

A survey map of the lot or acreage will have all measurements needed for planning your garden; the north point will have been indicated; and structures, fences, and hedges will have been located. Using such a map simplifies the drawing of an overall plan. If no

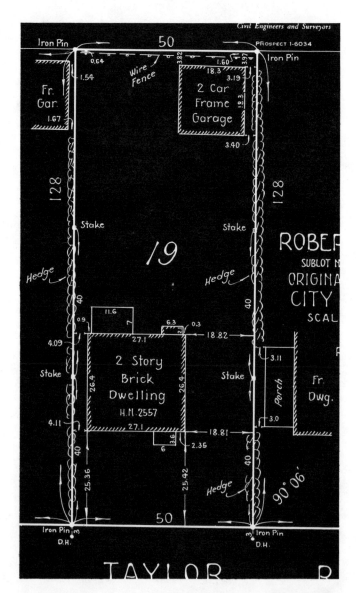

Survey map of property with precise measurements indicating dimensions of the lot and locations of all structures, fences, and hedges. Here, measurements are in engineer's scale, which is in tenths and hundredths of an inch.

survey map is available, the first step is to determine as nearly as possible where the lot lines are. Next, measure to locate the house, other significant structures, and the driveway. Two people working at measuring speed up the job and ensure greater accuracy of the measurements. A deed description, such as the one illustrated here, will give the lot or acreage measurements. In this example, to locate the house, measure from the front or back iron pin—whichever is nearer the house—to a point on the lot line well past the house. To determine the distance between the house and lot line, one person should hold the tape at a point (A) approximately twelve feet from the corner

(B) of the house while a second person establishes (C) on the lot line in a line as straight as can be sighted. This process can be repeated to determine space available around the house. Existing trees pertinent to the planning should be located on the drawing, too.

A drawing that will be useful as an overall plan must be executed on a small scale. For some areas a scale of one-eighth inch equals one foot may be suitable. Other areas may require a smaller scale. The object is to create an overall view of the property with structures and existing trees, shrubs, enclosures, paths, driveway, and unusual land features noted. The smaller the scale, the easier it is to visualize the relationship between structures and the areas being considered for the herb garden.

The tools needed for drawing are few, but essential:

architects' scale—a scale or rule usually of triangular section made of boxwood (currently, plastic is more easily found) with a variety of gradations on its edges, one edge usually graduated in inches and sixteenths of an inch, the other edges graduated in twelfths and fractions.

triangle—of inexpensive plastic, a right triangle to rest on T square for drawing perpendicular lines, lines at an angle, and parallel lines.

compass—an instrument for describing circles or transferring measurements that consists of two pointed branches joined at the top by a pivot, one of the branches generally having a pencil point.

T square—a ruler with a crosspiece or head at one end used in making parallel lines or as a support for triangles used in drawing lines at different angles to the ruler.

graph paper—for use under tracing paper.

roll of yellow tracing paper—for preliminary drawings.

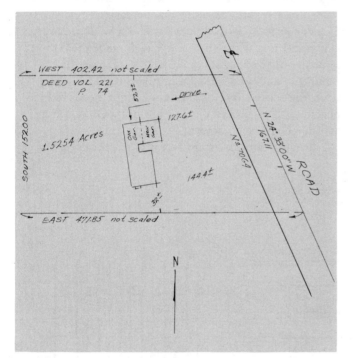

Survey of property with less precise measurements, but with all needed information. Here, too, measurements are in engineer's scale.

described premises, situated in the **Township** _of_ **Bainbridge**

County of **Geauga** and State of Ohio:

and known as being part of Lot No. 42, Tract No. 1 in said Township, and further described as follows:

Beginning at a point in the center line of Cats Den Road, at its intersection with the Northerly line of a parcel of land conveyed to J. Cipra and A. Coombs as recorded in Volume 22, Page 74 of Geauga County Deed Records.

Course #1 thence West along said Northerly line of land conveyed to J. Cipra and A. Coombs 402.42 feet, to an iron pipe;

Course #2 thence South 152.00 feet to an iron pipe;

Course #3 thence East 471.85 feet to the center line of Cats Den Road;

Course #4 thence North 24° 33' 00" West, 167.11 feet along the center line of Cats Den Road, to the place of beginning.

Containing 1.5254 acres of land, according to the survey of W. E. Holland Engineering Co., Chagrin Falls, Ohio, October, 1958.

In the absence of a survey map, a deed description indicates all measurements of the property required to make a drawing.

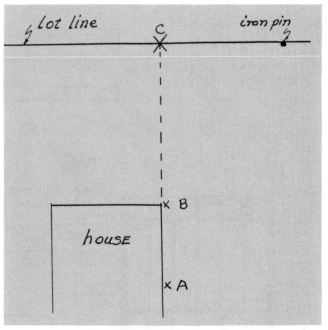

Locating the house on your drawing once the property line has been established.

white tracing paper—of better quality for finished drawing to copy mechanically or for black line print.

drawing board—inexpensive scrap plywood covered with poster board or masonite or the kitchen cutting board.

With the plan on paper, it is time to consider where to locate the herb garden. To place the garden in relation to a structure that can frame it in some way is one of the most satisfying arrangements. A toolhouse, garage, greenhouse, old smokehouse, gazebo, or summer kitchen is ideal. In the absence of a structure, a hedge or specially designed fence can be used. If the herb garden is to be related to a house or some similar structure, the location of the structure's doors and windows needs to be considered if balance and unity are to be achieved.

ENCLOSURES

The choice of an enclosure is an important part of achieving this total effect desired. The enclosure serves both to tie the garden into the surrounding landscape and to frame the space in a special way. In the designs that follow, a variety of enclosures is shown: fences of wood, iron, brick, and stone, and hedges of hemlock, yew, bayberry, and holly. In some cases, the type of enclosure may be determined by cost or availability of materials. Another important consideration is the height of the enclosure in relation to the height of the related structure. There are dual-purpose enclosures such as a low "sitting wall," an ideal spot for displaying potted plants. Upkeep, which may include the staining or preserving of a wood fence or the clipping of a hedge, must be included in assessing maintenance demands.

As important as the appearance of a wall enclosure is its hidden construction. How well made the concealed construction is has a direct bearing on the durability of the wall. One basic rule is the higher the wall, the more substantial its foundation needs to be. However, few should tackle a job of this magnitude as a do-it-yourself project.

Climate is an important factor when choosing the

Three examples of the many possible fence designs, along with two styles of gates

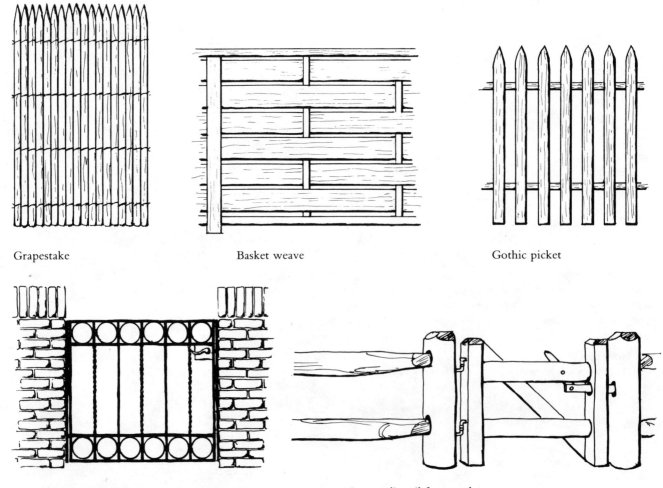

Grapestake

Basket weave

Gothic picket

Wrought-iron gate fittingly combined with a brick wall

Low, split-rail fence and gate

4 / Herb Garden Design

material for a wall. Reference books devoted exclusively to the subject of walls offer detailed information. For example, a masonry wall needs drainage tile or weep holes, and their spacing depends on the amount of precipitation. Adobe may be troublesome in a wet climate. In a cold climate where there is alternate freezing and thawing, concrete blocks shift position unless mortar is used to build the wall. Where air circulation is much needed, concrete blocks in openwork design can be ideal. Concrete blocks are often regarded as too cold and institutional, but they may gain in favor as more imaginative ways of softening their severity or camouflaging their Spartan, gray surfaces are found. Lower cost is an advantage, however.

Brick is the all-time favorite material. The elegance of a serpentine wall of brick delighted our forefathers, but it is unfortunately a luxury rarely seen today.

Wood may present greater opportunities for variety in design than any other material. It is especially useful to have a variety of designs to choose from when trying to select the right enclosure to reinforce the desired image of the garden. When this reinforcement is understated, the garden design is not overshadowed by the enclosure. When the reinforcement also complements the architecture of the house or related structure, the garden design is most attractive. Styles are legion, ranging from the simplest form of plain picket associated with colonial times to contemporary designs, as in outdoor room dividers. Stained, painted, or natural, the possibilities with wood are so great that many types of appropriate enclosures can be fashioned.

Stone, used for dry wall or masonry construction, can vary from irregular rock to precisely cut stone. Using a range of sizes in the rocks or stones for the wall adds interest without the necessity of planning an exacting design. Generally, rock or stone indigenous to an area is less costly and is more integrated with the surrounding area.

Iron was used for fences more often in the past than it is today. Designs from the most severe to the most ornate are available. If desired, they can be made to order. In some climates, annual painting is a necessity. This can be avoided by using preformed vinyl constructed in sections to simulate wrought iron. The vinyl costs relatively little and can be extremely useful for, as an example, a temporary garden that may be changed later.

Hedges make handsome enclosures and can be created from a variety of genera and species, some deciduous and some evergreen, such as bayberry, holly, yew, box, and rosemary. Consider the growing qualities and requirements before making a choice. Rosemary, for example, works well in a climate like that of the southwestern United States. Would you prefer to plant the deciduous bayberry (sometimes evergreen) in order to have the fruit for herb crafts? Or does the slow-growing, elegant box, deeply evergreen, meet the priority for infrequent pruning? Space for the width or thickness of a hedge must be allowed at the outset, keeping in mind that a plant can be cut back just so much. Allow adequate room within the row, too. At first, it will seem too sparsely planted, but the results will confirm this course.

Gates are part of the enclosure, and their styles are countless. If used, a gate needs to be fashioned in a style similar at least to the structural enclosure. When used with a hedge, the green of the enclosure presents a striking contrast with a gate painted white.

Once the enclosure for the herb garden is established, it is there for many years if thoughtfully conceived and well constructed. The decisions made ought to be carefully thought out.

STRUCTURAL EDGINGS

Availability of materials necessarily plays a part in the decision of which to choose, whether it will be rocks, cut stones, bricks, landscape timbers, railroad ties, or pressure-treated lumber. Any edging of treated wood will serve admirably if the chemicals used are nontoxic to plants.

Equally important is proportion. A small herb garden would call for a brick-size edging, or, if wood is the material of choice, something smaller than railroad ties or large landscape timbers. Pressure-treated lumber is available in various sizes easily accommodating a wide range of needs.

The structural edging may be chosen for neatness, for reinforcing the design, or for raising the beds to improve drainage. Whatever the reason, compatibility with and proportion to related structures should be the foremost consideration. Structural edgings are long-lasting and not easily changed, so give them much thought.

STEPS

When constructing steps, there is a necessary, logical ratio to be observed between the depth of the tread and the height of the riser. If the planner is unaware of or ignores this ratio, the steps created will be forever an annoyance, awkward and unsafe. Conversely, if the ratio is observed the steps will likely not be noticed—a sign of success.

The relationship between the riser and tread is exaggerated for steps outdoors in contrast to the ratio

A variety of borders for brick walks

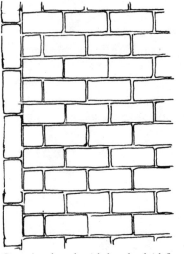

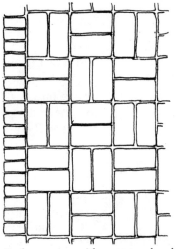

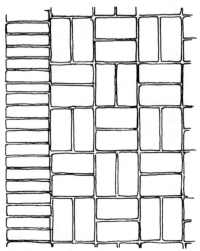

Running bond with border laid flat, edges perpendicular to ends

Basket weave with a narrow border

Basket weave with a wide border and brick on edge

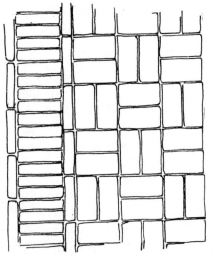

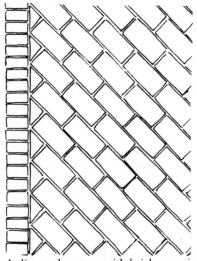

Basket weave with a much wider and more complex border for a walk six feet or more in width

Basket weave with a complex but narrower border, for walks less than six feet in width

A diagonal pattern with bricks meeting at a forty-five-degree angle and a narrow border of bricks on edge

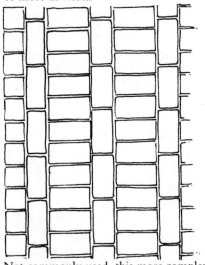

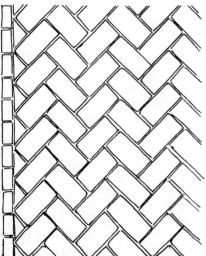

Not commonly used, this more complex pattern is for an ambitious bricklayer

A herringbone pattern is more obvious when laid so that the bricks strike the border of headers at a forty-five-degree angle

A brick pattern often used in old Spanish gardens

for those indoors. It is a general rule that the less the riser, the greater the tread. These are some suggested measurements for outdoor steps:

Height of Riser	Depth of Tread
4"	20"
4½"	18"
5"	16"
5½"	15"
6"	14"

A four-inch riser and twenty-inch tread may be considered ideal for a garden. There are, however, few situations in which outdoor steps should have a tread less than fourteen inches and a riser greater than six inches. Consider this matter carefully when moving from one level to another in the herb garden and related areas. Step materials need not be the same as, but should be compatible with, materials used in constructing the rest of the herb garden.

PATHS

In addition to their obvious utility, paths show off the separate beds to advantage, making the design more evident. Their width needs to be no less than adequate; their use no less than comfortable. The requirements for paths must be kept in mind from the very beginning of the design planning.

Paths must be wide enough to accommodate a large garden cart. A width of four feet allows room for turning, too. Although paths other than those for the use of a cart are sometimes less in width, remember they will be used by family and friends to enjoy the herb garden. A width of five feet is thought by some to be necessary for two people to walk comfortably side by side. Access paths, because they are just that, need to be only the width required for the gardener to work easily within the beds.

The requirements for paths in public gardens are quite another matter. Paths must be ample, for *public* implies that the gardens are open for tours. If groups are walking through, these paths may need to be as wide as six feet or more. Do not skimp—unless it means there will be no herb garden.

Choose the path material equally for comfort, appearance, cost, and maintenance. If the choice is crushed stone or pebbles, smaller sizes are noticeably more comfortable for any activity. Heavy black plastic laid under crushed stone or pebbles discourages weeds and eases maintenance. The depth of the stones or pebbles depends on the type of material used and the underlying soil. Grass provides a good contrast for the beds of herbs and is a pleasure to walk on. But do not overlook the mowing and trimming it requires.

Brick creates an illusion of warmth that is important in colder climates. The colors are various: terracotta, rosy pink, or red, for example. Be aware that the colder temperate zones will require a frost-proof brick to prevent shattering with extremes of temperature. Even more varied than their colors are the patterns to be composed with brick. Be mindful of other patterns that are a part of the herb garden area, so that the brick contributes to the unity of the overall plan.

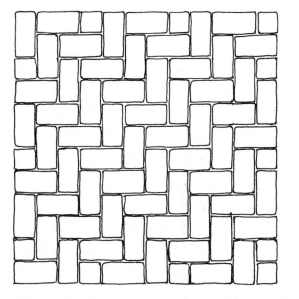

A less obvious herringbone pattern, in which the brick is laid flush with the edge

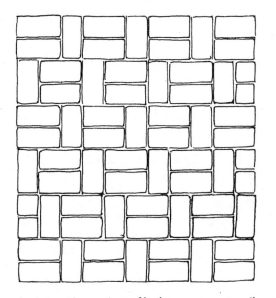

An interesting variant of basket weave, not easily counted

A variety of designs for flagstone walks

Irregular, flat stones laid in random fashion, but forming a path of uniform width for an informal effect

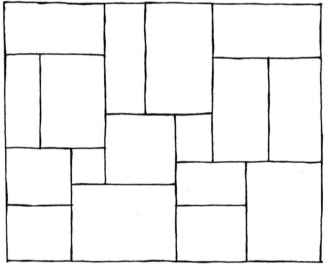

Stone dressed to create right angles, allowing closely laid joints for a formal effect

Dressed edge, random-shaped flagstones laid in an organized manner

Flagstone makes a substantial, lasting surface. In generally wet areas or humid climates even partial shade cast on flagstone and brick can cause the formation of algae and mosses on the surface, a result being hazardous footing. The same is true if wooden slabs—cross-cut sections of tree trunks—are used. (These are tempting to use in a naturalized area or adjacent to a woodland site.) To avoid having a slippery surface, bark or pine needles can be used. They are easily renewed as they break down, and they are relatively inexpensive and readily obtained.

TREES AND SHRUBS

Working out the design plan can be one of the most enjoyable parts of the project. It is important to know the growth habits of the trees and shrubs if any are to be planted within the garden or near it. When they mature, they should not shade the herbs too much. It must be practical to maintain trees and shrubs in proper scale to the garden. Here are examples that are suitable for such use:

TREES

Amelanchier, serviceberry, shad
Malus coronaria, sweet-scented crab
Cornus florida, dogwood
Crataegus phaenopyrum, Washington thorn
Magnolia virginiana, sweet bay
any of the dwarf fruit trees

SHRUBS

Hamamelis virginiana, witch hazel
Lindera benzoin, spicebush
Viburnum carlesii
Calluna, heather
Chaenomeles speciosa, flowering quince

In a historic garden the selection of trees needs to be made with historical accuracy in mind if the garden is to be judged authentic. A bit of research is in order for the planner unfamiliar with the characteristics of herbs, shrubs, or trees to be considered. This, too, is an enjoyable experience, and many good references are available.

THE PLANTING PLAN

A planting plan needs to be drawn on a larger scale than the overall plan. If the garden is made up of separate beds, prepare a planting plan for each, keeping in mind the growth habits and requirements of the herbs to be used. With these recommendations in mind, a soft-lead pencil in hand, and a few sheets of graph paper ready, begin work on the "skeleton" of the herb garden. Use the graph paper under tracing paper so that the planting plan can easily be read without the distraction of the grid of the graph paper. It is the graph paper that furnishes a constant reminder of the space being used for each plant. Do use a soft-lead pencil; it is easily read and easily erased, and there may be much erasure needed! The scale to be used will depend on the size of the garden and the size of the paper and may be one-fourth inch equals one foot, one-half inch equals one foot, or whatever is best in your case.

The "skeleton" of the plan is established with perennials that will sustain the design throughout the year, allowing the garden to remain interesting even when the annuals are spent. The skeleton thus stabilizes the form of the finished creation. It needs, however, the complement of the annuals to create the desired image. Seek out favorites among the perennial herbs, noting well their growth habits, whether they are invasive or tall growing, for example. What are their colors and textures? Which provide contrast?

To help develop a planting plan that takes fully into account the seasonal bloom and the height of plants and their maturity, prepare a chart of the plants to be used, such as the one illustrated here. The time taken to make a chart of this sort is well spent because in the process you may identify a number of unanticipated problems. It can be done when the weather is not fit for gardening and is best done well in advance of planting time.

Plants that serve a particular function such as edging are an aid in establishing the design, too. Lemon thyme and germander are two much-used examples. Individual interests will dictate which to choose; for example, someone strongly interested in culinary herbs may choose *Thymus × citriodorus*, lemon thyme. Other herbs function ideally when used to create the rhythm of a garden designed in the form of a knot. The variety of hues and textures of herbs helps to establish the contrast necessary to define a pattern as well as to avoid monochromatic monotony.

ARTIFACTS

As with other gardens, the herb garden's balance may be achieved symmetrically or asymmetrically. In whatever manner this aspect of the design is carried out, a focal point is customarily used. Often this center of interest is a sundial. It may be of the simplest sort with gnomon on a horizontal plate or of the more complex armillary sphere kind. Artifacts such as an old hand pump, statuary—sometimes of Saint Fiacre,

Chart for Height and Bloom

Season	Low	Medium	High
April	snowdrops primrose 'Alba'	daff. 'Mount Hood' daff. 'Cassata'	
May	sweet violet lily-of-the-valley sweet woodruff columbine 'Alba' pink 'White Lace'R	tulip 'White Trumpeter' tulip 'Blizzard' orris	flowering crab 'Guiding Star'
June	white miniature rose 'Cinderella'C lamb's-ears petunia C	gray santolina clary fraxinella yarrow 'The Pearl' honesty lavender 'Alba'	foxglove 'Alba' rose 'Schneezwerg' (snowdwarf) R
July	silver mound	feverfew C rocket nicotiana C 'Grandiflora' stock, white C	yucca absinthe
Aug.		horehound Western mugwort silver-king artemisia	white mugwort moonflower C
Sept.			tuberose

C-continuous bloom
R-recurrent bloom

the patron saint of gardeners—and birdbaths are frequently used. Again, scale is of prime importance in determining whether these features add to the final effect of the herb garden or whether they strike an incongruous note. If a statue less than life-size is used, a niche of its own should be created. It is then in scale with its frame, and a good sense of proportion is achieved. It is this aspect of design that some consider most important. Whether it is the size of artifacts in relation to the garden, the height of a fence to the house, or the width of a border to the total width of a walk, respect for good proportion can make the difference between a very pleasing herb garden and one less than satisfying.

PART II HERB GARDEN DESIGNS

The herb garden designs that follow are grouped for the convenience of those who have special interests or special needs. However, a design feature from one plan generally can be used in another, with one basic rule always needing to be observed, that of good proportion. It is expected that these designs will serve to inspire their adaptation for use in any situation and will serve further to stimulate the imagination and foster individual creativity. It is worthwhile to note the geographical location of these herb gardens so that the perennial or annual quality of the plant material can be gauged according to the area where it will be used. Except for two, the designs have a decorative north point, a stylized drawing of an ovary, which is the ovule-bearing part of a pistil in the flower of a seed plant.

For easy reference, here is the key to the symbols used consistently throughout the designs:

Symbols

◎	flowerpot	▨	hedge
▱	planter	∿	vine
◎	plant hoop	▭	fence
✺	bee skep	✿	deciduous shrub
◉	existing tree	✾	evergreen shrub
+	proposed tree	❀	deciduous tree
▃	edging	❋	evergreen tree

FOR THE NOVICE

A BEGINNING

For the beginner this plan is valuable as an introduction to herb gardens and their design. The rules of symmetry are observed, and the novice is afforded a variety of herbs with which to become acquainted. Three paths allow adequate access to the garden and to the working path that runs the length of it. Lavenders accent the front corners, which permit room for their full maturation and bloom. Perennials have been deliberately placed to keep a semblance of the design apparent throughout the months when annuals are spent. With color and texture considered for contrast, taller herbs were used at the back to form a pleasing background for those of intermediate height. The edgings in variety are herbs much prized for harvest. Clipping for that purpose helps maintain the design, which is used here in relation to a garage. This appealing plan is uncomplicated and will be equally suitable used in relation to a hedge, a fence, or other structure.

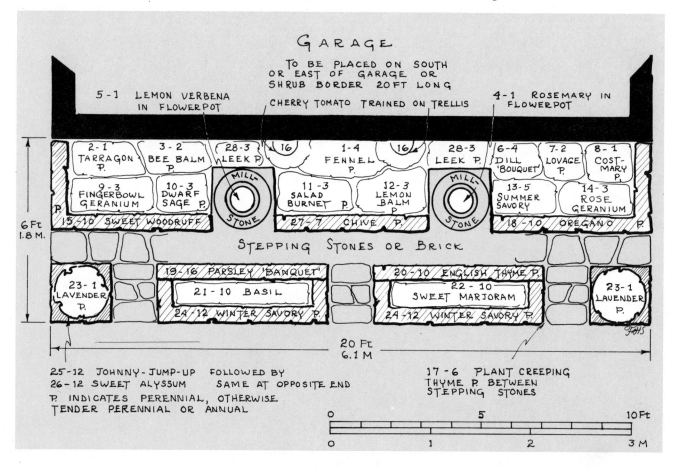

Ohio

Lucile Teeter Kissack, Landscape Architect, A.S.L.A.

The first number in each planting area is the key number, the second shows the quantity of plants to be used.

1. *Foeniculum vulgare*, fennel
2. *Artemisia dracunculus* var. *sativa*, French tarragon
3. *Monarda didyma*, bee balm
4. *Rosmarinus officinalis*, rosemary
5. *Aloysia triphylla*, lemon verbena
6. *Anethum graveolens* 'Bouquet', dill
7. *Levisticum officinale*, lovage
8. *Chrysanthemum balsamita*, costmary
9. *Pelargonium* × *limoneum*, English finger-bowl geranium
10. *Salvia officinalis*, dwarf garden sage
11. *Poterium sanguisorba*, salad burnet
12. *Melissa officinalis*, lemon balm
13. *Satureja hortensis*, summer savory
14. *Pelargonium graveolens*, rose geranium
15. *Galium odoratum*, sweet woodruff
16. *Lycopersicon lycopersicum* var. *cerasiforme*, cherry tomato
17. *Thymus praecox* subsp. *arcticus* 'Albus', white creeping thyme
18. *Origanum heracleoticum*, Greek oregano
19. *Petroselinum crispum* var. *crispum* 'Banquet', curly parsley
20. *Thymus* 'Broad-leaf English', English thyme
21. *Ocimum basilicum*, sweet basil
22. *Origanum majorana*, sweet marjoram
23. *Lavandula angustifolia*, English lavender
24. *Satureja montana*, winter savory
25. *Viola tricolor*, Johnny-jump-up
26. *Lobularia maritima*, sweet alyssum
27. *Allium schoenoprasum*, chive
28. *Allium ampeloprasum*, Porrum Group, leek

A POCKET-SIZE SPOT OF GREEN

Sometimes there is a corner or a niche in a village or town that is unused, perhaps overgrown with weeds. A few civic-minded herb growers can transform it into a delightful spot of green fragrant with herbs, as was done here. Even in this situation the need to enclose a garden was observed—if only on three sides. The fourth is open for passersby to admire the overall effect. It serves as entrance and exit for those who might choose to walk in to inspect more closely an individual herb. Volunteers for a project like this need to keep in mind that the hedge would require more than one trimming annually. Although this brick-paved area has an interesting basket-weave pattern, there are numerous other designs of equal appeal to consider. This plan can be used in the home environment just as easily, and the enclosure can be extended around the fourth side as desired.

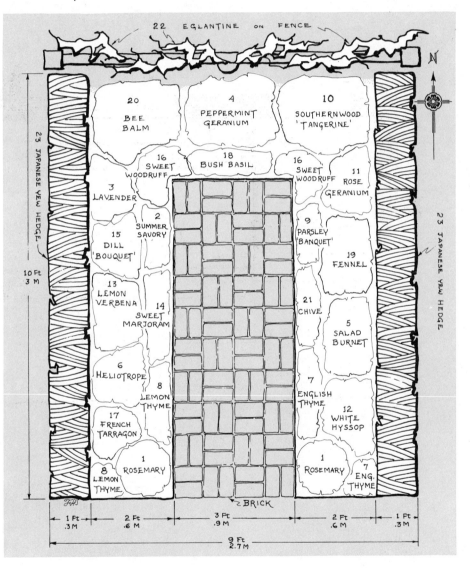

Pennsylvania

Designed by Contributor

The number in each planting area is the key number.

1. *Rosmarinus officinalis*, rosemary
2. *Satureja hortensis*, summer savory
3. *Lavandula angustifolia*, English lavender
4. *Pelargonium tomentosum*, peppermint geranium
5. *Poterium sanguisorba*, salad burnet
6. *Heliotropium arborescens*, heliotrope
7. *Thymus* 'Broad-leaf English', English thyme
8. *Thymus* × *citriodorus*, lemon thyme
9. *Petroselinum crispum* var. *crispum* 'Banquet', curly parsley
10. *Artemisia abrotanum* 'Tangerine', southernwood
11. *Pelargonium graveolens*, rose geranium
12. *Hyssopus officinalis* 'Alba', white hyssop
13. *Aloysia triphylla*, lemon verbena
14. *Origanum majorana*, sweet marjoram
15. *Anethum graveolens* 'Bouquet', dill
16. *Galium odoratum*, sweet woodruff
17. *Artemisia dracunculus* var. *sativa*, French tarragon
18. *Ocimum basilicum* 'Minimum', bush basil
19. *Foeniculum vulgare*, fennel
20. *Monarda didyma*, bee balm
21. *Allium schoenoprasum*, chive
22. *Rosa eglanteria*, eglantine
23. *Taxus cuspidata* 'Columnaris', Japanese yew

Herb Garden Design / 15

THAT DOORYARD HERB GARDEN

"Lilliputian" might come to mind at first sight of this garden. The image would soon give way to other considerations, however. The garden is conveniently located. An extremely small space—six feet by ten feet—makes narrow paths a necessity. Even in limited space, however, rules of good design can be observed with circles or an arc to soften the more severe rectangles or squares. Only the width of the paths needs to be sacrificed. Herbs grown especially for fragrance may be substituted for the culinary herbs, and the plan could be used at a front door. It would be a refreshing change from the standard foundation planting so commonly used. Then the design might need to be expanded, making the beds larger and the paths wider, still observing a scale.

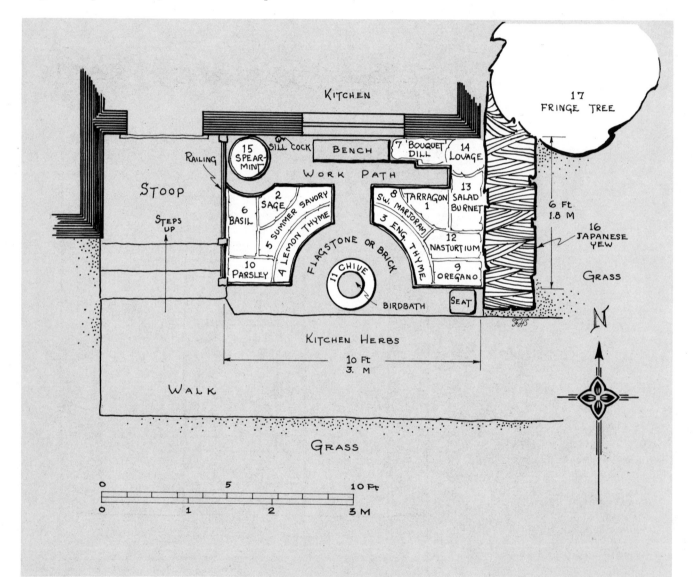

Connecticut

Margaret Osborn Holt, A.S.L.A.

The number in each planting area is the key number.

1. *Artemisia dracunculus* var. *sativa*, French tarragon
2. *Salvia officinalis*, garden sage
3. *Thymus* 'Broad-leaf English', English thyme
4. *Thymus × citriodorus*, lemon thyme
5. *Satureja hortensis*, summer savory
6. *Ocimum basilicum*, sweet basil
7. *Anethum graveolens* 'Bouquet', dill
8. *Origanum majorana*, sweet marjoram
9. *Origanum heracleoticum*, Greek oregano
10. *Petroselinum crispum*, parsley
11. *Allium schoenoprasum*, chive
12. *Tropaeolum majus*, nasturtium
13. *Poterium sanguisorba*, salad burnet
14. *Levisticum officinale*, lovage
15. *Mentha spicata*, spearmint
16. *Taxus cuspidata*, Japanese yew
17. *Chionanthus virginicus*, fringe tree

IN PARTIAL SHADE

It is not always the smaller city lot that offers a challenge for the herb enthusiast who anticipates planning and planting an herb garden. It may be a more spacious lot where too great a portion of the private area in the rear is shaded by mature trees not to be sacrificed. If the only area remaining is alongside the house and is a long, narrow strip dominated by a hedge, the challenge is obvious. The hedge is needed for privacy and establishes the property line. The garden is easily accessible from the kitchen and the garage, and a gate provides access to the front of the property. This is an intimate garden, a feeling heightened by the herringbone pattern of the brick paving. A brick edging raises the beds slightly. Edgings of herbs further delineate the beds. The sun warms and illuminates only the culinary beds of this area for a few hours of the day. The remainder is brightened by reflected light from the house-garage. The long, shady bed with ferns at the base of the hedge adds to the width of the narrow garden as viewed from the kitchen window.

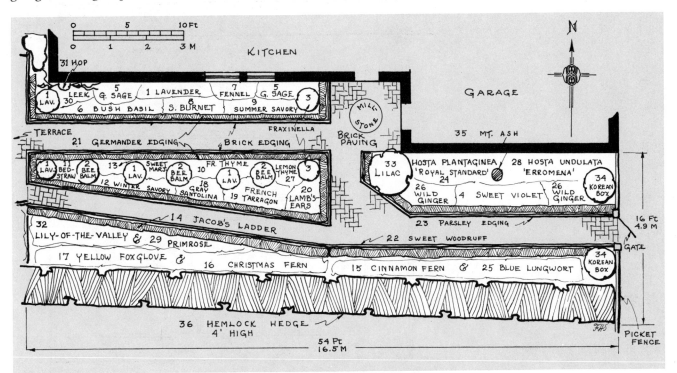

Ohio

Lucile Teeter Kissack, Landscape Architect, A.S.L.A.

The number in each planting area is the key number.

1. *Lavandula angustifolia* subsp. *angustifolia* 'Munstead', lavender
2. *Monarda didyma*, bee balm
3. *Dictamnus albus*, fraxinella
4. *Viola odorata*, sweet violet
5. *Salvia officinalis*, garden sage
6. *Ocimum basilicum* 'Minimum', bush basil
7. *Foeniculum vulgare*, fennel
8. *Poterium sanguisorba*, salad burnet
9. *Satureja hortensis*, summer savory
10. *Thymus vulgaris* 'Narrow-leaf French', French thyme
11. *Galium verum*, yellow bedstraw
12. *Satureja montana*, winter savory
13. *Origanum majorana*, sweet marjoram
14. *Polemonium reptans*, Jacob's-ladder
15. *Osmunda cinnamomea*, cinnamon fern
16. *Polystichum acrostichoides*, Christmas fern
17. *Digitalis grandiflora*, yellow foxglove
18. *Santolina chamaecyparissus*, gray santolina
19. *Artemisia dracunculus* var. *sativa*, French tarragon
20. *Stachys byzantina*, lamb's-ears
21. *Teucrium chamaedrys*, germander
22. *Galium odoratum*, sweet woodruff
23. *Petroselinum crispum* var. *crispum*, curly parsley
24. *Hosta plantaginea* 'Royal Standard', fragrant plantain lily
25. *Pulmonaria officinalis*, blue lungwort
26. *Asarum canadense*, wild ginger
27. *Thymus × citriodorus*, lemon thyme
28. *Hosta undulata* 'Erromena', mid-summer plantain lily
29. *Primula vulgaris*, primrose in variety
30. *Allium ampeloprasum*, Porrum Group, leek
31. *Humulus lupulus*, hop
32. *Convallaria majalis*, lily-of-the-valley
33. *Syringa vulgaris* 'Ellen Willmott', lilac
34. *Buxus microphylla* var. *koreana*, Korean box
35. *Sorbus americana*, mountain ash
36. *Tsuga canadensis*, Canada hemlock

THE DIMINUTIVE AND UNADORNED

If limited time and limited space are prime factors when planning an herb garden, this design can be an inspiration. Surprisingly, twenty-six herbs thrive in this tiny garden. To be placed near the kitchen, it became part of the patio. This necessarily limited the size of the garden. Even so, it added interest and fragrance to the atmosphere and a fine view of growing herbs from the kitchen window. The low wall enclosing the patio is an ideal spot for displaying specimen plants in pots. Redwood dividers form the beds and were constructed as a weekend project. It is a pleasing, geometric design, and its pattern is made more apparent with the contrasting leaf textures and colors of the herbs arranged with that purpose in mind. One of the beds, devoted to a "yearly surprise," is a splendid idea to encourage experimenting with unfamiliar herbs.

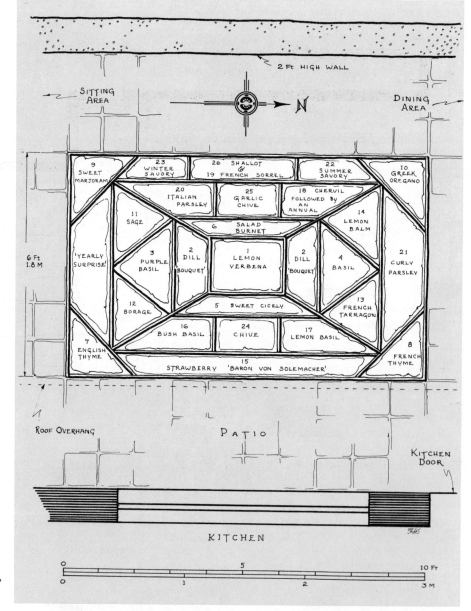

California

Designed by Owner

The number in each planting area is the key number.

1. *Aloysia triphylla*, lemon verbena
2. *Anethum graveolens* 'Bouquet', dill
3. *Ocimum basilicum* 'Purpurascens', purple basil
4. *Ocimum basilicum*, sweet basil
5. *Myrrhis odorata*, sweet cicely
6. *Poterium sanguisorba*, salad burnet
7. *Thymus* 'Broad-leaf English', English thyme
8. *Thymus vulgaris* 'Narrow-leaf French', French thyme
9. *Origanum majorana*, sweet marjoram
10. *Origanum heracleoticum*, Greek oregano
11. *Salvia officinalis*, garden sage
12. *Borago officinalis*, borage
13. *Artemisia dracunculus* var. *sativa*, French tarragon
14. *Melissa officinalis*, lemon balm
15. *Fragaria vesca* 'Baron von Solemacher', Alpine strawberry
16. *Ocimum basilicum* 'Minimum', bush basil
17. *Ocimum basilicum* 'Citriodorum', lemon basil
18. *Anthriscus cerefolium*, chervil
19. *Rumex scutatus*, French sorrel
20. *Petroselinum crispum* var. *neapolitanum*, Italian parsley
21. *Petroselinum crispum* var. *crispum*, curly parsley
22. *Satureja hortensis*, summer savory
23. *Satureja montana*, winter savory
24. *Allium schoenoprasum*, chive
25. *Allium tuberosum*, garlic chive
26. *Allium cepa* Aggregatum group, shallot

AS A GEOMETRIC FORM

Originally this herb garden was designed for a horticultural display at the National Arboretum in Washington, D.C. A planting plan was prepared for it that named not only the plants used but also the number of each kind. It is a plan that can be used in whole or in part. As a whole, it is full of interesting angles. Created in an orderly way, it is an unusual, geometric design. A thumbnail sketch shows the manner in which a design can be developed from a geometric figure. Unusual shapes for beds and work paths can become apparent by extending lines through the vertices of the angles in the figure. Then additional lines are drawn parallel and equidistant to them, so that the location of an entrance or a niche can be more easily and logically determined. The center beds here were established in this way; so, too, was the inverted *V* of gray santolina established. To increase the planting area, the work paths could be eliminated, resulting in a still attractive bed featured centrally in the plan.

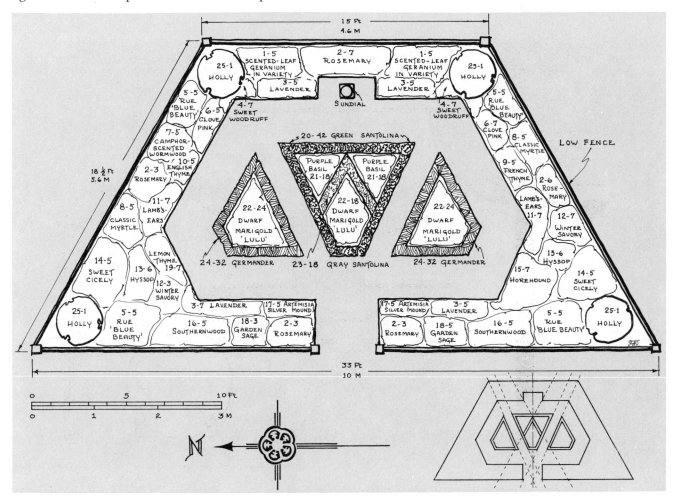

New York

Designed by Contributor

The first number in each planting area is the key number; the second shows the quantity of plants to be used.

1. *Pelargonium* in variety, scented-leaf geranium
2. *Rosmarinus officinalis*, rosemary
3. *Lavandula angustifolia*, English lavender
4. *Galium odoratum*, sweet woodruff
5. *Ruta graveolens* 'Blue Beauty', rue
6. *Dianthus caryophyllus*, clove pink
7. *Artemisia camphorata*, camphor-scented wormwood
8. *Myrtus communis*, classic myrtle
9. *Thymus vulgaris* 'Narrow-leaf French', French thyme
10. *Thymus* 'Broad-leaf English', English thyme
11. *Stachys byzantina*, lamb's-ears
12. *Satureja montana*, winter savory
13. *Hyssopus officinalis*, blue hyssop
14. *Myrrhis odorata*, sweet cicely
15. *Marrubium vulgare*, horehound
16. *Artemisia abrotanum*, southernwood
17. *Artemisia schmidtiana* 'Nana', silver mound artemisia
18. *Salvia officinalis*, garden sage
19. *Thymus* × *citriodorus*, lemon thyme
20. *Santolina virens*, green santolina
21. *Ocimum basilicum* 'Purpurascens', purple basil
22. *Tagetes tenuifolia* 'Lulu', dwarf marigold
23. *Santolina chamaecyparissus*, gray santolina
24. *Teucrium chamaedrys*, germander
25. *Ilex opaca*, American holly

SOME SECLUDED SPOT

Although only a few steps from the front door, this herb garden is secluded. A redwood fence seven feet high secures its privacy. This is a basket-weave fence that allows some air circulation but at times becomes an effective windbreak, too. The path from the front gate needs to lead to something of particular interest. Here it is a reading nook or an aged rosemary in a special container. Sometimes space is limited, and if an herb garden is to be created at all, the paths must be narrower than may be recommended. In this case no casual herb edging but rather a clipped one such as the *Santolina chamaecyparissus* used here should be selected. Maximum width thus is left clear for walking. The gray of the *Santolina* is a good color alongside the brick, which adds its impression of warmth, seeming to extend the season of enjoyment in colder climates. Brick is repeated in the base for the focal point. This center of interest is of particular note, an equatorial sundial with its hour lines on a curved metal strip depicting the equator. Its arrow points north and, being perpendicular to the symbolic equator, casts the shadow for the hour.

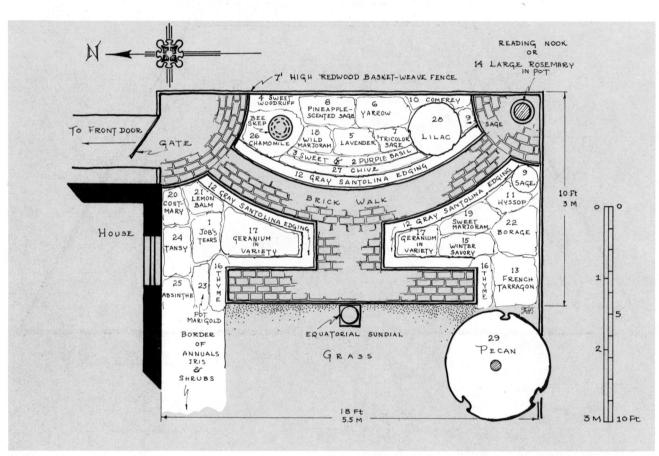

Kansas

Designed by Owner

The number in each planting area is the key number.

1. *Coix lacryma-jobi*, Job's tears
2. *Ocimum basilicum* 'Purpurascens', purple basil
3. *Ocimum basilicum*, sweet basil
4. *Galium odoratum*, sweet woodruff
5. *Lavandula angustifolia*, English lavender
6. *Achillea millefolium*, yarrow
7. *Salvia officinalis* 'Tricolor', variegated garden sage
8. *Salvia elegans*, pineapple-scented sage
9. *Salvia officinalis*, garden sage
10. *Symphytum officinale*, comfrey
11. *Hyssopus officinalis*, blue hyssop
12. *Santolina chamaecyparissus*, gray santolina
13. *Artemisia dracunculus* var. *sativa*, French tarragon
14. *Rosmarinus officinalis*, rosemary
15. *Satureja montana*, winter savory
16. *Thymus praecox* subsp. *arcticus* 'Albus', white creeping thyme
17. *Pelargonium* in variety, scented-leaf geranium
18. *Origanum vulgare*, wild marjoram
19. *Origanum majorana*, sweet marjoram
20. *Chrysanthemum balsamita*, costmary
21. *Melissa officinalis*, lemon balm
22. *Borago officinalis*, borage
23. *Calendula officinalis*, pot marigold
24. *Tanacetum vulgare*, tansy
25. *Artemisia absinthium*, absinthe
26. *Chamaemelum nobile*, chamomile
27. *Allium schoenoprasum*, chive
28. *Syringa*, lilac
29. *Carya illinoinensis*, pecan

WITH HERBS IN SUNKEN POTS

Originally planned with herbs potted, sunken into the ground, and heavily mulched with cocoa bean hulls, this design could be used with herbs planted directly in the ground. The more invasive ones, for example lemon balm and spearmint, need to be planted in confining tiles or flue liners to contain them. When controlled in this way, the members of the mint family become rootbound and must be cut apart with sections of new growth replanted each spring if they are to survive. The neatness of this design makes good use of limited space, and it is this limited space that dictates the narrow work paths. Potted herbs can be held in readiness to replace one doing poorly, resulting in a very trim herb garden that always looks its best. This trimness is accentuated by the germander edgings and the Japanese yew hedge—in this case *Taxus cuspidata* 'Densa'—used as a partial enclosure.

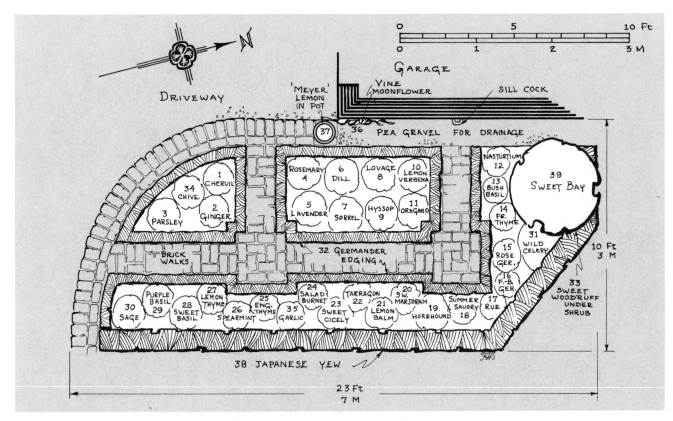

Ohio

Designed by Owner

The number in each planting area is the key number.

1. *Anthriscus cerefolium*, chervil
2. *Zingiber officinale*, true ginger
3. *Petroselinum crispum*, parsley
4. *Rosmarinus officinalis*, rosemary
5. *Lavandula angustifolia*, English lavender
6. *Anethum graveolens*, dill
7. *Rumex scutatus*, French sorrel
8. *Levisticum officinale*, lovage
9. *Hyssopus officinalis*, blue hyssop
10. *Aloysia triphylla*, lemon verbena
11. *Origanum heracleoticum*, Greek oregano
12. *Tropaeolum minus*, dwarf nasturtium
13. *Ocimum basilicum* 'Minimum', bush basil
14. *Thymus vulgaris* 'Narrow-leaf French', French thyme
15. *Pelargonium graveolens*, rose geranium
16. *Pelargonium × limoneum*, English finger-bowl geranium
17. *Ruta graveolens*, rue
18. *Satureja hortensis*, summer savory
19. *Marrubium vulgare*, horehound
20. *Origanum majorana*, sweet marjoram
21. *Melissa officinalis*, lemon balm
22. *Artemisia dracunculus* var. *sativa*, French tarragon
23. *Myrrhis odorata*, sweet cicely
24. *Poterium sanguisorba*, salad burnet
25. *Thymus* 'Broad-leaf English', English thyme
26. *Mentha spicata*, spearmint
27. *Thymus × citriodorus*, lemon thyme
28. *Ocimum basilicum*, sweet basil
29. *Ocimum basilicum* 'Purpurascens', purple basil
30. *Salvia officinalis*, garden sage
31. *Apium graveolens*, wild celery
32. *Teucrium chamaedrys*, germander
33. *Galium odoratum*, sweet woodruff
34. *Allium schoenoprasum*, chive
35. *Allium sativum*, garlic
36. *Ipomoea alba*, moonflower
37. *Citrus limon* 'Meyer', Meyer lemon
38. *Taxus cuspidata* 'Densa', Japanese yew
39. *Magnolia virginiana*, sweet bay

AT A SUMMER COTTAGE

A word or two from Thoreau, "Simplify, simplify!," may have been the key to the inspiration for this plan at a summer cottage. Here are the indispensable culinary herbs, the insect-repellent pennyroyal, and "first-aid" necessities such as jewelweed for poison ivy country and aloe for minor burns or skin abrasions. Interest and charm were not sacrificed for utility, however. Compass points in the center of the flag-stone terrace and the rail fence are elements of appeal and are easily adaptable to other situations. The planting beds were raised using two-by-six-inch boards, a quick way to ensure good drainage. It may not be a summer cottage that limits gardening time, but, whatever the reason, this casual plan devised for this casual place can be an inspiration with its simplicity.

New Jersey

Designed by Owner

The number in each planting area is the key number.

1. *Petroselinum crispum*, parsley
2. *Lactuca sativa*, lettuce
3. *Lycopersicon lycopersicum*, tomato
4. *Anethum graveolens*, dill
5. *Capsicum frutescens*, Grossum Group, bell pepper
6. *Ocimum basilicum*, sweet basil
7. *Thymus praecox* subsp. *arcticus*, mother-of-thyme
8. *Galium odoratum*, sweet woodruff
9. *Artemisia absinthium*, absinthe
10. *Tanacetum vulgare*, tansy
11. *Monarda didyma*, bee balm
12. *Mentha spicata*, spearmint
13. *Melissa officinalis*, lemon balm
14. *Mentha* × *piperita*, peppermint
15. *Impatiens capensis*, jewelweed
16. *Origanum majorana*, sweet marjoram
17. *Rosmarinus officinalis*, rosemary
18. *Thymus vulgaris* 'Narrow-leaf French', French thyme
19. *Ruta graveolens*, rue
20. *Salvia officinalis*, garden sage
21. *Hedeoma pulegioides*, American pennyroyal
22. *Artemisia dracunculus* var. *sativa*, French tarragon
23. *Aloe barbadensis*, aloe
24. *Satureja hortensis*, summer savory
25. *Allium schoenoprasum*, chive
26. *Allium fistulosum*, Welsh onion
27. *Lindera benzoin*, spicebush

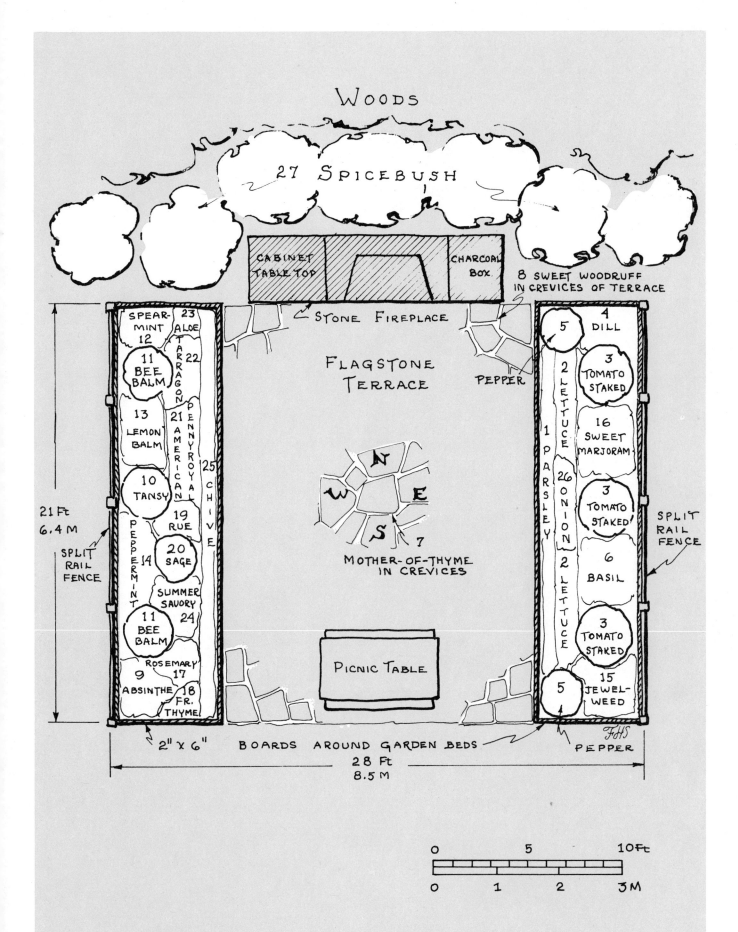

WOODS

27 SPICEBUSH

CABINET TABLE TOP · CHARCOAL BOX

STONE FIREPLACE

8 SWEET WOODRUFF IN CREVICES OF TERRACE

FLAGSTONE TERRACE

PEPPER

N
W · E
S
7

MOTHER-OF-THYME IN CREVICES

PICNIC TABLE

21 Ft
6.4 M

SPLIT RAIL FENCE

SPEARMINT 12
23 ALOE
11 BEE BALM
22 TARRAGON
13 LEMON BALM
21 AMERICAN PENNYROYAL
10 TANSY
25 CHIVE
19 RUE
20 SAGE
14 PEPPERMINT
SUMMER SAVORY 24
11 BEE BALM
ROSEMARY 17
9 ABSINTHE
18 FR. THYME

5
4 DILL
2 LETTUCE
3 TOMATO STAKED
1 PARSLEY
16 SWEET MARJORAM
26 ONION
3 TOMATO STAKED
2 LETTUCE
6 BASIL
3 TOMATO STAKED
5
15 JEWEL-WEED
PEPPER

SPLIT RAIL FENCE

2" X 6" BOARDS AROUND GARDEN BEDS

28 Ft
8.5 M

0   5   10 Ft
0   1   2   3 M

MORE AMBITIOUS

AS A PATTERNED ENTRANCE

This patterned entrance has been treated asymmetrically. The deep green germander arcs lay out the design clearly, and the pattern is made more evident with contrasting leaf textures and leaf colors. A different retaining device is used for the slightly raised beds to keep soil and mulch in place. It is heavy nylon marine rope held in place with pegs. A low wall of brick, faced and capped with random, horizontally laid bluestone, encloses this plan. Blue-gray crushed stone eight inches deep and retained by galvanized soil barriers provides a direct approach to the screened porch and house. The directness of the path is softened by the arcs created on the one side, and the stone also helps this patterned entrance complement the architecture of the house. The late autumn yellow flowers and foliage of witch hazel are placed to add to the view from the house. The color is good with the blue-gray of the stone used in this plan, too.

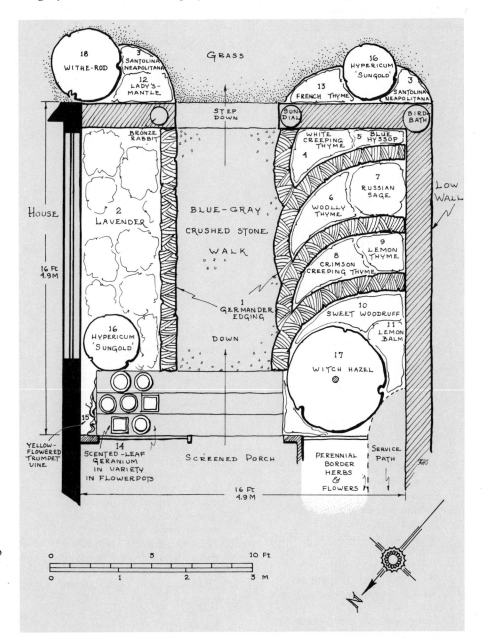

Massachusetts

Designed by Owner

The number in each planting area is the key number.

1. *Teucrium chamaedrys*, germander
2. *Lavandula angustifolia* subsp. *angustifolia*, lavender
3. *Santolina neapolitana*
4. *Thymus praecox* subsp. *arcticus* 'Albus', white creeping thyme
5. *Hyssopus officinalis*, blue hyssop
6. *Thymus praecox* subsp. *arcticus* 'Lanuginosus', woolly thyme
7. *Perovskia abrotanoides*, Russian sage
8. *Thymus praecox* subsp. *arcticus* 'Coccineus', crimson creeping thyme
9. *Thymus × citriodorus*, lemon thyme
10. *Galium odoratum*, sweet woodruff
11. *Melissa officinalis*, lemon balm
12. *Alchemilla vulgaris*, lady's-mantle
13. *Thymus vulgaris* 'Narrow-leaf French', French thyme
14. *Pelargonium* in variety, scented-leaf geranium
15. *Campsis radicans*, trumpet vine
16. *Hypericum patulum* 'Sungold', St.-John's-wort
17. *Hamamelis virginiana*, witch hazel
18. *Viburnum cassinoides*, withe-rod

FOR A CONTEMPORARY HOUSE

Often there is a need to soften the stark lines of a contemporary house by using plantings. To serve that purpose and in a manner quite out of the ordinary, a relatively small herb garden is situated two steps down from the terrace. A Japanese holly hedge repeats the curves of the brick walk, which is treated with patches of various cultivars of *Thymus praecox* subsp. *arcticus* and encloses the herb garden. These curves alone might have produced the softening effect desired. However, bays and niches were created with the inner walk of marble chips. The bays result in a greater border area for a wider variety of border

herbs. The niches are an ideal way to make a place for a birdbath and to tuck in a garden seat. Germander is a proper edging here. Its dark green color is good contrast for the path of marble chips. The gravel walkway is a useful device to move the garden from under the roof overhang into the sun. It is, however, the shrubs—yew, box, holly, lilac, privet—that back up the germander and structure the design for the entire year. Although this is not a large garden, with this planting plan it provides an abundance of herbs for many uses.

Connecticut

Eloise & Jo Ray, Landscape Architects

The number in each planting area is the key number.

1. *Myrrhis odorata*, sweet cicely
2. *Marrubium vulgare*, horehound
3. *Viola odorata*, sweet violet
4. *Alchemilla vulgaris*, lady's-mantle
5. *Lavandula angustifolia* subsp. *angustifolia* 'Hidcote', lavender
6. *Thymus praecox* subsp. *arcticus* 'Lanuginosus', woolly thyme
7. *Heliotropium arborescens*, heliotrope
8. *Mentha requienii*, Corsican mint
9. *Thymus praecox* subsp. *arcticus* 'Splendens', red creeping thyme
10. *Santolina chamaecyparissus*, gray santolina
11. *Santolina virens*, green santolina
12. *Rosmarinus officinalis* 'Prostratus', prostrate rosemary
13. *Satureja montana*, winter savory
14. *Salvia sclarea*, clary
15. *Artemisia frigida*, fringed wormwood
16. *Artemisia ludoviciana* var. *albula*, silver-king artemisia
17. *Dianthus plumarius* 'Mrs. Simkins', cottage pink
18. *Hyssopus officinalis*, blue hyssop
19. *Hyssopus officinalis* 'Alba', white hyssop
20. *Chamaemelum nobile*, chamomile
21. *Borago officinalis*, borage
22. *Ruta graveolens*, rue
23. *Fragaria vesca* 'Baron von Solemacher', alpine strawberry
24. *Artemisia schmidtiana* 'Nana', silver mound artemisia
25. *Anemone pulsatilla*, pasqueflower
26. *Artemisia camphorata*, camphor-scented wormwood
27. *Dianthus alpinus* 'Petite', alpine pink
28. *Chrysanthemum coccineum*, painted daisy
29. *Salvia leucophylla*, gray sage
30. *Thymus praecox* subsp. *arcticus* 'Coccineus', crimson creeping thyme
31. *Dictamnus albus*, fraxinella
32. *Comptonia peregrina*, sweet fern
33. *Santolina pinnata*
34. *Stachys byzantina*, lamb's-ears
35. *Teucrium chamaedrys*, germander
36. *Thymus praecox* subsp. *arcticus* 'Albus', white creeping thyme
37. *Iris × germanica* var. *florentina*, orris
38. *Iris cristata*, dwarf crested iris
39. *Cytisus supinus*, broom
40. *Buxus microphylla* 'Nana', dwarf box
41. *Ilex crenata* 'Stokesii', Japanese holly
42. *Taxus × media* 'Hicksii', columnar yew
43. *Taxus cuspidata* 'Densa', Japanese yew
44. *Syringa patula*, lilac
45. *Potentilla fruticosa* 'Katherine Dykes', shrubby cinquefoil
46. *Ilex crenata* 'Bullata', Japanese holly
47. *Ligustrum vulgare* 'Nanum', dwarf privet
48. *Myrtus communis*, classic myrtle

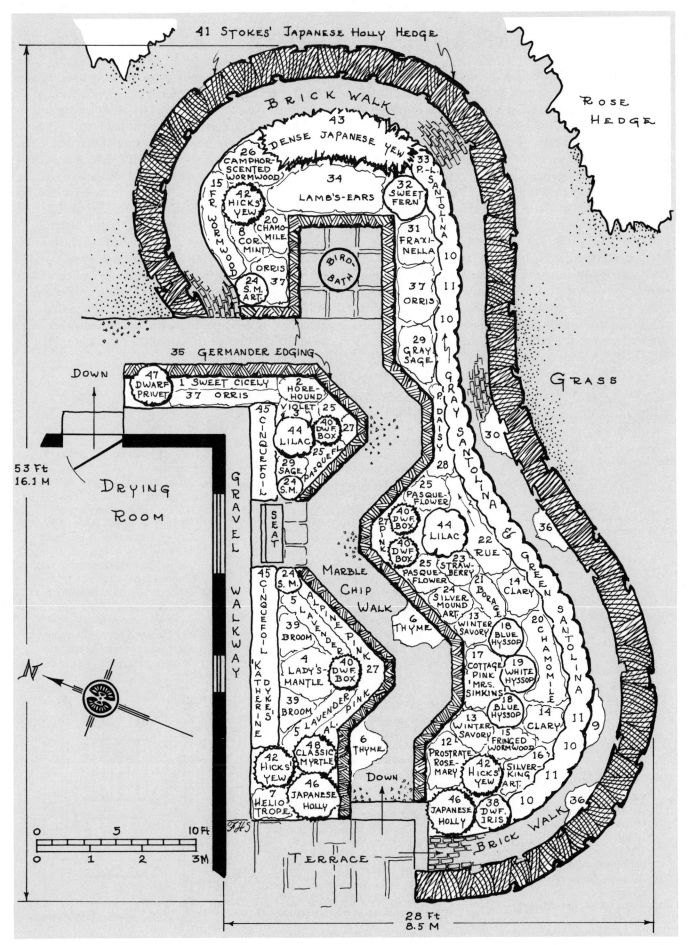

41 STOKES' JAPANESE HOLLY HEDGE

BRICK WALK

ROSE HEDGE

43 DENSE JAPANESE YEW

26 CAMPHOR-SCENTED WORMWOOD

15 FR. WORMWOOD

42 HICKS' YEW

34 LAMB'S-EARS

33 P.-L. SANTOLINA

32 SWEET FERN

20 CHAMOMILE

8 COR. MINT

31 FRAXINELLA 10

24 S. M. ART.

37 ORRIS

BIRD-BATH

37 ORRIS 11

10

29 GRAY SAGE

35 GERMANDER EDGING

DOWN

47 DWARF PRIVET

1 SWEET CICELY
37 ORRIS

2 HORE-HOUND

45 CINQUEFOIL

3 VIOLET 25

44 LILAC

40 DWF. BOX 27

GRASS

29 SAGE

25

P. DAISY

24 S.M.

PASQUEF.

30

53 Ft
16.1 M

DRYING ROOM

SEAT

28

25 PASQUE-FLOWER

GRAY SANTOLINA & GREEN SANTOLINA

40 DWF. BOX 27

44 LILAC

36

MARBLE CHIP WALK

PINK

40 DWF. BOX

22 RUE

45 CINQUEFOIL KATHERINE DYKES'

24 S.M.

5 ALPINE PINK

25 PASQUE-FLOWER

23 STRAW-BERRY

21 BORAGE

14 CLARY

39 BROOM

LAVENDER

24 SILVER MOUND ART.

13 WINTER SAVORY

18 BLUE HYSSOP

20 CHAMOMILE

6 THYME

4 LADY'S MANTLE

40 DWF. BOX 27

17 COTTAGE PINK 'MRS. SIMKINS'

19 WHITE HYSSOP

N

39 BROOM

5 LAVENDER

A. PINK

18 BLUE HYSSOP

15 CLARY

14

42 HICKS' YEW

48 CLASSIC MYRTLE

6 THYME

13 WINTER SAVORY

15 FRINGED WORMWOOD

11 9

DOWN

12 PROSTRATE ROSEMARY

16

10

7 HELIO-TROPE

46 JAPANESE HOLLY

42 HICKS' YEW

SILVER-KING ART.

11

46 JAPANESE HOLLY

38 DWF. IRIS

10

36

0   5   10 Ft
0   1   2   3M

TERRACE

BRICK WALK

28 Ft
8.5 M

GRAVEL WALKWAY

IN MORE THAN AN HERB GARDEN

This long narrow melding of gardens is composed of a perennial garden, an herb garden, a cutting garden, and a vegetable garden. The varied shapes of the beds add interest, and one has an inset for a garden seat. The herb garden itself could be considered a focal point. This is an area of more than one hundred square feet with paths running diagonally across the square. These paths are random flagstone that are compatible with the raised stone slab of an old well, the center of interest for the herb garden. Other paths are brick, a running bond pattern, which requires less brick and merges nicely with the flagstone. The several beds create an opportunity to use a variety of edgings, and here there are nine for the exterior edges of the beds. All were selected to fit the purposes of the beds, and the alpine strawberry edging is a good choice for continuity between the herb garden area and the vegetable garden. A white fence of wood is the enclosure for two sides of this sunny garden area and serves as a handsome support for grape vines. The second seventy-five-foot side is served by an alpine currant hedge and is a fine transition to the lawn area. This hedge, while adding to the enclosure of the area, does not accentuate the narrowness of the garden as enclosing it entirely with the white fence would have. The direction a path takes can add interest, as is true here in the vegetable garden, more pleasing for having taken a turn to one of two openings in the hedge, allowing adequate access to the lawn area. The house with its flagstone terrace is the final portion of the enclosure. A gate provides access to the garden from the driveway and is wood painted white in keeping with the fence. Its charm is well illustrated in the sketch and is varied only by the seasonal changes of the herbal blooms or foliage in the container on the gate.

Ohio

Lucile Teeter Kissack, Landscape Architect, A.S.L.A.

The number in each planting area is the key number.

1. *Iberis sempervirens* 'Little Gem', candytuft
2. *Fragaria vesca* 'Baron von Solemacher', alpine strawberry
3. *Rosmarinus officinalis*, rosemary
4. *Anethum graveolens* 'Bouquet', dill
5. *Aquilegia chrysantha*, yellow columbine
6. *Dianthus plumarius* 'Her Majesty', cottage pink
7. *Dictamnus albus*, fraxinella
8. *Campanula persicifolia*, blue peach-bells
9. *Achillea taygetea*, pale yellow yarrow
10. *Aloysia triphylla*, lemon verbena
11. *Paeonia lactiflora* 'Festiva Maxima', double white peony
12. *Stokesia laevis*, Stokes' aster
13. *Chrysanthemum* × *superbum*, shasta daisy
14. *Epimedium* × *versicolor* 'Sulphureum', yellow epimedium
15. *Satureja hortensis*, summer savory
16. *Digitalis grandiflora*, yellow foxglove
17. *Platycodon grandiflorus* 'Mariesii', balloon flower
18. *Hemerocallis* × *luteola*, yellow daylily
19. *Phlox paniculata* 'Mary Louise', white phlox
20. *Hosta plantaginea* 'Royal Standard', plantain lily
21. *Limonium latifolium*, statice
22. *Helenium autumnale* 'Riverton Gem', helenium
23. *Torenia fournieri* 'Alba', white wishbone flower
24. *Tagetes patula* 'Petite Yellow', dwarf marigold
25. *Thymus vulgaris* 'Narrow-leaf French', French thyme
26. *Teucrium chamaedrys*, germander
27. *Salvia sclarea*, clary
28. *Polystichum acrostichoides*, Christmas fern
29. *Helleborus niger*, Christmas rose
30. *Stachys byzantina*, lamb's-ears
31. *Artemisia schmidtiana* 'Nana', silver mound artemisia
32. *Galium odoratum*, sweet woodruff
33. *Origanum heracleoticum*, Greek oregano
34. *Petroselinum crispum* var. *crispum*, curly parsley
35. *Ocimum basilicum* 'Purpurascens', purple basil
36. *Lavandula angustifolia* subsp. *angustifolia* 'Munstead', lavender
37. *Salvia officinalis*, garden sage
38. *Thymus* 'Broad-leaf English', English thyme
39. *Thymus* × *citriodorus*, lemon thyme
40. *Ocimum basilicum* 'Minimum', bush basil
41. *Santolina virens*, green santolina
42. *Hyssopus officinalis*, blue hyssop
43. *Satureja montana*, winter savory
44. *Origanum majorana*, sweet marjoram
45. *Artemisia dracunculus* var. *sativa*, French tarragon
46. *Iris* × *germanica* 'Great Lakes', blue iris
47. *Pelargonium* in variety, scented-leaf geranium
48. *Allium schoenoprasum*, chive
49. *Allium christophii*, stars-of-Persia
50. *Tulipa* 'General de Wet', early tawny orange tulip
51. *Tulipa* 'Sweet Harmony', pale yellow Darwin tulip
52. *Lilium candidum*, Madonna lily
53. *Rosa damascena* 'Versicolor', York-and-Lancaster rose
54. *Ilex crenata* 'Hetzii', Japanese holly
55. *Ribes alpinum*, alpine currant
56. *Magnolia virginiana*, sweet bay

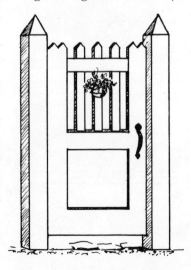

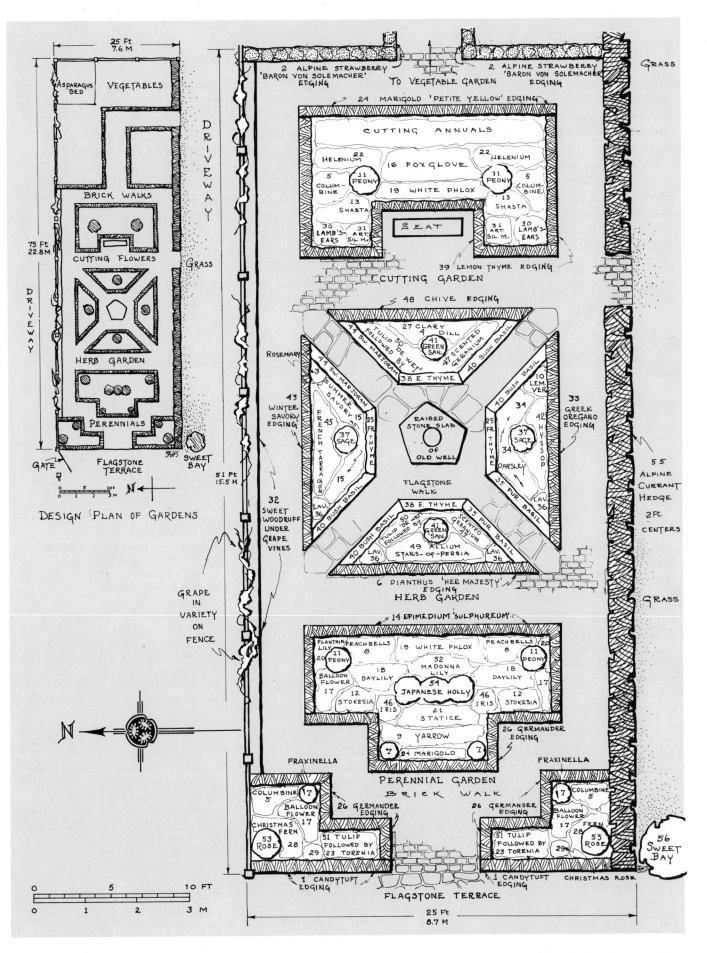

ON A TERRACED HILLSIDE

When confronted with a hillside location for an herb garden, as in this case, a retaining wall or walls are needed. It is highly unlikely that a plan could be conceived that would be workable or durable without this kind of preparation. The stone wall at the back of this garden is good background for the textures and colors of the herbs. While serving as a soil retainer, it confines the carpet bugleweed that softens the line of the wall. This wall and the holly hedge lend a feeling of enclosure on two sides of the garden. The other two are unenclosed for visibility from the house and pool area. A bench alcove is located for the best overall view of the herb garden. Flagstone paths used throughout unify the garden and related pool area. The entrance to the herb garden is enlarged by setting back the bed at the top of the steps from the house. An area nearly twelve square feet is gained this way to be used to better advantage as entry space. Four rectangular beds are altered on their central corners to expand the area where the more narrow work paths intersect. An air of spaciousness results from opening up the center in this manner. The edgings of thyme relieve the severity of the straight lines and right angles.

Arkansas

Neil Hamill Park, Landscape Architect, F.A.A.R.

The number in each planting area is the key number.

1. *Artemisia schmidtiana* 'Nana', silver mound artemisia
2. *Melissa officinalis*, lemon balm
3. *Ocimum basilicum*, sweet basil
4. *Monarda didyma*, bee balm
5. *Stachys byzantina*, lamb's-ears
6. *Borago officinalis*, borage
7. *Ajuga reptans*, carpet bugleweed
8. *Rosmarinus officinalis*, rosemary
9. *Poterium sanguisorba*, salad burnet
10. *Nepeta cataria*, catnip
11. *Ruta graveolens*, rue
12. *Satureja hortensis*, summer savory
13. *Chrysanthemum balsamita*, costmary
14. *Anethum graveolens*, dill
15. *Foeniculum vulgare*, fennel
16. *Salvia officinalis*, garden sage
17. *Marrubium vulgare*, horehound
18. *Salvia elegans*, pineapple-scented sage
19. *Cassia marilandica*, wild senna
20. *Artemisia absinthium*, absinthe
21. *Mentha spicata*, spearmint
22. *Solanum pseudocapsicum*, Jerusalem cherry
23. *Alchemilla vulgaris*, lady's-mantle
24. *Lavandula angustifolia*, English lavender
25. *Tanacetum vulgare* var. *crispum*, fern-leaf tansy
26. *Aloysia triphylla*, lemon verbena
27. *Origanum majorana*, sweet marjoram
28. *Mentha* × *piperita* var. *citrata*, orange mint
29. *Mentha spicata* 'Crispata', curly mint
30. *Artemisia abrotanum*, southernwood
31. *Verbascum thapsus*, mullein
32. *Artemisia dracunculus* var. *sativa*, French tarragon
33. *Origanum heracleoticum*, Greek oregano
34. *Mentha pulegium*, pennyroyal
35. *Dianthus caryophyllus*, clove pink
36. *Petroselinum crispum* var. *crispum* 'Banquet', curly parsley
37. *Petroselinum crispum* var. *neapolitanum*, Italian parsley
38. *Vinca minor*, myrtle
39. *Capsicum frutescens*, tabasco pepper
40. *Thymus* 'Broad-leaf English', English thyme
41. *Thymus* × *citriodorus*, lemon thyme
42. *Viola odorata*, sweet violet
43. *Galium odoratum*, sweet woodruff
44. *Iris cristata*, dwarf crested iris
45. *Iris pseudacorus*, yellow flag
46. *Allium schoenoprasum*, chive
47. *Allium tuberosum*, garlic chive
48. *Allium ampeloprasum*, Porrum Group, leek
49. *Allium sativum*, garlic
50. *Allium cepa*, Proliferum Group, Egyptian onion
51. *Rosa* × *rehderana*, polyantha rose
52. *Ilex cornuta* 'Burfordii', holly
53. *Elaeagnus pungens*, thorny elaeagnus
54. *Cornus florida*, flowering dogwood
55. *Crataegus arkansana*, hawthorn
56. *Quercus stellata*, post oak
57. *Cercis canadensis* 'Alba', white eastern redbud
58. *Ilex vomitoria* 'Nana', dwarf yaupon

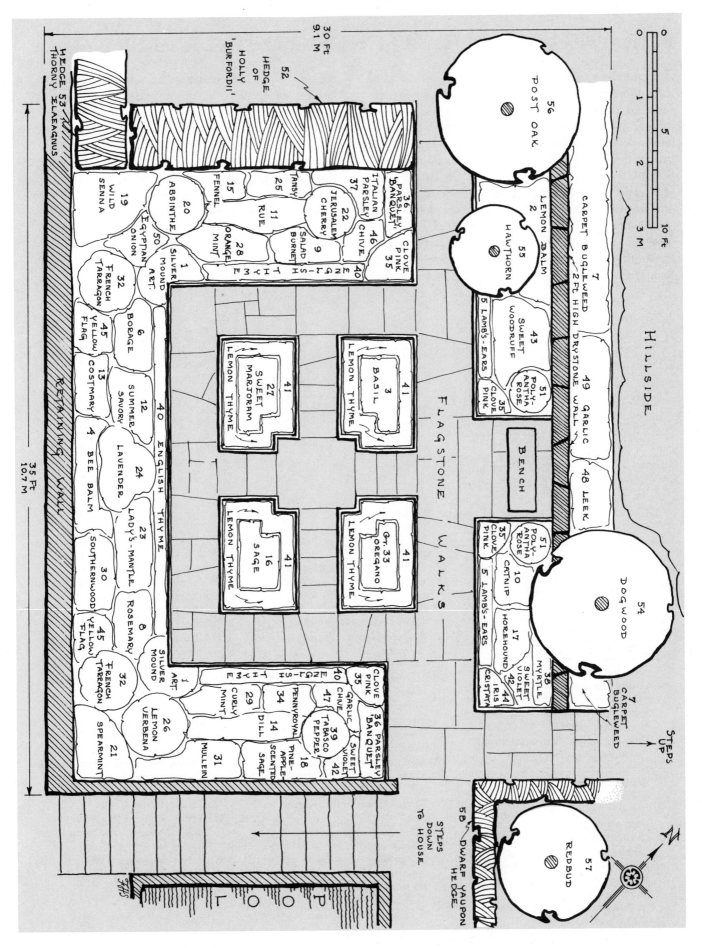

FOR AN OUTDOOR KITCHEN WORK CENTER

A sheltered, inside corner of the house—bordered by the kitchen on one side, a drying room and a garden room on the other—makes an ideal spot for an herb garden. Although this is a northeast exposure, the hemlock hedge and slight slope provide some weather relief from that direction. All this protection makes possible a climate that supports an open-air kitchen atmosphere. It is here that all preparation of vegetables from a large vegetable garden takes place and that herb harvest procedures are completed. A useful dipping well makes a break in the long curved bed in front of the fence and hedge that enclose the back of the garden. A number of potted plants and hanging baskets requiring less sun spend summer in the two lathhouses, which are a good way to supply controlled shade. Pebbled areas such as found here ensure use of fresh herbs even in rainy weather. A relatively small portion of the area is used for herb plantings, but it is more than adequate for potpourri, sleep pillows, mothproofing bags, and vinegars. It is a quarter of a circle that forms this design—this intimate herb garden and convenient outdoor kitchen and work center. However, it has a feeling of spaciousness because the pebbled area is so large. The kitchen and the garden room have splendid views of this pleasing design in its sheltered climate.

Massachusetts

Edmund G. Wilcox, Landscape Architect

The number in each planting area is the key number.

1. *Thymus × citriodorus*, lemon thyme
2. *Petroselinum crispum* var. *crispum*, curly parsley
3. *Artemisia pontica*, Roman wormwood
4. *Artemisia schmidtiana* 'Nana', silver mound artemisia
5. *Poterium sanguisorba*, salad burnet
6. *Lavandula angustifolia* subsp. *angustifolia* 'Hidcote', lavender
7. *Santolina chamaecyparissus*, gray santolina
8. *Lactuca*, lettuce in variety
9. *Ruta graveolens*, rue
10. *Ocimum basilicum* 'Purpurascens', purple basil
11. *Calendula officinalis*, pot marigold
12. *Satureja montana*, winter savory
13. *Monarda didyma*, bee balm
14. *Melissa officinalis*, lemon balm
15. *Tanacetum vulgare*, tansy
16. *Iris × germanica* var. *florentina*, orris
17. *Hyssopus officinalis*, blue hyssop
18. *Salvia officinalis* 'Holt's Mammoth', garden sage
19. *Alchemilla vulgaris*, lady's-mantle
20. *Galium odoratum*, sweet woodruff
21. *Chrysanthemum balsamita*, costmary
22. *Levisticum officinale*, lovage
23. *Mentha spicata*, spearmint
24. *Rumex scutatus*, French sorrel
25. *Artemisia abrotanum*, southernwood
26. *Artemisia dracunculus* var. *sativa*, French tarragon
27. *Salvia officinalis*, garden sage
28. *Salvia elegans*, pineapple-scented sage
29. *Salvia officinalis*, dwarf garden sage
30. *Agastache foeniculum*, anise hyssop
31. *Valeriana officinalis*, valerian
32. *Pelargonium graveolens*, rose geranium
33. *Rosmarinus officinalis*, rosemary
34. *Rosmarinus officinalis* 'Prostratus', prostrate rosemary
35. *Aloysia triphylla*, lemon verbena
36. *Tropaeolum minus*, dwarf nasturtium
37. *Pelargonium × limoneum*, English finger-bowl geranium
38. *Pelargonium fragrans*, nutmeg geranium
39. *Pelargonium tomentosum*, peppermint geranium
40. *Hemerocallis*, daylily in variety
41. *Allium cepa*, Proliferum Group, Egyptian onion
42. *Allium schoenoprasum*, chive
43. *Allium moly*, lily leek
44. *Allium sativum* var. *ophioscorodon* rocambole
45. *Allium sphaerocephalum*, round-headed garlic
46. *Allium pulchellum*
47. *Laurus nobilis*, bay
48. *Syringa vulgaris* 'Addie V. Hallock', 'Monge', 'President Poincare', lilac
49. *Tsuga canadensis*, Canada hemlock
50. *Thuja occidentalis*, American arborvitae

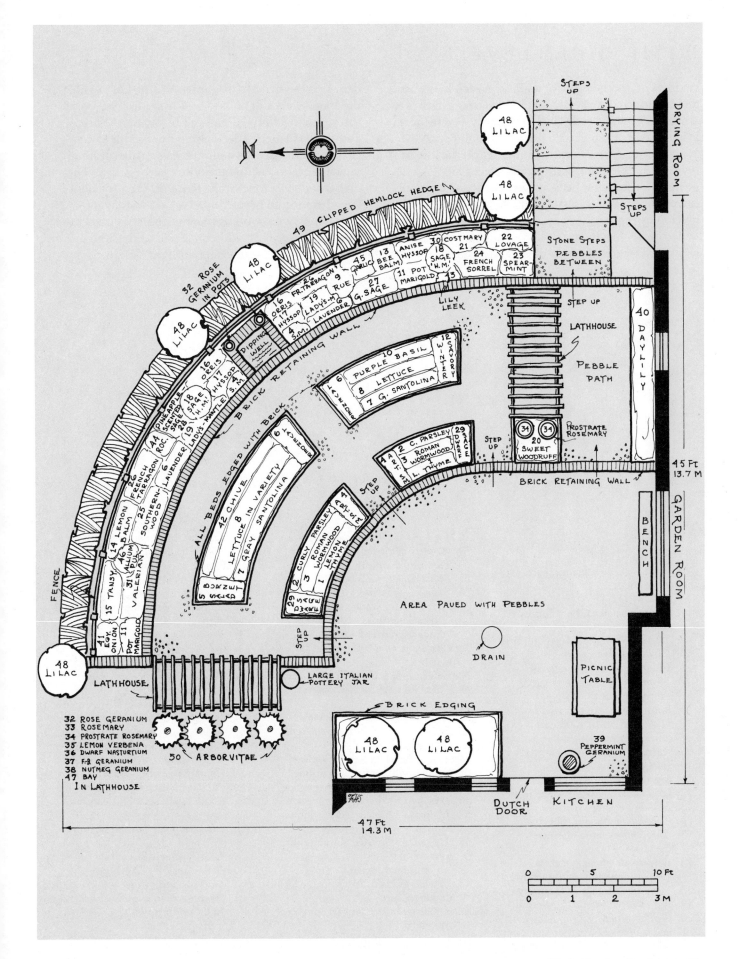

WITH THREE LEVELS

A site with three levels for an herb garden is almost an invitation to treat each level as a separate entity. A stone wall retains each level in this fifty-seven-foot-long garden. Each garden has a focal point with the knot of dwarf box a center of interest on the lowest level. A simple knot, with its ribbons of hyssop and germander forming beds for saffron crocus to be followed by suitable annuals, is the focus of the middle level. The highest level has a rectangular bed of lavender for its focal point. The varied treatment of these centers of interest adds to the appeal of the total garden. It is the size of this garden that makes possible the long sweeps of color—a pleasing feature—used throughout. Unity is achieved by laying the brick paths and the herb house porch floor in the same basket-weave pattern and by using a natural-wood picket fence to enclose the entire herb garden. The driftwood gray tone of the fence makes a splendid backdrop for all herbs. Invasive, shade-tolerant sweet cicely and sweet woodruff are purposely placed outside the fence at the white pine end of the herb garden where they cannot interfere with the design.

Pennsylvania

Designed by Owner

The number in each planting area is the key number.

1. *Satureja montana* 'Nana', dwarf winter savory
2. *Thymus* 'Long-leaf Gray', thyme
3. *Digitalis purpurea*, foxglove
4. *Valeriana officinalis*, valerian
5. *Mentha suaveolens* 'Variegata', pineapple mint
6. *Isatis tinctoria*, dyer's woad
7. *Dictamnus albus*, fraxinella
8. *Salvia sclarea*, clary
9. *Angelica archangelica*, angelica
10. *Ruta graveolens*, rue
11. *Myrrhis odorata*, sweet cicely
12. *Foeniculum vulgare*, bronze fennel
13. *Echium vulgare*, viper's bugloss
14. *Calendula officinalis*, pot marigold
15. *Chrysanthemum parthenium*, feverfew
16. *Galium odoratum*, sweet woodruff
17. *Anemone pulsatilla*, pasqueflower
18. *Symphytum officinale*, comfrey
19. *Agrimonia eupatoria*, agrimony
20. *Galium verum*, yellow bedstraw
21. *Salvia officinalis*, garden sage
22. *Poterium sanguisorba*, salad burnet
23. *Armeria maritima*, white thrift
24. *Foeniculum vulgare*, fennel
25. *Monarda didyma*, bee balm
26. *Satureja hortensis*, summer savory
27. *Levisticum officinale*, lovage
28. *Thymus vulgaris* 'Narrow-leaf French', French thyme
29. *Origanum majorana*, sweet marjoram
30. *Salvia viridis*, annual clary
31. *Lavandula angustifolia*, English lavender
32. *Artemisia absinthium*, absinthe
33. *Ocimum basilicum* 'Purpurascens', purple basil
34. *Thymus praecox* subsp. *arcticus* 'Albus', white creeping thyme
35. *Teucrium chamaedrys*, germander
36. *Hyssopus officinalis*, blue hyssop
37. *Hyssopus officinalis* 'Alba', white hyssop
38. *Hyssopus officinalis* 'Rosea', pink hyssop
39. *Sium sisarum*, skirret
40. *Salvia officinalis* 'Albiflora', white-flowered sage
41. *Dictamnus albus* 'Rubra', pink fraxinella
42. *Ocimum basilicum*, sweet basil
43. *Artemisia dracunculus* var. *sativa*, French tarragon
44. *Sempervivum tectorum*, houseleek
45. *Marrubium vulgare*, horehound
46. *Salvia elegans*, pineapple-scented sage
47. *Thymus* 'Clear Gold', golden thyme
48. *Rosmarinus officinalis*, rosemary
49. *Fragaria vesca* 'Alpine', alpine strawberry
50. *Alchemilla vulgaris*, lady's-mantle
51. *Helleborus orientalis*, Lenten rose
52. *Helleborus niger*, Christmas rose
53. *Lilium candidum*, Madonna lily
54. *Crocus sativus*, saffron crocus
55. *Eranthis hyemalis*, winter aconite
56. *Allium schoenoprasum*, chive
57. *Rosa* 'Tausendschön', climbing rose
58. *Rosa centifolia* 'Muscosa', moss rose
59. *Rosa eglanteria*, eglantine
60. *Rosa chinensis*, China rose
61. *Laurus nobilis*, bay
62. *Buxus sempervirens* 'Suffruticosa', dwarf edging box

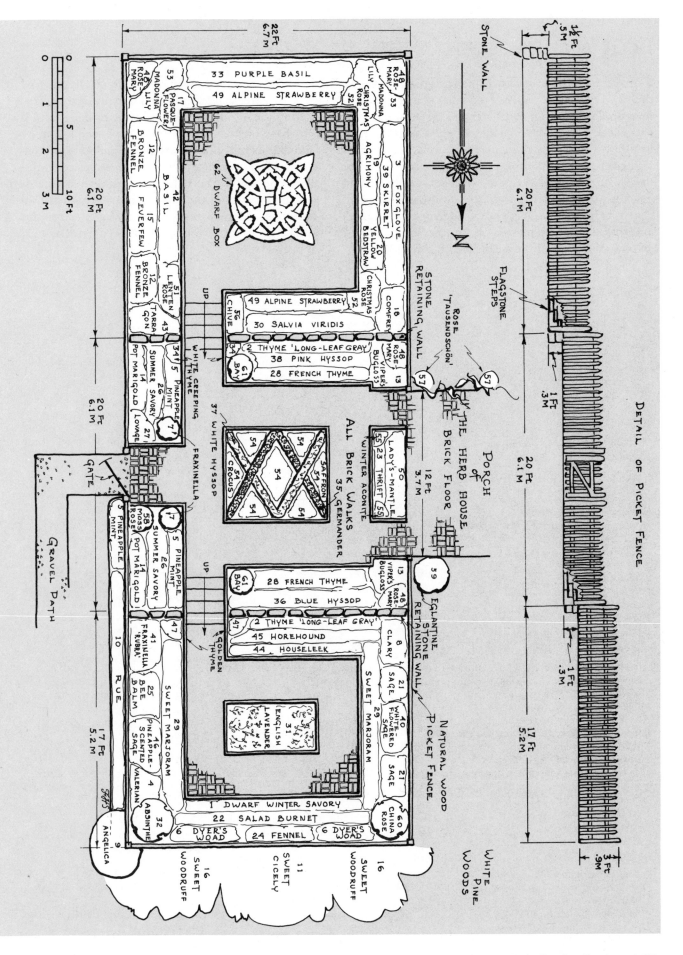

FOR A CITY LOT

To have an herb garden on a smaller city lot may present a challenge. Privacy is a chief concern in a metropolitan setting, and shrubs and trees are used for that advantage here. However, the size of the lot prohibits using only these for that purpose, and so a white board fence completes the enclosure. There is variety in this plan, even though space is limited. Old brick is used for paths to add its warmth of color and charm. The herb beds are raised and edged with brick and further edged with diverse trimmed herbs. Varying the treatment of the areas on each side of the central walk adds greatly to the interest in this garden. The trees and shrubs add dimensional contrast. Thought needs to be given to their pruning, and the shagbark hickory, *Carya ovata*, may need lower branches removed to allow more sunlight into the garden. Thymes in variety ease the severe line of grass and walk. The Baltic ivy makes an arc that softens the severity of the squares and rectangles of the herb beds. Many ideas quite easily adapted to other situations are to be found in this herb garden of great appeal.

Pennsylvania

William C. Paxton, Landscape Architect

BED I

Artemisia absinthium, absinthe
Salvia officinalis, garden sage
Artemisia dracunculus var. *sativa*, French tarragon
Ocimum basilicum, sweet basil
Satureja montana, winter savory
Borago officinalis, borage
Poterium sanguisorba, salad burnet
Allium pulchellum
Allium neapolitanum, daffodil garlic
Buxus sempervirens, box

BED II

Santolina chamaecyparissus, gray santolina
Santolina virens, green santolina
Santolina pinnata
Rosmarinus officinalis, rosemary
Aloysia triphylla, lemon verbena
Lavandula angustifolia subsp. *angustifolia* 'Hidcote', lavender
Lavandula dentata, French lavender
Mentha × *piperita* var. *citrata*, orange mint
Linum usitatissimum, flax
Ruta graveolens, rue
Salvia sclarea, clary

BED III

Teucrium chamaedrys, germander
Agastache foeniculum, anise hyssop
Artemisia camphorata, camphor-scented wormwood
Nepeta mussinii, catmint
Hyssopus officinalis, blue hyssop

Galium verum, yellow bedstraw
Symphytum officinale, comfrey
Marrubium vulgare, horehound

BED IV

Petroselinum crispum, parsley
Monarda didyma, bee balm
Narcissus in variety
Hedera helix, English ivy
Buxus sempervirens, box
Carya ovata, shagbark hickory

BED V

Primula veris, cowslip
Anchusa officinalis, bugloss
Aloe barbadensis, aloe
Asarum canadense, wild ginger
Galium odoratum, sweet woodruff
Adiantum pedatum, maidenhair fern
Buxus sempervirens, box
Cornus florida, dogwood

BED VI

Thymus 'Clear Gold', golden thyme
Thymus herba-barona, caraway thyme
Thymus 'Argenteus', silver thyme
Thymus × *citriodorus*, lemon thyme

BED VII

Stachys byzantina, lamb's-ears
Stachys officinalis, betony
Baptisia australis, blue false indigo
Isatis tinctoria, dyer's woad
Mentha suaveolens, apple mint
Mentha spicata 'Crispii', crisp-leaved spearmint
Mentha × *gentilis*, red mint
Saponaria officinalis, bouncing Bet

BED VIII

Fragaria 'Baron von Solemacher', alpine strawberry
Pelargonium in variety, scented-leaf geranium
Calendula officinalis, pot marigold
Perilla frutescens, perilla
Artemisia schmidtiana, wormwood

BED IX

Myrrhis odorata, sweet cicely
Ajuga reptans, carpet bugleweed
Allium schoenoprasum, chive
Ilex opaca, American holly

BED X

Angelica archangelica, angelica
Mondarda didyma, bee balm
Melissa officinalis, lemon balm
Aconitum napellus, monkshood
Asclepias tuberosa, butterfly weed
Dictamnus albus, fraxinella
Valeriana officinalis, valerian
Rosa damascena, damask rose

BED XI

Chrysanthemum parthenium, feverfew
Chrysanthemum balsamita, costmary
Eupatorium rugosum, white snakeroot
Rosa centifolia, cabbage rose

UNDER HEMLOCK

Osmunda cinnamomea, cinnamon fern
Sanguinaria canadensis, bloodroot
Helleborus foetidus
Arisaema triphyllum, jack-in-the-pulpit
Arisaema triphyllum subsp. *stewardsonii*, jack-in-the-pulpit
Hedera helix 'Baltica', Baltic ivy
Tsuga canadensis, Canada hemlock

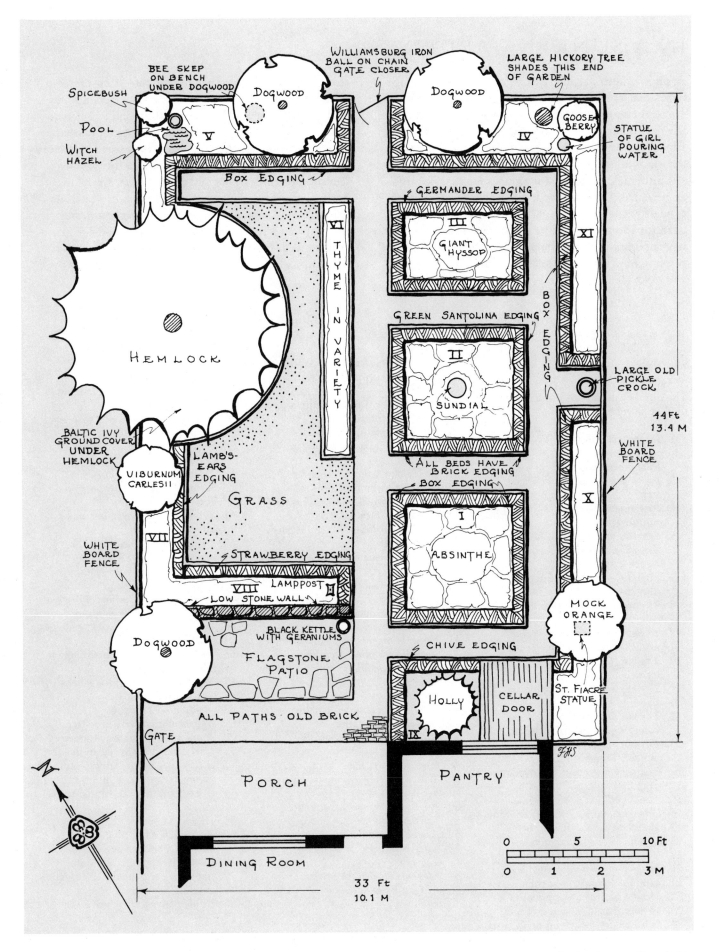

SPICEBUSH

BEE SKEP ON BENCH UNDER DOGWOOD

POOL

WITCH HAZEL

DOGWOOD

WILLIAMSBURG IRON BALL ON CHAIN GATE CLOSER

DOGWOOD

LARGE HICKORY TREE SHADES THIS END OF GARDEN

GOOSE BERRY

STATUE OF GIRL POURING WATER

V

BOX EDGING

GERMANDER EDGING

III

GIANT HYSSOP

XI

VI

THYME IN VARIETY

GREEN SANTOLINA EDGING

II

SUNDIAL

BOX EDGING

HEMLOCK

LARGE OLD PICKLE CROCK

BALTIC IVY GROUND COVER UNDER HEMLOCK

VIBURNUM CARLESII

LAMB'S-EARS EDGING

GRASS

ALL BEDS HAVE BRICK EDGING

BOX EDGING

WHITE BOARD FENCE

X

WHITE BOARD FENCE

VII

STRAWBERRY EDGING

I

ABSINTHE

VIII

LOW STONE WALL

LAMPPOST

XII

BLACK KETTLE WITH GERANIUMS

DOGWOOD

FLAGSTONE PATIO

CHIVE EDGING

MOCK ORANGE

ALL PATHS OLD BRICK

HOLLY

CELLAR DOOR

ST. FIACRE STATUE

GATE

IX

FHS

N

PORCH

PANTRY

DINING ROOM

33 Ft
10.1 M

44 Ft
13.4 M

0   5   10 Ft

0   1   2   3 M

IN A SUNKEN GARDEN

A sunken herb garden? It is an unlikely situation for herbs that are known to require good drainage if they are to thrive. However, this excavation, first intended for the construction of a cottage, is on a sandy knoll. Embraced on three sides by the slope resulting from the excavating, it is open on the side facing the house. An informal, unplanned look was desired. For this appearance, a plan is needed as much as for any other type of garden. So this garden was planned with regard for the casual outline the slope created, and lack of constraint dictated the paths and beds. A clump of birch here, a dipping pool there, and random river-

stone paths work together to generate an impression of pleasing informality. The sloped sides enclose the herb garden and add interest with varied plant material in a range of foliage and texture. A singular statue of St. Francis—less than life-size—was correctly placed in a rustic niche on a post to serve as a focal point. Ceramic plant markers add their appeal, too. This herb garden is a good example of what can be done using imagination and ingenuity to create a design when given a set of unusual and unplanned-for circumstances. It could be called an herb garden of serendipity.

Ontario

Designed by Owner

The number in each planting area is the key number.

1. *Rosmarinus officinalis* 'Prostratus', prostrate rosemary
2. *Ruta graveolens*, rue
3. *Iris* × *germanica* var. *florentina*, orris
4. *Artemisia schmidtiana* 'Nana', silver mound artemisia
5. *Sempervivum tectorum*, houseleek
6. *Artemisia dracunculus* var. *sativa*, French tarragon
7. *Thymus* 'Broad-leaf English', English thyme
8. *Thymus* × *citriodorus*, lemon thyme
9. *Thymus praecox* subsp. *arcticus*, mother-of-thyme
10. *Thymus* 'Clear Gold', golden thyme
11. *Thymus herba-barona*, caraway thyme
12. *Thymus praecox* subsp. *arcticus* 'Lanuginosus', woolly thyme
13. *Thymus vulgaris* 'Narrow-leaf French', French thyme
14. *Glechoma hederacea*, gill-over-the-ground
15. *Althaea officinalis*, marsh mallow
16. *Origanum vulgare*, wild marjoram
17. *Melissa officinalis*, lemon balm
18. *Mentha spicata*, spearmint
19. *Mentha pulegium*, pennyroyal
20. *Mentha* × *piperita*, peppermint
21. *Mentha* × *gentilis*, red mint
22. *Mentha suaveolens*, apple mint
23. *Mentha* 'Eau de Cologne', mint
24. *Monarda fistulosa*, wild bergamot
25. *Teucrium canadense*, germander
26. *Lavandula angustifolia*, English lavender
27. *Viola tricolor*, Johnny-jump-up
28. *Armeria maritima*, thrift
29. *Salvia officinalis*, garden sage
30. *Santolina chamaecyparissus*, gray santolina
31. *Consolida orientalis*, larkspur
32. *Anethum graveolens*, dill
33. *Satureja hortensis*, summer savory
34. *Ocimum basilicum*, sweet basil
35. *Ocimum basilicum* 'Purpurascens', purple basil
36. *Origanum majorana*, sweet marjoram
37. *Coriandrum sativum*, coriander
38. *Hyssopus officinalis*, blue hyssop
39. *Origanum onites*, pot marjoram
40. *Anthriscus cerefolium*, chervil
41. *Poterium sanguisorba*, salad burnet
42. *Digitalis purpurea*, foxglove
43. *Digitalis grandiflora*, yellow foxglove
44. *Myrrhis odorata*, sweet cicely
45. *Petroselinum crispum*, parsley
46. *Nepeta cataria*, catnip
47. *Artemisia abrotanum*, southernwood
48. *Levisticum officinale*, lovage
49. *Tanacetum vulgare* var. *crispum*, fern-leaf tansy
50. *Angelica archangelica*, angelica
51. *Valeriana officinalis*, valerian
52. *Achillea tomentosa*, woolly yarrow
53. *Chrysanthemum parthenium*, feverfew
54. *Monarda didyma*, bee balm
55. *Chrysanthemum balsamita*, costmary
56. *Pulmonaria officinalis*, blue lungwort
57. *Salvia elegans*, pineapple-scented sage
58. *Pelargonium graveolens*, rose geranium
59. *Pelargonium crispum*, lemon geranium
60. *Pelargonium* × *domesticum* 'Clorinda', eucalyptus-scented geranium
61. *Pelargonium quercifolium*, oak-leaved geranium
62. *Pelargonium odoratissimum*, apple geranium
63. *Pelargonium graveolens* 'Rober's Lemon Rose', rose geranium
64. *Pelargonium* × *citrosum* 'Prince of Orange', orange geranium
65. *Pelargonium denticulatum*, pine geranium
66. *Pelargonium tomentosum*, peppermint geranium
67. *Pelargonium* 'Concolor Filbert', filbert geranium
68. *Vinca minor*, myrtle
69. *Marrubium vulgare*, horehound
70. *Ajuga reptans*, carpet bugleweed
71. *Chelidonium majus*, celandine
72. *Stachys byzantina*, lamb's-ears
73. *Satureja montana*, winter savory
74. *Convallaria majalis*, lily-of-the-valley
75. *Allium flavum*
76. *Allium schoenoprasum*, chive
77. *Urginea maritima*, sea onion
78. *Rosa* 'Merry England', rose
79. *Juniperus horizontalis* 'Bar Harbor', creeping juniper
80. *Betula papyrifera*, white birch

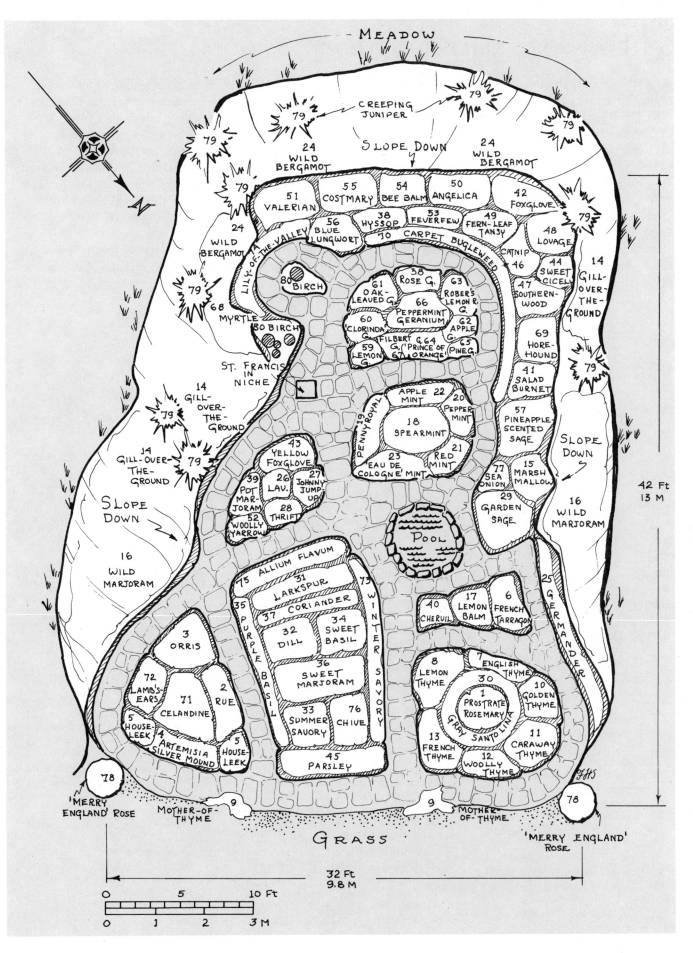

FOR AN 1850 SMOKEHOUSE

If a smokehouse doesn't exist, perhaps a gazebo or other structure could be built and an herb garden related to it—placed in the sun for advantage. Foundation stone, the same as the smokehouse construction, is used for the wall, handsomely enclosing the herb garden. Interest is created by varying the outline of the walk of flagstones with brick and by edging it. A niche across from the smokehouse balances the entrance path to it and expands the entrance to the garden. Four large rosemary plants emphasize it nicely. The area devoted to a walkway is generous here, made so by enlarging it to nearly forty-nine square feet as it changes direction. A boxlike effect is avoided by cutting the inside corner diagonally. Edging of the beds adds to the air of roominess as thyme and Corsican mint place the dwarf edging box farther from the walk. A small plum tree provides light shade for herbs needing it, and an English hawthorn features the entrance without dominating it. Some of the more invasive herbs are prudently located outside the herb garden enclosure. They are clustered around the smokehouse, making it more a part of the herb garden. Because of the edging box, the accents of the six large box, and the two small trees, there is appealing design to enjoy even in the months of winter dormancy.

Ohio

Elsetta Gilchrist Barnes, Landscape Architect, A.S.L.A.

The number in each planting area is the key number.

1. *Origanum majorana*, sweet marjoram
2. *Rosmarinus officinalis*, rosemary
3. *Asarum europaeum*, European ginger
4. *Dictamnus albus*, fraxinella
5. *Pelargonium graveolens*, rose geranium in pots
6. *Lavandula angustifolia*, English lavender
7. *Symphytum officinale*, white comfrey
8. *Ocimum basilicum* 'Purpurascens', purple basil
9. *Satureja hortensis*, summer savory
10. *Ocimum basilicum*, sweet basil
11. *Tanacetum vulgare* var. *crispum*, fern-leaf tansy
12. *Chrysanthemum balsamita*, costmary
13. *Monarda didyma*, bee balm
14. *Ocimum basilicum* 'Citriodorum', lemon basil
15. *Hyssopus officinalis* 'Alba', white hyssop
16. *Ocimum basilicum* 'Minimum', bush basil
17. *Mentha requienii*, Corsican mint
18. *Melissa officinalis*, lemon balm
19. *Angelica archangelica*, angelica
20. *Aloysia triphylla*, lemon verbena
21. *Galium odoratum*, sweet woodruff
22. *Alchemilla vulgaris*, lady's-mantle
23. *Mentha spicata* 'Crispata', curly mint
24. *Artemisia dracunculus* var. *sativa*, French tarragon
25. *Mentha* × *piperita*, peppermint
26. *Satureja montana*, winter savory
27. *Artemisia frigida*, fringed wormwood
28. *Digitalis purpurea* 'Alba', white foxglove
29. *Myrrhis odorata*, sweet cicely
30. *Levisticum officinale*, lovage
31. *Artemisia abrotanum*, southernwood
32. *Mentha spicata*, spearmint
33. *Mentha suaveolens* 'Variegata', pineapple mint
34. *Mentha* × *piperita* var. *citrata*, orange mint
35. *Pulmonaria officinalis*, blue lungwort
36. *Thymus* 'Broad-leaf English', English thyme
37. *Viola tricolor*, Johnny-jump-up
38. *Viola cornuta* 'Alba', horned violet
39. *Allium schoenoprasum*, chive
40. *Allium giganteum*, ornamental onion
41. *Lilium candidum*, Madonna lily
42. *Fritillaria imperialis*, crown-imperial
43. *Crocus*, species in variety
44. *Clematis lanuginosa* 'Alba', white clematis
45. *Buxus sempervirens* 'Suffruticosa', dwarf edging box
46. *Buxus sempervirens*, box
47. *Prunus domestica*, plum
48. *Crataegus laevigata*, English hawthorn

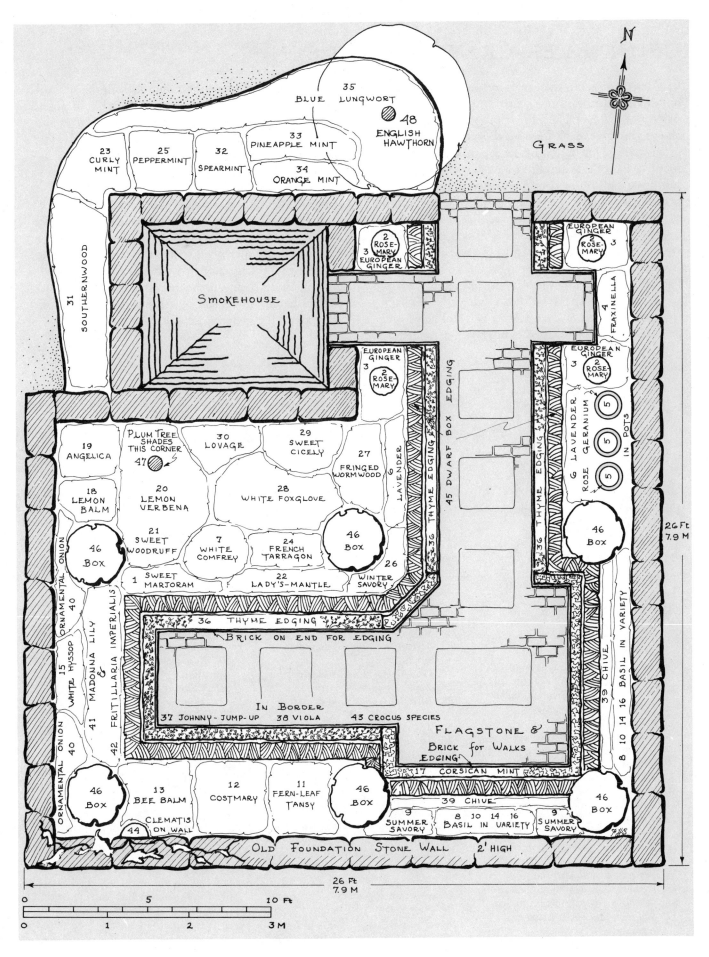

N

GRASS

35
BLUE LUNGWORT

48
ENGLISH HAWTHORN

23 CURLY MINT
25 PEPPERMINT
32 SPEARMINT
33 PINEAPPLE MINT
34 ORANGE MINT

SMOKEHOUSE

31 SOUTHERNWOOD

2 ROSE-MARY
3 EUROPEAN GINGER

EUROPEAN GINGER
2 ROSE-MARY
3

EUROPEAN GINGER
3
2 ROSE-MARY

4 FRAXINELLA

EUROPEAN GINGER
3
2 ROSE-MARY

3 EUROPEAN GINGER
2 ROSE-MARY

45 DWARF BOX EDGING

36 THYME EDGING

36 THYME EDGING

6 LAVENDER
ROSE GERANIUM
5
5
5
IN POTS

19 ANGELICA

PLUM TREE SHADES THIS CORNER
47

30 LOVAGE

29 SWEET CICELY

27 FRINGED WORMWOOD

18 LEMON BALM

20 LEMON VERBENA

28 WHITE FOXGLOVE

6 LAVENDER

46 BOX

46 BOX

21 SWEET WOODRUFF

7 WHITE COMFREY

24 FRENCH TARRAGON

46 BOX

26 WINTER SAVORY

46 BOX

26 Ft 7.9 M

1 SWEET MARJORAM
22 LADY'S-MANTLE

36 THYME EDGING

BRICK ON END FOR EDGING

IN BORDER

37 JOHNNY-JUMP-UP   38 VIOLA   43 CROCUS SPECIES

FLAGSTONE & BRICK FOR WALKS EDGING

17 CORSICAN MINT

39 CHIVE

8 10 14 16 BASIL IN VARIETY

15 WHITE HYSSOP
40 ORNAMENTAL ONION
41 MADONNA LILY &
42 FRITILLARIA IMPERIALIS

46 BOX

13 BEE BALM

12 COSTMARY

11 FERN-LEAF TANSY

46 BOX

39 CHIVE

46 BOX

44 CLEMATIS ON WALL

9 SUMMER SAVORY

8 10 14 16 BASIL IN VARIETY

9 SUMMER SAVORY

OLD FOUNDATION STONE WALL 2' HIGH

26 Ft 7.9 M

0   5   10 Ft
0   1   2   3 M

USING EVER-GRAY, EVER-GREEN

In a departure from the usual, this kitchen entrance is not devoted primarily to culinary herbs. Instead, a palette of the purple of *Heliotropium*, pink of *Dianthus*, and lavender of *Lavandula* with foliage of grays and greens highlights its asymmetrical treatment. Balance is achieved in the ever-green garden with two millstones circled with a variety of appropriate plantings. Stepping stones allow access to millstones in each plan and are compatible with the entrance walk and porch paving. This is true also of the stone curbing, a soil retainer. Low-growing, creeping thymes in variety soften the rigid line of the curbing and effect a widening of the walk, although it is ample at four feet. The dwarf box edging thus set back from the entrance walk still accents it and helps to enclose the gardens. The dipping bowl, arranged for convenience with a trough filling it from the sill cock, is especially useful when there are a number of potted plants to be watered. Plant stands are half-circles and with the round millstones relieve the rectangular shapes in the plan. Bayberry makes a splendid background for the ever-green garden. This hedge, the dwarf box edging, two specimen shrubs, and millstones contribute to a design of appeal in winter, too. The Christmas rose in a more protected spot near the house and the witch hazel afford blooms during the seasons when other plant material is dormant. Either of these two plans could be used alone for a smaller garden. Noteworthy is the intensive use of space, accomplished by interplantings that make the most of and extend the growing season.

Ohio

Elsetta Gilchrist Barnes, Landscape Architect, A.S.L.A.

The number in each planting area is the key number.

1. *Santolina chamaecyparissus*, gray santolina
2. *Salvia officinalis*, dwarf garden sage
3. *Dianthus gratianopolitanus* 'Nanus Compactus', cheddar pink
4. *Ruta graveolens* 'Blue Beauty', rue
5. *Lavandula angustifolia* subsp. *angustifolia* 'Nana', dwarf lavender
6. *Origanum majorana*, sweet marjoram
7. *Stachys byzantina*, lamb's-ears
8. *Thymus doerfleri*, thyme
9. *Thymus praecox* subsp. *arcticus* 'Albus', white creeping thyme
10. *Borago officinalis*, borage
11. *Salvia sclarea*, clary
12. *Thymus × citriodorus*, lemon thyme
13. *Thymus praecox* subsp. *arcticus* 'Lanuginosus', woolly thyme
14. *Nepeta mussinii*, catmint
15. *Heliotropium arborescens*, heliotrope
16. *Santolina virens*, green santolina
17. *Teucrium canadense*, American germander
18. *Satureja montana*, winter savory
19. *Dianthus plumarius* 'Essex witch', cottage pink
20. *Thymus* 'Clear Gold', golden thyme
21. *Hyssopus officinalis* 'Albus', white hyssop
22. *Digitalis purpurea* 'Alba', foxglove
23. *Dicentra spectabilis*, bleeding heart
24. *Digitalis grandiflora*, yellow foxglove
25. *Mertensia virginica*, Virginia bluebells
26. *Ocimum basilicum*, sweet basil
27. *Mentha spicata*, spearmint
28. *Mentha × piperita* var. *citrata*, orange mint
29. *Mentha × piperita*, peppermint
30. *Levisticum officinale*, lovage
31. *Angelica archangelica*, angelica
32. *Helleborus niger*, Christmas rose
33. *Helleborus lividus* subsp. *corsicus*
34. *Galium odoratum*, sweet woodruff
35. *Cimicifuga racemosa*, black cohosh
36. *Convallaria majalis*, lily-of-the-valley
37. *Thymus herba-barona*, caraway thyme
38. *Rosmarinus officinalis* 'Prostratus', prostrate rosemary
39. *Aloysia triphylla*, lemon verbena
40. *Pelargonium* in variety, scented-leaf geranium
41. *Pelargonium* in variety, scented-leaf dwarf geranium
42. *Lilium candidum*, Madonna lily
43. *Sternbergia lutea*, winter daffodil
44. *Crocus speciosus* 'Albus', crocus
45. *Crocus tomasinianus*, crocus
46. *Crocus speciosus*, crocus
47. *Crocus kotschyanus*, crocus
48. *Crocus angustifolius*, crocus
49. *Tulipa clusiana*, tulip
50. *Tulipa kaufmanniana*, water-lily tulip
51. *Allium rosenbachianum*
52. *Allium giganteum*
53. *Allium karataviense*
54. *Allium christophii*, stars-of-Persia
55. *Galanthus nivalis*, snowdrop
56. *Anemone blanda*, windflower
57. *Endymion hispanicus* 'Alba', Spanish bluebell
58. *Narcissus triandrus* var. *albus*, angel's-tears
59. *Narcissus asturiensis*, miniature daffodil
60. *Leucojum aestivum*, snowflake
61. *Myrica pensylvanica*, bayberry
62. *Hamamelis virginiana*, witch hazel
63. *Buxus sempervirens* 'Suffruticosa', dwarf edging box

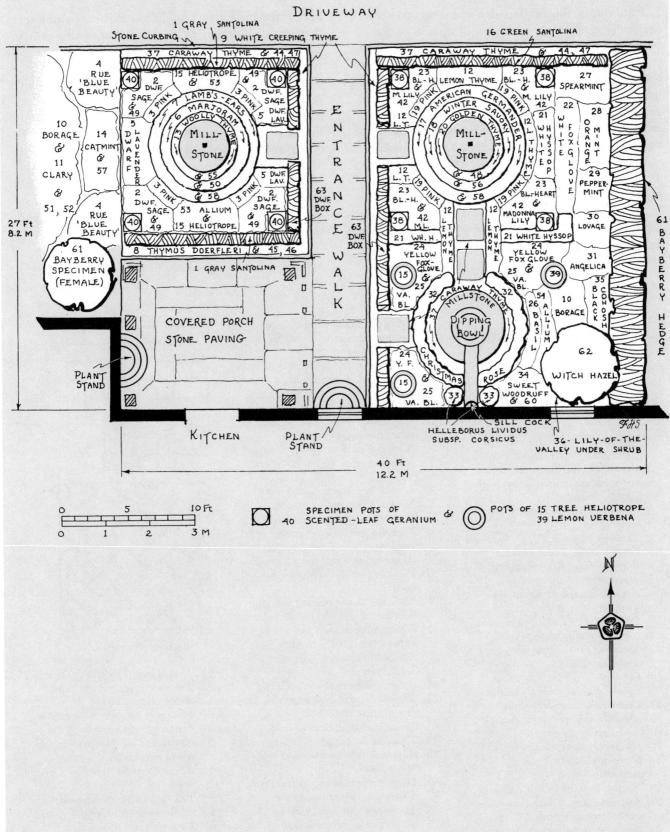

WITH A BRICK TERRACE

Uncommonly, this herb garden was designed before the house was built. There were blueprints of the house at hand to assure the proper relationship of plan to house. The results have been most satisfying. First, the site was given an eastern exposure so that daylong use is comfortable. Morning sun warms it early; late afternoon heat is tempered by shade from the house and the Washington hawthorn. Second, enclosing the garden with a yew hedge three feet high created an outdoor room and afforded a surprise for newcomers. The garden's existence is not obvious until the visitor has nearly reached the front entrance of the house. Views of the herb garden from the expanse of windows of the kitchen and the dining room are enjoyed in all seasons. Edging material creates "boxes" that border the brick terrace. The succession plantings in these provide masses of color for the growing season. The brick pattern of the terrace is herringbone, its pattern not apparent because the side of the brick is laid square with the edges of the planting beds. This is an optical illusion demonstrated below. Herbs can be tended or harvested any time, for the brick paving makes the garden accessible soon after a shower. Accent plants are used to extend the months of visibility of the design. Fruiting shrubs and trees for this area and the remainder of the grounds were selected with birds in mind. This is an altogether pleasing and serviceable herb garden, very livable and profoundly satisfying.

Ohio

Lucile Teeter Kissack, Landscape Architect, A.S.L.A.

The number in each planting area is the key number.

1. *Thymus × citriodorus*, lemon thyme
2. *Thymus praecox* subsp. *arcticus* 'Lanuginosus', woolly thyme
3. *Ocimum basilicum*, sweet basil
4. *Artemisia absinthium* 'Lambrook Silver', absinthe
5. *Origanum heracleoticum*, Greek oregano
6. *Digitalis purpurea* 'Alba', foxglove
7. *Viola odorata*, sweet violet
8. *Fragaria vesca* 'Rugen', alpine strawberry
9. *Lavandula angustifolia*, English lavender
10. *Dianthus × allwoodii*, pink
11. *Lobelia siphilitica*, great lobelia
12. *Santolina chamaecyparissus*, gray santolina
13. *Lobularia maritima* 'Carpet of Snow', dwarf sweet alyssum
14. *Levisticum officinale*, lovage
15. *Monarda didyma* 'Snow White', bee balm
16. *Dictamnus albus*, fraxinella
17. *Origanum majorana*, sweet marjoram
18. *Hyssopus officinalis*, blue hyssop
19. *Artemisia camphorata*, camphor-scented wormwood
20. *Santolina virens*, green santolina
21. *Salvia sclarea*, clary
22. *Ruta graveolens* 'Blue Beauty', rue
23. *Salvia officinalis*, garden sage
24. *Artemisia dracunculus* var. *sativa*, French tarragon
25. *Artemisia lactiflora*, white mugwort
26. *Tagetes* 'Lulu', marigold
27. *Asclepias tuberosa*, butterfly weed
28. *Galium mollugo*, white bedstraw
29. *Tropaeolum minus*, pale yellow dwarf nasturtium
30. *Aloysia triphylla*, lemon verbena
31. *Nicotiana alata* 'Green Sherbert', green nicotiana
32. *Stachys byzantina*, lamb's-ears
33. *Nepeta × faassenii*, catmint
34. *Rosmarinus officinalis*, rosemary
35. *Digitalis grandiflora*, yellow foxglove
36. *Aconitum napellus*, monkshood
37. *Viola cornuta* 'Scottish Yellow', viola
38. *Nicotiana alata* 'Affinis', white nicotiana
39. *Petroselinum crispum* var. *crispum* 'Paramount', curly parsley
40. *Achillea filipendula* 'Coronation Gold', yarrow
41. *Apium graveolens*, wild celery
42. *Thymus* 'Broad-leaf English', English thyme
43. *Crocus sieberi*, crocus
44. *Tulipa tarda*, tulip
45. *Allium ampeloprasum*, Porrum Group, leek
46. *Allium neapolitanum*, daffodil garlic
47. *Allium schoenoprasum*, chive
48. *Allium senescens* var. *glaucum*
49. *Ipomoea alba*, moonflower
50. *Clematis* 'Mrs. Robert Brydon', clematis

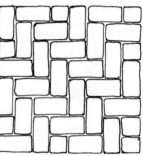

Herringbone brick patterns

51. *Hedera helix* 'Baltica', Baltic ivy
52. *Ribes sativum*, red currant
53. *Viburnum plicatum*
54. *Sambucus canadensis* 'Acutiloba', American elderberry
55. *Rhododendron* 'Marie's Choice', white evergreen azalea
56. *Taxus × media* 'Kelseyi', upright yew
57. *Ilex opaca*, American holly
58. *Malus hupehensis*, crab
59. *Cornus florida*, dogwood
60. *Crataegus phaenopyrum*, Washington hawthorn

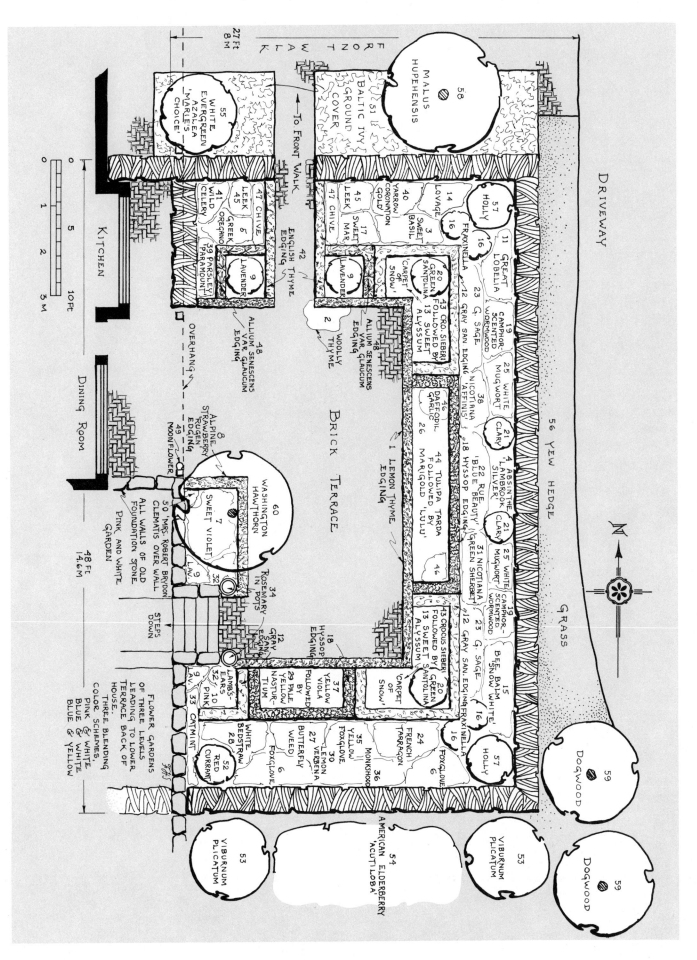

A TOUCH OF FORMALITY

IN OCTAGONAL FORM

It may have been a natural impulse to repeat pleasing lines that prompted the re-creation of the octagonal form of the toolhouse in the design of this garden of herbs. Or it may have been done in lieu of relating the garden directly to the toolhouse or some other structure. A birdbath of copper, an impression of Sol in it, repeats again the octagonal form. A variation of sunburst brick pattern makes an interesting walk circling the focal point and shows how different brick patterns can meet in a pleasing fashion. The four herb beds, created by the four brick paths of basket-weave pattern, are raised with bricks on edge. Well-drained as they are, these beds situated in full sun provide an abundance of herbs for many uses, even though the growing area is not extensive. A perennial border and shrubs and small trees afford a feeling of enclosure while located at a discreet distance. The design plan illustrates how an herb garden placed in full sun and away from a structure can be made to give an illusion of being related. Repetition of the toolhouse form and the slate walk leading from that structure to the herb garden help give that impression.

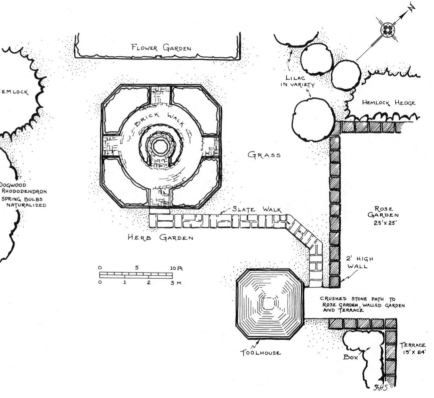

Design plan of herb garden area

Pennsylvania

Joan E. Semple, Landscape Architect

The number in each planting area is the key number.

1. *Thymus* 'Broad-leaf English', English thyme
2. *Stachys byzantina*, lamb's-ears
3. *Anethum graveolens*, dill
4. *Artemisia abrotanum*, southernwood
5. *Artemisia absinthium*, absinthe
6. *Artemisia dracunculus* var. *sativa*, French tarragon
7. *Artemisia schmidtiana* 'Nana', silver mound artemisia
8. *Galium odoratum*, sweet woodruff
9. *Dianthus caryophyllus* 'Snowflake', clove pink
10. *Heliotropium arborescens*, heliotrope
11. *Lavandula dentata*, French lavender
12. *Lavandula angustifolia* subsp. *angustifolia*, lavender
13. *Lavandula angustifolia*, English lavender
14. *Lavandula angustifolia* subsp. *angustifolia* 'Munstead', lavender
15. *Aloysia triphylla*, lemon verbena
16. *Marrubium vulgare*, horehound
17. *Mentha spicata* 'Crispii', curly mint
18. *Mentha × piperita*, peppermint
19. *Mentha spicata*, spearmint
20. *Nepeta mussinii*, catmint
21. *Ocimum basilicum*, sweet basil
22. *Ocimum basilicum* 'Minimum', bush basil
23. *Ocimum basilicum* 'Purpurascens', purple basil

24. *Thymus × citriodorus*, lemon thyme
25. *Pelargonium × citrosum* 'Prince of Orange', orange geranium
26. *Pelargonium crispum*, lemon geranium
27. *Pelargonium denticulatum*, pine geranium
28. *Pelargonium graveolens*, rose geranium
29. *Pelargonium odoratissimum*, apple geranium
30. *Pelargonium tomentosum*, peppermint geranium
31. *Petroselinum crispum* var. *crispum*, curly parsley
32. *Rosmarinus officinalis*, rosemary

33. *Rosmarinus officinalis* 'Prostratus', prostrate rosemary
34. *Ruta graveolens*, rue
35. *Salvia officinalis* 'Purpurea', purple variegated garden sage
36. *Salvia officinalis* 'Tricolor', variegated garden sage
37. *Salvia officinalis*, golden variegated garden sage
38. *Salvia sclarea*, clary
39. *Poterium sanguisorba*, salad burnet
40. *Santolina chamaecyparissus*, gray santolina
41. *Thymus praecox* subsp. *arcticus* 'Albus', white creeping thyme
42. *Allium schoenoprasum*, chive
43. *Allium tuberosum*, garlic chive

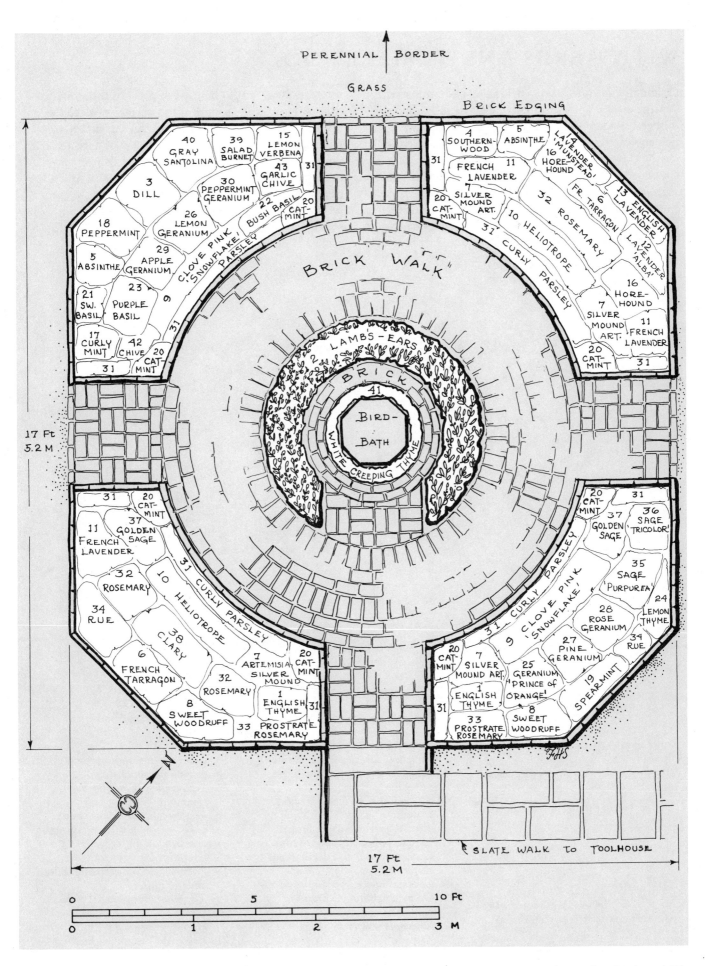

PERENNIAL | BORDER

GRASS

BRICK EDGING

40 GRAY SANTOLINA · 39 SALAD BURNET · 15 LEMON VERBENA · 43 GARLIC CHIVE · 31 · 4 SOUTHERN-WOOD · 5 ABSINTHE · LAVENDER 'MUNSTEAD' · 31 · FRENCH LAVENDER · 11 · 16 HORE-HOUND · 13 ENGLISH LAVENDER · 3 DILL · 30 PEPPERMINT GERANIUM · 22 BUSH BASIL · 20 CAT-MINT · 7 SILVER MOUND ART. · FR. TARRAGON 6 · 12 LAVENDER 'ALBA' · 18 PEPPERMINT · 26 LEMON GERANIUM · CLOVE PINK 'SNOWFLAKE' · 20 CAT-MINT · 32 ROSEMARY · 10 HELIOTROPE · 16 HOREHOUND · 5 ABSINTHE · 29 APPLE GERANIUM · PARSLEY · 31 CURLY PARSLEY · 21 SW. BASIL · 23 PURPLE BASIL · 9 · 31 · 7 SILVER MOUND ART. · 11 FRENCH LAVENDER · 17 CURLY MINT · 42 CHIVE · 20 CAT-MINT · 20 CAT-MINT · 31 · 31

17 Ft 5.2 M

BRICK WALK

LAMBS-EARS

BRICK

41 BIRD-BATH

WHITE CREEPING THYME

31 · 20 CAT-MINT · 11 FRENCH LAVENDER · 37 GOLDEN SAGE · 32 ROSEMARY · 10 HELIOTROPE · 31 CURLY PARSLEY · 34 RUE · 38 CLARY · 7 ARTEMISIA SILVER MOUND · 20 CAT-MINT · 6 FRENCH TARRAGON · 32 ROSEMARY · 1 ENGLISH THYME · 31 · 8 SWEET WOODRUFF · 33 PROSTRATE ROSEMARY

20 CAT-MINT · 31 · 37 GOLDEN SAGE · 36 SAGE TRICOLOR · 35 SAGE PURPUREA · 31 CURLY PARSLEY · 9 CLOVE PINK 'SNOWFLAKE' · 28 ROSE GERANIUM · 24 LEMON THYME · 20 CAT-MINT · 7 SILVER MOUND ART. · 25 GERANIUM 'PRINCE OF ORANGE' · 27 PINE GERANIUM · 34 RUE · 1 ENGLISH THYME · 31 · 33 PROSTRATE ROSEMARY · 8 SWEET WOODRUFF · 19 SPEARMINT

FHS

N

SLATE WALK TO TOOLHOUSE

17 Ft 5.2 M

0 · 5 · 10 Ft
0 · 1 · 2 · 3 M

WITH HERBS AND A SMALL POOL

Originally designed for an exhibit at a fair, this strictly symmetrical plan—although small—is full of possibilities for adaptation and substitutions to fit the interests and circumstances of the individual. A suitable fence, a toolhouse, or a garage wall may serve as a background instead of a holly hedge. In a warm climate *Myrtus communis* with a white picket fence could be an alternative. Grindstones may be more easily found than millstones; if neither is available, flagstone or brick could be used—the latter laid in a pattern of interest. Brick could be used in place of the stone for the retaining wall, too. A birdbath may replace the pool. The standards in tubs make an important contribution to the structure of the design. There are a number of plants suitable for such use; lemon verbena, rose geranium, rose, and lantana are a few. One of several cultivars of *Thymus praecox* subsp. *arcticus* would do nicely in the area allowed for grass. This is a symmetrical plan sure to please when a touch of formality is desired for a small herb garden.

Ohio

Elsetta Gilchrist Barnes, Landscape Architect, A.S.L.A.

The number in each planting area is the key number.

1. *Tanacetum vulgare* var. *crispum*, fern-leaf tansy
2. *Lavandula angustifolia* subsp. *angustifolia* 'Munstead', lavender
3. *Aloysia triphylla*, lemon verbena
4. *Artemisia absinthium* 'Lambrook Silver', absinthe
5. *Santolina virens*, green santolina
6. *Santolina chamaecyparissus*, gray santolina
7. *Thymus praecox* subsp. *arcticus* 'Lanuginosus', woolly thyme
8. *Thymus praecox* subsp. *arcticus* 'Albus', white creeping thyme
9. *Ocimum basilicum* 'Purpurascens', purple basil
10. *Chenopodium botrys*, ambrosia
11. *Ocimum basilicum* 'Minimum', bush basil
12. *Origanum majorana*, sweet marjoram
13. *Chamaemelum nobile*, chamomile
14. *Rosmarinus officinalis*, rosemary
15. *Pelargonium × blandfordianum*, geranium
16. *Pelargonium capitatum* 'Attar of Roses', rose-scented geranium
17. *Pelargonium frutetorum*, zonal geranium
18. *Pelargonium × hortorum* 'Jubilee', zonal geranium
19. *Thymus × citriodorus*, lemon thyme
20. *Heliotropium arborescens*, heliotrope
21. *Ilex opaca* 'Rotunda', holly

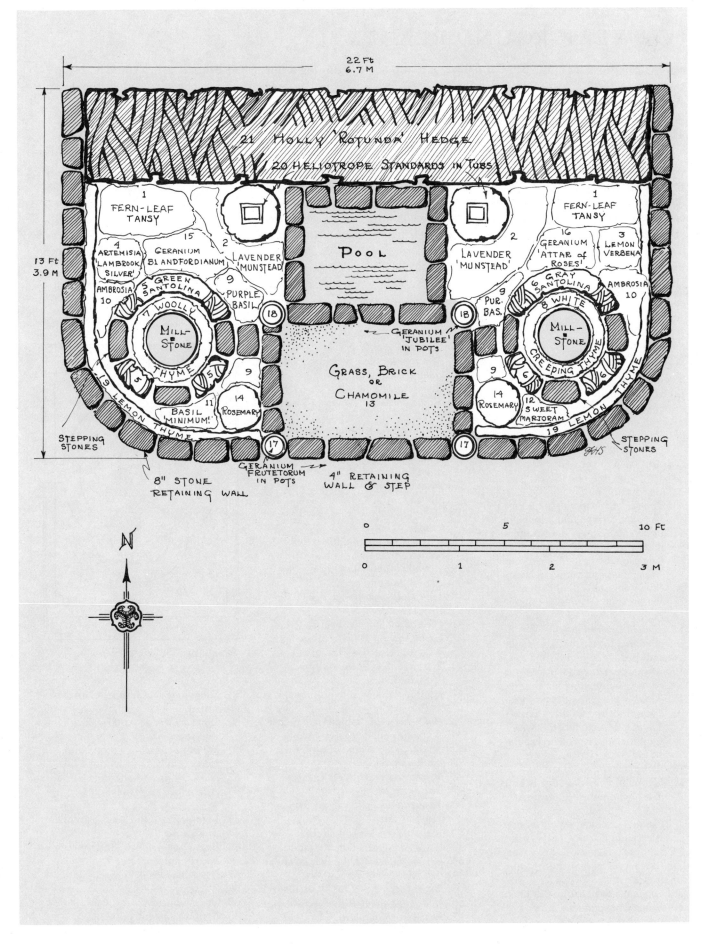

22 Ft
6.7 M

13 Ft
3.9 M

21 HOLLY 'ROTUNDA' HEDGE

20 HELIOTROPE STANDARDS IN TUBS

1 FERN-LEAF TANSY

POOL

2 LAVENDER 'MUNSTEAD'

1 FERN-LEAF TANSY

15

16 GERANIUM 'ATTAR OF ROSES'

3 LEMON VERBENA

4 ARTEMISIA 'LAMBROOK SILVER'

GERANIUM 'BLANDFORDIANUM'

AMBROSIA 10

3 GREEN SANTOLINA

2 LAVENDER 'MUNSTEAD'

9 PUR. BAS.

6 GRAY SANTOLINA

8 WHITE

AMBROSIA 10

7 WOOLLY THYME

PURPLE BASIL

MILL-STONE

18

18

MILL-STONE

CREEPING THYME

19 LEMON THYME

5

5

9

GRASS, BRICK OR CHAMOMILE 13

GERANIUM 'JUBILEE' IN POTS

9

14 SWEET MARJORAM

19 LEMON THYME

11 BASIL 'MINIMUM'

14 ROSEMARY

14 ROSEMARY

12

6

STEPPING STONES

17

17

STEPPING STONES

8" STONE RETAINING WALL

GERANIUM FRUTETORUM IN POTS

4" RETAINING WALL & STEP

N

0   5   10 Ft

0   1   2   3 M

FOR YEAR-ROUND BEAUTY

Specialized interests in medicine and pharmacy influenced the choice of plant material in this herb garden. At times the herbs used in the central circles were varied, but the design itself has endured forty years. The few changes made were effected only after viewing from the window of the barn loft studio. Wise planning relegated the largest and invasive herbs to the borders and cutting gardens. Angelica, mints, artemisias, and coltsfoot are only a few of them. These can easily obliterate a design. While most of the culinary herbs have been planted in the vegetable garden here, spring-flowering bulbs have been used to round out the year's enjoyment of the herb garden. In a cold climate even the rigors of winter contribute beauty, bringing a burnished-bronze cast to some herbs, a deep mauve to others. As the snows melt, the design is clearly traced. The dwarf box frames the focal point, a sundial. Hyssop hedges define the circles. The germander and santolina edgings repeat the pleasing arcs. At first this pleasing shape appears elliptical, but it is developed by constructing three circles as illustrated in the drawing. Not to be overlooked is the unusual brick pattern and the manner in which it is merged with stepping stones used in the central area. Judicious use of shrubs—lilac, box, apothecary's rose, and lavender—for accent gives character to the design. Box and holly enclose it all. It is an herb garden particularly structured for year-round beauty.

Rhode Island

James D. Graham, Landscape Architect

The number in each planting area is the key number.

1. *Santolina virens*, green santolina
2. *Rosmarinus officinalis*, rosemary
3. *Ocimum basilicum* 'Minimum', bush basil
4. *Origanum majorana*, sweet marjoram
5. *Tropaeolum majus*, nasturtium
6. *Dianthus caryophyllus*, clove pink
7. *Pelargonium* in variety, scented-leaf geranium
8. *Chamaemelum nobile*, chamomile
9. *Satureja montana*, winter savory
10. *Stachys byzantina*, lamb's-ears
11. *Artemisia absinthium*, absinthe
12. *Asclepias tuberosa*, butterfly weed
13. *Santolina neapolitana*
14. *Santolina chamaecyparissus*, gray santolina
15. *Thymus praecox* subsp. *arcticus* 'Albus', white creeping thyme
16. *Thymus praecox* subsp. *arcticus* 'Lanuginosus', woolly thyme
17. *Thymus praecox* subsp. *arcticus* 'Coccineus', crimson creeping thyme
18. *Armeria maritima*, thrift
19. *Hyssopus officinalis*, blue hyssop
20. *Teucrium chamaedrys*, germander
21. *Paeonia officinalis*, piney
22. *Galium odoratum*, sweet woodruff
23. *Alchemilla vulgaris*, lady's-mantle
24. *Arisaema dracontium*, green-dragon
25. *Asarum europaeum*, European ginger
26. *Lamium album*, white dead nettle
27. *Pulmonaria officinalis*, blue lungwort
28. *Perilla frutescens*, perilla
29. *Monarda fistulosa*, wild bergamot
30. *Sium sisarum*, skirret
31. *Reseda luteola*, weld
32. *Salvia officinalis* 'Albiflora', garden sage
33. *Sempervivum tectorum*, houseleek
34. *Iris pallida* 'Dalmatica', orris
35. *Lavandula angustifolia*, English lavender
36. *Mentha spicata* 'Crispata', curly mint
37. *Alchemilla alpina*, alpine lady's-mantle
38. *Thymus vulgaris* 'Narrow-leaf French', French thyme
39. *Artemisia camphorata*, camphor-scented wormwood
40. *Lavandula angustifolia* 'Alba', English lavender
41. *Foeniculum vulgare*, bronze fennel
42. *Lavandula angustifolia* subsp. *angustifolia* 'Hidcote', lavender
43. *Symphytum officinale*, white comfrey
44. *Iris* × *germanica* var. *florentina*, orris
45. *Ruta graveolens* 'Blue Beauty', rue
46. *Astrantia major*, masterwort
47. *Artemisia abrotanum* 'Tangerine', southernwood
48. *Myrrhis odorata*, sweet cicely
49. *Sedum telephium*, orpine
50. *Tanacetum vulgare* var. *crispum*, fern-leaf tansy
51. *Valeriana officinalis*, valerian
52. *Origanum onites*, pot marjoram
53. *Lavandula dentata*, French lavender
54. *Isatis tinctoria*, dyer's woad
55. *Helleborus niger*, Christmas rose
56. *Helleborus orientalis*, Lenten rose
57. *Helleborus atrorubens*

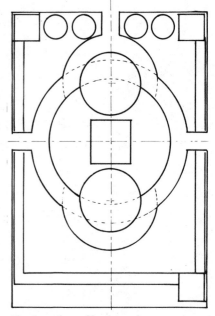

Design plan of herb garden

58. *Sanguisorba canadensis*, Canadian burnet
59. *Chrysanthemum parthenium*, feverfew
60. *Melissa officinalis*, lemon balm
61. *Lilium candidum*, Madonna lily
62. *Narcissus pseudonarcissus*, daffodil
63. *Allium schoenoprasum*, chive
64. *Vitis*, grape
65. *Rosa gallica* 'Officinalis', apothecary's rose
66. *Buxus sempervirens* 'Suffruticosa', dwarf edging box
67. *Buxus sempervirens*, box
68. *Taxus*, yew
69. *Syringa*, lilac
70. *Pyrus communis*, pear

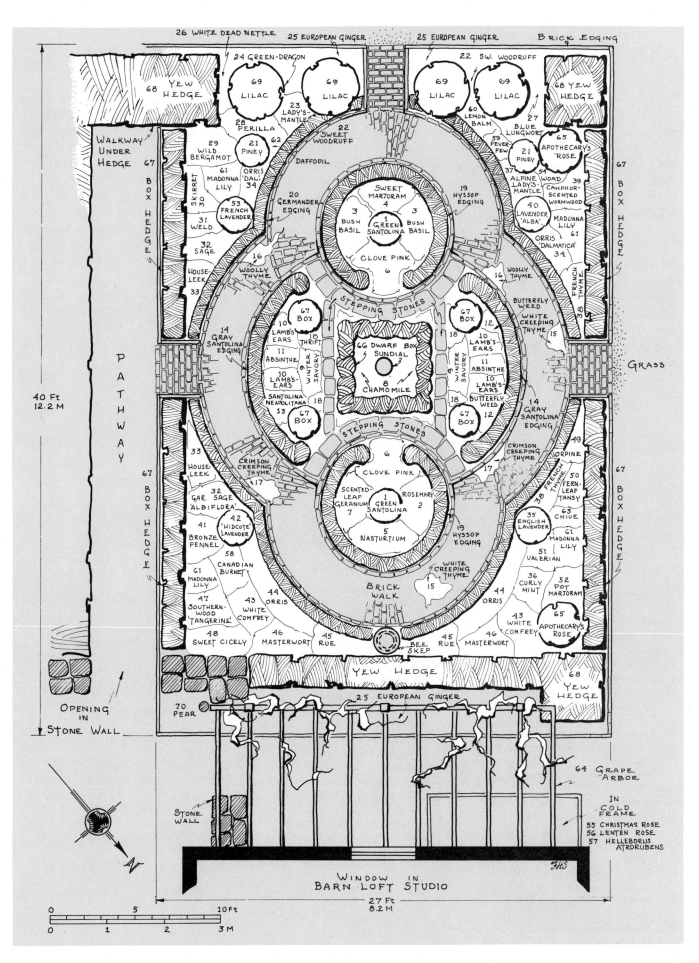

26 WHITE DEAD NETTLE   25 EUROPEAN GINGER   25 EUROPEAN GINGER   BRICK EDGING

68 YEW HEDGE

24 GREEN-DRAGON

69 LILAC   69 LILAC   69 LILAC   69 LILAC

22 SW. WOODRUFF

68 YEW HEDGE

WALKWAY UNDER HEDGE   67

BOX HEDGE

23 LADY'S MANTLE
28 PERILLA
62
22 SWEET WOODRUFF
60 LEMON BALM
27 BLUE LUNGWORT
59 FEVER-FEW
65 APOTHECARY'S ROSE

29 WILD BERGAMOT
21 PINEY
DAFFODIL
21 PINEY
37 ALPINE LADY'S-MANTLE
54 WOAD
39 CAMPHOR-SCENTED WORMWOOD

61 MADONNA LILY
31 WELD
30 SKIRRET
ORRIS 'DAL.' 34
20 GERMANDER EDGING
SWEET MARJORAM 4
3   1 GREEN SANTOLINA   3
BUSH BASIL   BUSH BASIL
19 HYSSOP EDGING
40 LAVENDER 'ALBA'
61 MADONNA LILY
34 ORRIS 'DALMATICA'

53 FRENCH LAVENDER
32 SAGE
HOUSE-LEEK 33
16 WOOLLY THYME
CLOVE PINK 6
16 WOOLLY THYME
BUTTERFLY WEED
WHITE CREEPING THYME 15
38 FRENCH THYME

14 GRAY SANTOLINA EDGING
67 BOX
10 LAMB'S-EARS
18 THRIFT
67 BOX
12
10 LAMB'S-EARS
18

11 ABSINTHE
9 WINTER SAVORY
66 DWARF BOX SUNDIAL
9 WINTER SAVORY
11 ABSINTHE

10 LAMB'S-EARS
8 CHAMOMILE
10 LAMB'S-EARS
18 BUTTERFLY WEED

SANTOLINA NEAPOLITANA 13
67 BOX
67 BOX 12
14 GRAY SANTOLINA EDGING

STEPPING STONES

33 HOUSE-LEEK
CRIMSON CREEPING THYME 17
6
CLOVE PINK
17
CRIMSON CREEPING THYME
49 ORPINE
50 FERN-LEAF TANSY

32 GAR. SAGE 'ALBIFLORA'
42 'HIDCOTE' LAVENDER
41 BRONZE FENNEL
7 SCENTED-LEAF GERANIUM
1 GREEN SANTOLINA
2 ROSEMARY
5 NASTURTIUM
19 HYSSOP EDGING
38 FRENCH THYME
63 CHIVE
61 MADONNA LILY
35 ENGLISH LAVENDER
51 VALERIAN

58 CANADIAN BURNET
61 MADONNA LILY
43 WHITE COMFREY
44 ORRIS
WHITE CREEPING THYME 15
36 CURLY MINT
52 POT MARJORAM
44 ORRIS
43 WHITE COMFREY
65 APOTHECARY'S ROSE

47 SOUTHERN-WOOD 'TANGERINE'
48 SWEET CICELY
46 MASTERWORT
45 RUE
BRICK WALK
45 RUE
46 MASTERWORT
BEE SKEP

67 BOX HEDGE

PATHWAY

40 Ft
12.2 M

67 BOX HEDGE

GRASS

67 BOX HEDGE

YEW HEDGE

68 YEW HEDGE

OPENING IN STONE WALL

70 PEAR

25 EUROPEAN GINGER

64 GRAPE ARBOR

STONE WALL

IN COLD FRAME
55 CHRISTMAS ROSE
56 LENTEN ROSE
57 HELLEBORUS ATRORUBENS

N

WINDOW IN BARN LOFT STUDIO

0   5   10Ft
0   1   2   3 M

27 Ft
8.2 M

Herb Garden Design / 55

A HINT OF PARTERRE

Looking for something different—an out-of-the-ordinary plan? It appears at first glance that a formal garden quite in balance has been planned. However, on the right are extra beds that add a touch of asymmetry. At the top of the steps, rising from the courtyard, the main axis path is widened to accommodate a birdbath. This creates two identical beds of unusual shape on either side. At an appropriate distance farther along this path, interest is maintained with a standard of rose geranium. Again the path is expanded where two paths intersect to make room for this standard. Beds of such diverse shapes as found here create interest in themselves. They are small specialty beds, diverse in the herbs that are planted in them. In addition to the brick edging around each, an assortment of herbs trimly finishes them. Bordered and clipped as they are in the fashion of a parterre, this design is best viewed looking down from the windows of the house. The large, crescent-shaped bed at the back of the herb garden holds the beds together. This device and the dry stone wall at the courtyard combine to create the feeling of an enclosure. The roses in this garden are noteworthy "old roses," and the stone wall makes a fine background for the rambler, *Rosa* 'Albertine', with buds of red, pink, and gold that open to coppery-pink blooms that are intensely fragrant. If there is room for only one rambler rose, include this one. Care would have to be a major consideration for this large garden, even without the added features of a greenhouse and hotbeds. Grass walks to be mowed and trimmed and herb edgings to be clipped contribute their demands. The brick edging around each bed is a help, but no panacea for the maintenance required.

New Jersey
Barbara Capen, Landscape Designer
The number in each planting area is the key number.

1. *Angelica archangelica*, angelica
2. *Fragaria vesca* 'Fraises des Bois', alpine strawberry
3. *Lavandula angustifolia*, subsp. *angustifolia* 'Munstead', lavender
4. *Mentha suaveolens* 'Variegata', pineapple mint
5. *Carum carvi*, caraway
6. *Hyssopus officinalis*, blue hyssop
7. *Consolida ambigua*, rocket larkspur
8. *Thymus* 'Argenteus', silver thyme
9. *Pelargonium graveolens*, rose geranium
10. *Chrysanthemum*, chrysanthemum in variety
11. *Pelargonium*, geranium in variety
12. *Teucrium chamaedrys*, germander
13. *Thymus vulgaris* 'Narrow-leaf French', French thyme
14. *Lavandula dentata*, French lavender
15. *Salvia elegans*, pineapple-scented sage
16. *Mentha* × *piperita* var. *citrata*, orange mint
17. *Chrysanthemum balsamita*, costmary
18. *Origanum majorana*, sweet marjoram
19. *Dianthus caryophyllus* 'Snowflake', clove pink
20. *Rheum rhabarbarum*, rhubarb
21. *Tanacetum vulgare*, tansy
22. *Borago officinalis*, borage
23. *Thymus* × *citriodorus*, lemon thyme
24. *Digitalis purpurea* 'Alba', foxglove
25. *Artemisia dracunculus* var. *sativa*, French tarragon
26. *Marrubium vulgare*, horehound
27. *Chrysanthemum frutescens*, marguerite
28. *Anethum graveolens* 'Bouquet', dill
29. *Tagetes filifolia*, Irish-lace
30. *Satureja hortensis*, summer savory
31. *Calendula officinalis*, pot marigold
32. *Aloysia triphylla*, lemon verbena
33. *Dianthus gratianopolitanus* 'Tiny Rubies', cheddar pink
34. *Rosmarinus officinalis* 'Prostratus', prostrate rosemary
35. *Tagetes tenuifolia* 'Lulu', marigold
36. *Chenopodium ambrosioides*, Mexican tea
37. *Salvia officinalis* 'Tricolor', variegated garden sage
38. *Salvia officinalis* 'Holt's Mammoth', garden sage
39. *Salvia officinalis* 'Albiflora', garden sage
40. *Satureja montana*, winter savory
41. *Melissa officinalis*, lemon balm
42. *Ocimum basilicum* 'Minimum', bush basil
43. *Thymus* 'Broad-leaf English', English thyme
44. *Petroselinum crispum* var. *crispum* 'Bravour', curly parsley
45. *Poterium sanguisorba*, salad burnet
46. *Allium schoenoprasum*, chive
47. *Rosa* × *borboniana* 'Souvenir de la Malmaison', bourbon rose
48. *R.* 'Baronne Prevost', hybrid perpetual rose
49. *R. moschata* 'Bishop Darlington', musk rose
50. *R. centifolia*, crested moss rose
51. *R.* 'Frau Karl Druschki', hybrid perpetual
52. *R. borboniana* 'La Reine Victoria', bourbon rose
53. *R. centifolia* var. *muscosa* 'Salet', moss rose
54. *R. centifolia* 'Cristata', cabbage rose
55. *R.* 'Albertine', rambler rose
56. *Laurus nobilis*, bay

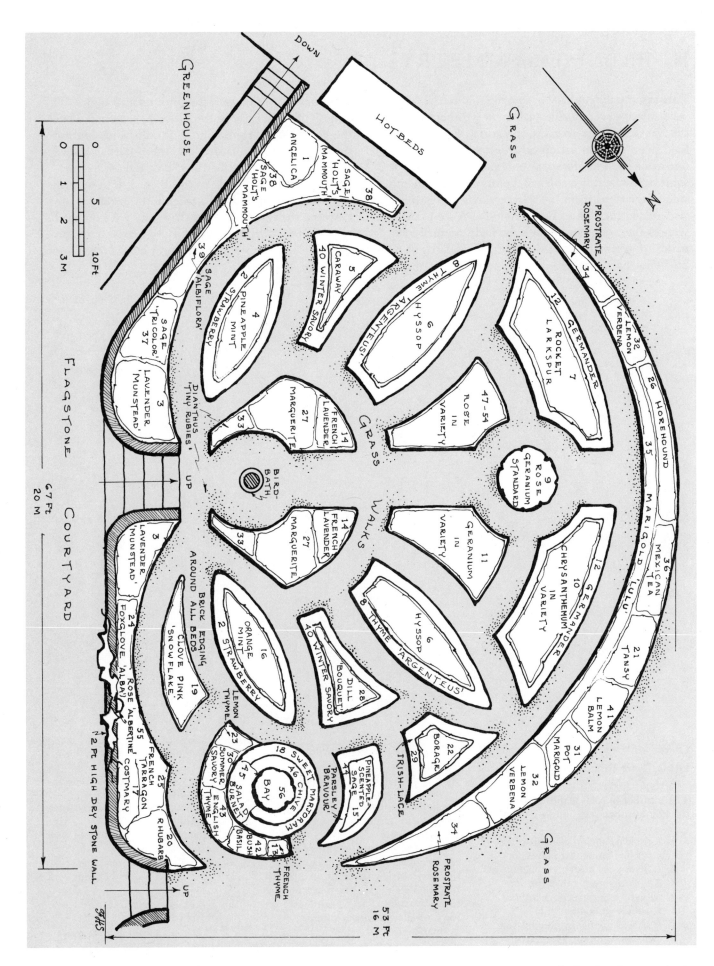

IN PRECISE SYMMETRY

This essentially culinary herb garden is sure to be used often—even during inclement weather. It is near the house, and the access to it is surfaced with brick. Laid in an unusual pattern, the design of the brick is one often used in old Spanish gardens. Symmetry was achieved with almost identical plots of herbs on either side of the steps from the terrace where the path is widened at their base, as it should be. A stone curb secures the bricks and retains the beds. Semicircular bands of green accented with potted standards of purple heliotrope reinforce the symmetrical look and make arcs to soften the straight lines and angles. The yellow of viola early in the growing season and later the yellow of marigolds provide color and contrast that emphasize the balance and the pattern. Balance is augmented, too, by the dwarf box and dwarf ninebark hedge on each side of this plan. It is good planning that creates an herb garden to utilize the space between the terrace and the driveway with one path to serve two purposes. Beautifully precise and symmetrical, this herb garden requires regular clipping to maintain its pattern.

Ohio

Lucile Teeter Kissack, Landscape Architect, A.S.L.A.

The number in each planting area is the key number.

1. *Lavandula angustifolia* subsp. *angustifolia* 'Munstead', lavender
2. *Heliotropium arborescens*, heliotrope
3. *Thymus praecox* subsp. *arcticus* 'Albus', white creeping thyme
4. *Anethum graveolens*, dill
5. *Hyssopus officinalis*, blue hyssop
6. *Ocimum basilicum*, sweet basil
7. *Santolina chamaecyparissus*, gray santolina
8. *Lobularia maritima* 'Purple Carpet', sweet alyssum
9. *Rosmarinus officinalis*, rosemary
10. *Thymus* 'Broad-leaf English', English thyme
11. *Satureja hortensis*, summer savory
12. *Poterium sanguisorba*, salad burnet
13. *Aloysia triphylla*, lemon verbena
14. *Santolina virens*, green santolina
15. *Salvia officinalis*, garden sage
16. *Origanum majorana*, sweet marjoram
17. *Viola lutea* 'Splendens', yellow viola
18. *Tagetes tenuifolia* 'Lulu', signet marigold
19. *Myosotis sylvatica*, garden forget-me-not
20. *Paeonia lactiflora* 'Festiva Maxima', double white peony
21. *Allium schoenoprasum*, chive
22. *Rosa* 'Mme. Louis Leveque', moss rose
23. *Buxus sempervirens* 'Suffruticosa', dwarf edging box
24. *Physocarpus opulifolius* 'Nanus', dwarf ninebark

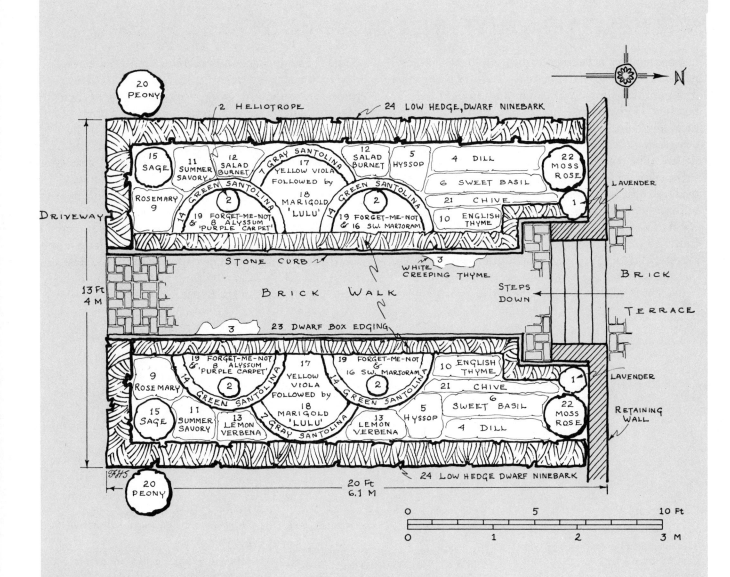

WITH A TAPESTRYLIKE FOCAL POINT

If a garden area is large enough, it can have another garden twenty-six feet square for its focal point. The design of this square was inspired by an old French tapestry. Herbs, selected for their contrasting leaf textures and colors, were used with bricks to create the design adaptation. The pattern is symmetrically geometric. The trim look of clipped germander and the brick edging form the arcs that soften the square. A birdbath circled with lavender is the center of interest within this focal point and adds to the softening effect. The brick patterns used here merge tastefully. Eight dwarf box accent the corner entrances to this tapestrylike focal point. A generous expanse of grass sets the focal point apart from a periphery of herb beds. The apple trees in each far corner provide welcome shade during summer, and a comfortable, well-designed bench encircles the trunk of one tree. Just as important is the interesting skeleton tracery of their branches on the snow in winter. This is a feature often overlooked when planning for small trees near the herb garden. The grape vines, winter pruned, and their arbor contribute their own particularly pleasing shadow patterns, too. Huge tubs of aged rosemary shrubs, potted lemon verbena, and scented-leaf geraniums serve as accents in the garden. Enclosure of all is effected by a stone wall, the fence with roses, and the grape arbor. The entrance to this raised garden is fortified with a box hedge—a fountain tucked into a curve of it. This is an appealing feature adding interest to the view from the house.

Connecticut

Vera Breed, Landscape Architect

The number in each planting area is the key number.

BED I

Althaea officinalis, marsh mallow
Galium odoratum, sweet woodruff
Myrrhis odorata, sweet cicely
Artemisia pontica, Roman wormwood
Aloysia triphylla, lemon verbena in pots at intervals
Digitalis purpurea 'Alba', foxglove
Potentilla tridentata, three-toothed cinquefoil
Rosa wichuraiana × *laevigata* 'Silver Moon', climbing rose
Taxus × *media* 'Hatfieldii', conical yew

BED II

Santolina virens, green santolina
Santolina chamaecyparissus, gray santolina
Artemisia schmidtiana 'Nana', silver mound artemisia
Lavandula angustifolia, English lavender
Chamaemelum nobile, chamomile
Teucrium chamaedrys, germander
Artemisia stellerana, beach wormwood
Symphytum officinale, comfrey
Melissa officinalis, lemon balm
Macleaya cordata, plume poppy

Chrysanthemum parthenium, feverfew
Monarda didyma 'Croftway Pink', pink bee balm
Rosa chinensis 'Minima', fairy rose
Rosa centifolia 'Muscosa', moss rose
Rosa 'Etoile de Hollande', climbing rose, deep crimson
Rosa 'Dame Edith Helen', climbing rose, pure rose-pink

BED III

Angelica archangelica, angelica
Pulmonaria officinalis, lungwort
Amsonia tabernaemontana, bluestar
Lamium maculatum 'Album', spotted dead nettle
Anchusa officinalis, alkanet
Rosmarinus officinalis, rosemary

BED IV

Salvia officinalis 'Purpurea', purple variegated garden sage
Poterium sanguisorba, salad burnet
Origanum majorana, sweet marjoram
Pelargonium in variety, scented-leaf geranium

BED V

Marrubium vulgare, horehound
Rosmarinus officinalis, rosemary
Anemone × *hybrida*, Japanese anemone

Baptisia australis, blue false indigo
Delphinium × *belladonna*, larkspur

BED VI

Myosotis sylvatica, garden forget-me-not
Alchemilla vulgaris, lady's-mantle
Rosmarinus officinalis, rosemary
Levisticum officinale, lovage
Consolida ambigua, rocket larkspur
Isatis tinctoria, dyer's woad
Linum perenne, flax
Filipendula vulgaris, dropwort
Valeriana officinalis, valerian
Iris cristata, dwarf crested iris
Aconitum napellus, monkshood
Taxus × *media* 'Hatfieldii', conical yew

BED VII   Knot Garden

1. *Teucrium chamaedrys*, germander
2. *Stachys byzantina*, lamb's-ears
3. *Nepeta mussinii*, catmint
4. *Nepeta faassenii* 'Six Hills Giant', catmint
5. *Nepeta tuberosa* subsp. *tuberosa*
6. *Sempervivum*, houseleek in variety
7. *Thymus*, creeping thyme in variety
8. *Thymus* × *citriodorus*, lemon thyme
9. *Lavandula angustifolia* subsp. *angustifolia* 'Munstead', lavender
10. *Buxus sempervirens* 'Myosotidifolia', dwarf box

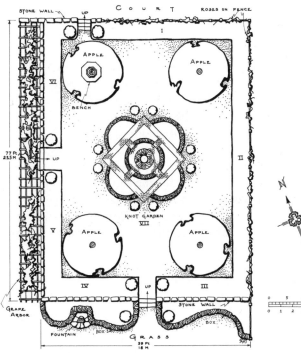

Design plan of herb garden

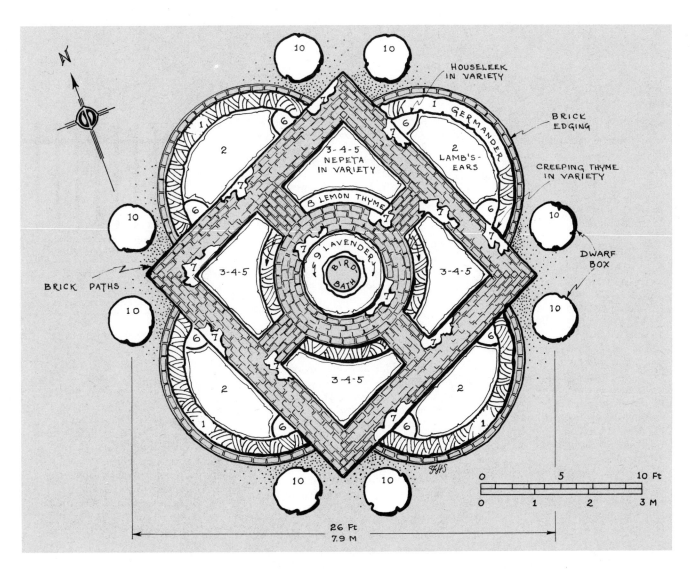

FOR A WILLIAMSBURG AIR

In a climate where summers are hot and humid, an impression of greenery and cool fragrances may be desired. Ivy, myrtle, magnolia, holly, and box of deep green color are excellent for contrast with the varying shades of gray, silver, blue green, and bright green in the herb beds. When this garden was designed a quarter of a century ago, the center ellipse was ringed with gray santolina. Later, this was replaced with "edging" box. Either it flourished too well, grew too large, or it may have been a mislabeled cultivar. A newer cultivar of more restrained growth will take its place. A truly dwarf edging box will let the design as a whole be better seen from the terrace. The steps from the terrace lead to paths of old and worn rose-colored brick. The pattern of the brick complements the center of interest, and its oval form results in beds of unusual shape. Herbs, planted in bands across these beds, tend to broaden the width of the garden. Another angle could be tried with these, perhaps repeating the curve of the oval, if desired. The accent plants are placed with thought for the months when much of the herbaceous material is dormant. This herb garden is enclosed with a wall of uncommon design. Of brick and unpretentious ironwork, its detail is shown below.

Virginia

Designed by Owner

The number in each planting area is the key number.

1. *Thymus* 'Broad-leaf English', English thyme
2. *Stachys byzantina*, lamb's-ears
3. *Ruta graveolens*, rue
4. *Tropaeolum minus*, dwarf nasturtium
5. *Ocimum basilicum* 'Minimum', bush basil
6. *Salvia officinalis* 'Purpurascens', purple garden sage
7. *Ocimum basilicum* 'Purpurascens', purple basil
8. *Salvia officinalis* 'Aurea', golden garden sage
9. *Borago officinalis*, borage
10. *Rumex scutatus*, French sorrel
11. *Rosmarinus officinalis*, rosemary
12. *Melissa officinalis*, lemon balm
13. *Monarda didyma*, bee balm
14. *Santolina chamaecyparissus*, gray santolina
15. *Lavandula angustifolia*, English lavender
16. *Marrubium vulgare*, horehound
17. *Origanum majorana*, sweet marjoram
18. *Chamaemelum nobile*, chamomile
19. *Pelargonium graveolens*, rose geranium
20. *Pelargonium × nervosum*, lime geranium
21. *Pelargonium fragrans*, nutmeg geranium
22. *Artemisia ludoviciana* var. *albula*, silver-king artemisia
23. *Artemisia abrotanum*, southernwood
24. *Satureja montana*, winter savory
25. *Mentha spicata*, spearmint
26. *Poterium sanguisorba*, salad burnet
27. *Artemisia dracunculus* var. *sativa*, French tarragon
28. *Tanacetum vulgare*, tansy
29. *Thymus × citriodorus*, lemon thyme
30. *Vinca minor*, myrtle
31. *Levisticum officinale*, lovage
32. *Anthriscus cerefolium*, chervil
33. *Teucrium chamaedrys*, germander
34. *Mentha suaveolens*, apple mint
35. *Galium odoratum*, sweet woodruff
36. *Thymus doerfleri*, thyme
37. *Thymus carnosus*, thyme
38. *Thymus vulgaris* 'Narrow-leaf French', French thyme
39. *Thymus herba-barona*, caraway thyme
40. *Thymus praecox* subsp. *arcticus* 'Albus', white creeping thyme

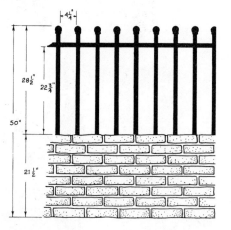

Detail of brick wall and iron fence

41. *Thymus praecox* subsp. *arcticus* 'Lanuginosus', woolly thyme
42. *Thymus* 'Argenteus', silver thyme
43. *Hedera helix*, English ivy
44. *Buxus sempervirens* 'Suffruticosa', dwarf edging box
45. *Laurus nobilis*, bay
46. *Myrica pensylvanica*, bayberry
47. *Ilex opaca*, American holly
48. *Buxus sempervirens* 'Myrtifolia', box
49. *Magnolia grandiflora*, southern magnolia

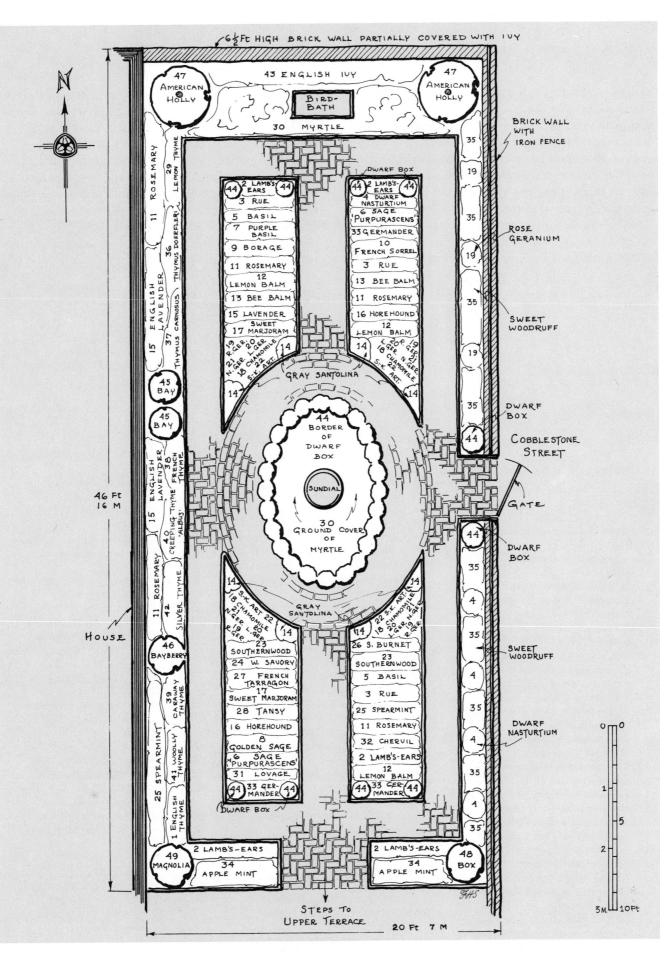

6½ FT HIGH BRICK WALL PARTIALLY COVERED WITH IVY

N

43 ENGLISH IVY

47 AMERICAN HOLLY

47 AMERICAN HOLLY

BIRD-BATH

30 MYRTLE

BRICK WALL WITH IRON FENCE

DWARF BOX

35

19

35

ROSE GERANIUM

11 ROSEMARY

29 LEMON THYME

36 THYMUS DOEFFLERI

37 THYMUS CARNOSUS

15 ENGLISH LAVENDER

44 — 2 LAMB'S-EARS — 44

3 RUE

5 BASIL

7 PURPLE BASIL

9 BORAGE

11 ROSEMARY

12 LEMON BALM

13 BEE BALM

15 LAVENDER

17 SWEET MARJORAM

19 R.GER. 20 L.GER.
21 N.GER. 22 S-K ART.
18 CHAMOMILE

14

44 — 2 LAMB'S-EARS — 44

4 DWARF NASTURTIUM

6 SAGE 'PURPURASCENS'

33 GERMANDER

10 FRENCH SORREL

3 RUE

13 BEE BALM

11 ROSEMARY

16 HOREHOUND

12 LEMON BALM

19 L.GER. 20 R.GER.
21 N.GER. 22 S-K ART.
18 CHAMOMILE

14

19

35

SWEET WOODRUFF

14

GRAY SANTOLINA

14

45 BAY

45 BAY

15 ENGLISH LAVENDER

38 FRENCH THYME

40 CREEPING THYME 'ALBUS'

44 BORDER OF DWARF BOX

SUNDIAL

30 GROUND COVER OF MYRTLE

35

44

COBBLESTONE STREET

GATE

DWARF BOX

46 FT 16 M

44

35

4

35

HOUSE

11 ROSEMARY

42 SILVER THYME

39 CARAWAY THYME

25 SPEARMINT

41 WOOLLY THYME

1 ENGLISH THYME

46 BAYBERRY

14

22 S-K ART. 18 CHAMOMILE
20 N.GER. 21
19 R.GER. L.GER.

14

23 SOUTHERNWOOD

24 W. SAVORY

27 FRENCH TARRAGON

17 SWEET MARJORAM

28 TANSY

16 HOREHOUND

8 GOLDEN SAGE

6 SAGE 'PURPURASCENS'

31 LOVAGE

44 — 33 GERMANDER — 44

14

22 S-K ART. 18 CHAMOMILE
20 L.GER. N.GER. 21
19 R.GER.

14

26 S. BURNET

23 SOUTHERNWOOD

5 BASIL

3 RUE

25 SPEARMINT

11 ROSEMARY

32 CHERVIL

2 LAMB'S-EARS

12 LEMON BALM

44 — 33 GERMANDER — 44

DWARF BOX

GRAY SANTOLINA

4

35

4

35

SWEET WOODRUFF

DWARF NASTURTIUM

4

35

49 MAGNOLIA

2 LAMB'S-EARS

34 APPLE MINT

2 LAMB'S-EARS

34 APPLE MINT

48 BOX

STEPS TO UPPER TERRACE

20 FT 7 M

0

1

5

2

3M. 10FT

USING STANDARDS AND MAYPOLES

Variety is a prime feature of this herb garden. It is a large garden, as it must be to accommodate a number of topiaries, standards, potted shrubs, maypoles, and trees—some of which are espaliered. There is variety in the walks, too. The use of flagstone, brick, and grass adds more interest than would result from using any one of these exclusively. The chief focal point is the ornamental lead pump on a bed of wild thyme. Adequate space for this artifact was made by rounding off the corners of the adjacent beds. Creeping thyme is used as an edging on these curves, adding to the space for walking. The four potted bay, *Laurus nobilis*, accent this prime focal point even more. Each of the four gardens has a center of interest, too, a maypole of cherry tomatoes. Work paths for these gardens are brick and are enhanced by widening at the halfway point of each. The marginal beds embrace all this by having a gazebo placed at the end of one of the main axes paths. It is located for the best viewing. Enclosure of this altogether pleasing design is completed with a white board fence, a splendid foil for the variety of herbs here.

New Jersey

Design from Contributor

The number in each planting area is the key number.

1. *Ocimum basilicum* 'Minimum', bush basil
2. *Thymus* 'Broad-leaf English', English thyme
3. *Satureja montana*, winter savory
4. *Origanum vulgare* 'Viride', wild marjoram
5. *Thymus × citriodorus*, lemon thyme
6. *Thymus × citriodorus* 'Aureus', golden lemon thyme
7. *Chamaemelum nobile*, chamomile
8. *Rosmarinus officinalis*, rosemary
9. *Hyssopus officinalis*, blue hyssop
10. *Salvia officinalis*, garden sage
11. *Petroselinum crispum*, parsley
12. *Anethum graveolens*, dill
13. *Origanum majorana*, sweet marjoram
14. *Foeniculum vulgare*, bronze fennel
15. *Lactuca sativa* 'Bibb', lettuce
16. *Lactuca sativa* 'Ruby', lettuce
17. *Lactuca sativa* 'Oak Leaf', lettuce
18. *Poterium sanguisorba*, salad burnet
19. *Thymus praecox* subsp. *arcticus* 'Albus', white creeping thyme
20. *Artemisia dracunculus* var. *sativa*, French tarragon
21. *Melissa officinalis*, lemon balm
22. *Marrubium vulgare*, horehound
23. *Aloysia triphylla*, lemon verbena
24. *Fragaria vesca*, strawberry
25. *Chenopodium botrys*, ambrosia
26. *Viola tricolor*, Johnny-jump-up
27. *Chrysanthemum balsamita*, costmary
28. *Calendula officinalis*, pot marigold
29. *Nigella damascena*, love-in-a-mist
30. *Thymus serpyllum*, wild thyme
31. *Lavandula angustifolia*, English lavender
32. *Salvia caerulea*, blue sage
33. *Artemisia abrotanum*, southernwood
34. *Tanacetum vulgare* var. *crispum*, fern-leaf tansy
35. *Artemisia schmidtiana* 'Nana', silver mound artemisia
36. *Achillea filipendula*, fern-leaf yarrow
37. *Mentha pulegium*, pennyroyal
38. *Origanum dictamnus*, dittany-of-Crete
39. *Monarda didyma*, bee balm
40. *Lycopersicon lycopersicum*, cherry tomato
41. *Pelargonium crispum*, lemon geranium
42. *P. graveolens*, rose geranium
43. *P. tomentosum*, peppermint geranium
44. *P. graveolens* 'Camphor Rose', camphor-scented geranium
45. *P. graveolens* 'Rober's Lemon Rose', lemon-rose geranium
46. *P. radens*, crowfoot geranium
47. *P. radens* 'Dr. Livingston', lemon geranium
48. *P. glutinosum*, pheasant's-foot geranium
49. *P. acerifolium*, maple-leaved geranium
50. *P. odoratissimum*, apple geranium
51. *P. quercifolium*, oak-leaved geranium
52. *P. quercifolium* 'Giganteum', musty oak-scented geranium
53. *P. fragrans*, nutmeg geranium
54. *P. × nervosum*, lime geranium
55. *P. crispum*, lemon geranium
56. *P. crispum* 'Prince Rupert', lemon geranium
57. *P. crispum* 'Minor', lemon geranium
58. *P. denticulatum*, pine geranium
59. *P. denticulatum* 'Filicifolium', fern-leaf geranium
60. *Viola odorata*, white sweet violet
61. *Mentha*, mint in variety
62. *Levisticum officinale*, lovage
63. *Acorus calamus*, sweet flag
64. *Allium schoenoprasum*, chive
65. *Allium senescens* var. *glaucum*
66. *Buxus sempervirens* 'Myrtifolia', box
67. *Forsythia*, forsythia
68. *Laurus nobilis*, bay
69. *Myrtus communis*, classic myrtle
70. *Poncirus trifoliata*, orange
71. *Malus angustifolia*, wild crab
72. *Malus*, dwarf apple

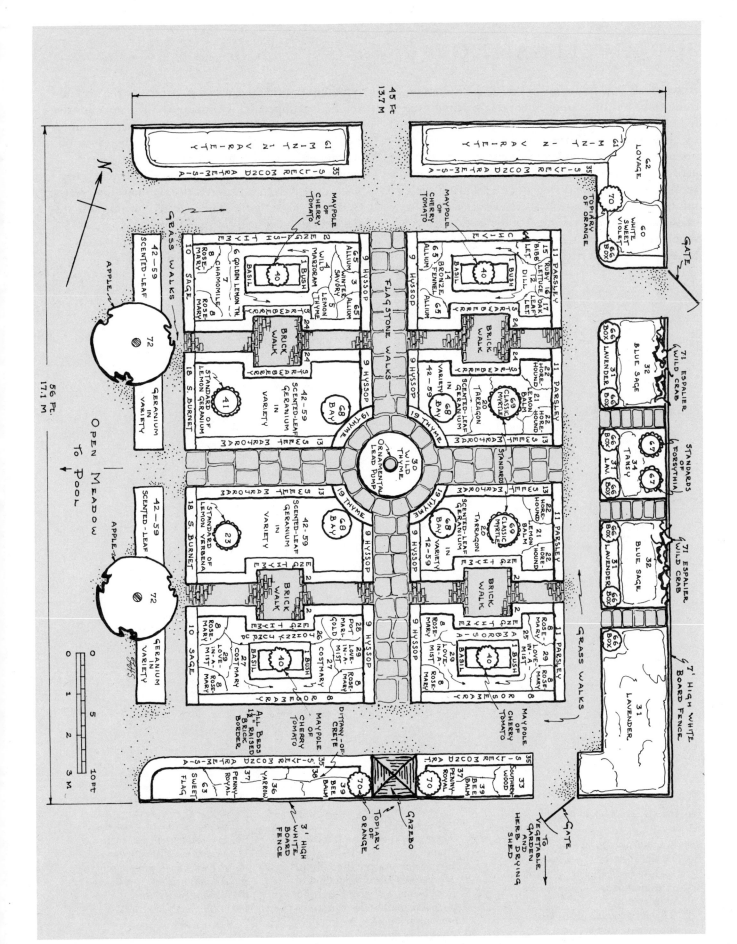

FOR AN ELEGANT OVAL

A genuinely stately design was needed here, something to be a fitting complement to a gracious estate. In keeping with this feeling, the herb garden is flanked by generous beds of roses enclosed with hedges of box. This is a large garden by any standard, with a natural stone birdbath of appropriate size being its focal point. The bath is ringed with aromatic apple mint, green santolina, and *Allium karataviense*. The main axes paths of grass meet at the brick walk in a sunburst pattern encircling this center of interest. Mother-of-thyme strips between the beds in each quadrant provide the access so necessary for keeping the herbs clipped. This clipping is mandatory for the fringed wormwood edging, too. It prevents its unremarkable bloom from developing and allows its full downy effect to be achieved. The result is one of sculptured elegance. The maximum is realized only with a great deal of maintenance. Perhaps the greatest impact is made by the frame created for this design—the delicately fringed foliage of *Artemisia frigida*—a pale, silvery green that sets the frame off from the surrounding darker green area of grass.

New York

Florence B. Baker, Landscape Architect

The number in each planting area is the key number.

1. *Artemisia frigida*, fringed wormwood
2. *Thymus praecox* subsp. *arcticus*, mother-of-thyme
3. *Satureja montana*, winter savory
4. *Santolina chamaecyparissus*, gray santolina
5. *Thymus* × *citriodorus*, lemon thyme
6. *Liriope muscari*, big blue lilyturf
7. *Mentha suaveolens*, apple mint
8. *Santolina virens*, green santolina
9. *Artemisia dracunculus* var. *sativa*, French tarragon
10. *Hyssopus officinalis*, blue hyssop
11. *Salvia officinalis*, dwarf garden sage
12. *Salvia officinalis*, garden sage
13. *Foeniculum vulgare*, fennel
14. *Levisticum officinale*, lovage
15. *Allium schoenoprasum*, chive
16. *Allium christophii*, stars-of-Persia
17. *Allium karataviense*
18. *Allium moly*, lily leek

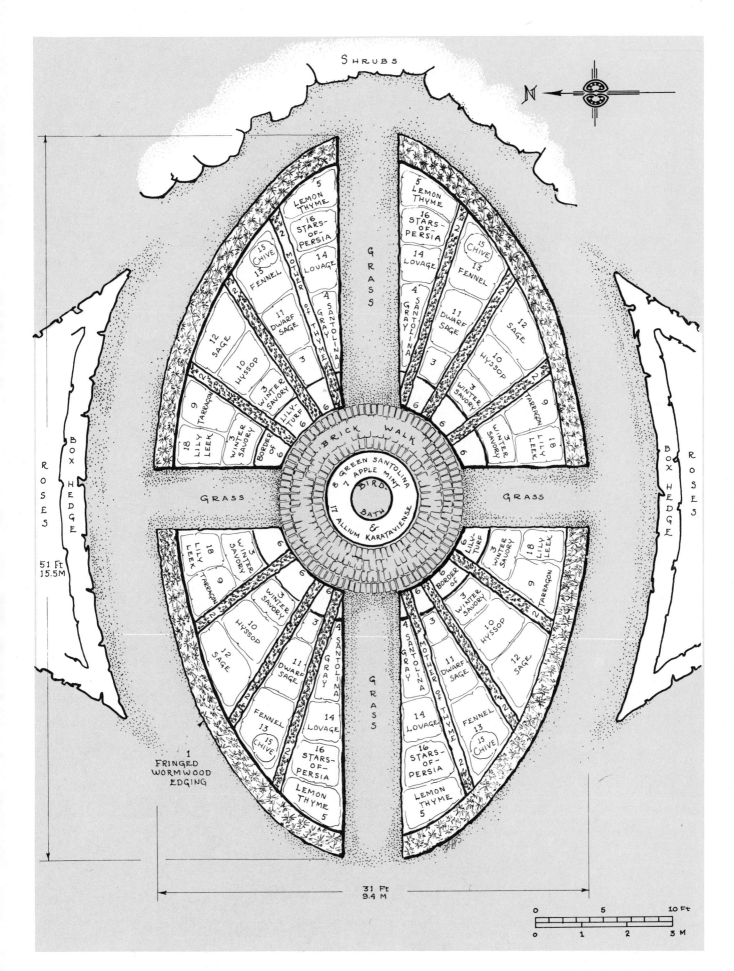

A SPECIALTY

DEVOTED TO FRAGRANCE

Desired for fragrance, this herb garden is situated on a hillside in a city and is the lowest of three levels. Its peak of fragrance occurs in June when the lavender blooms in profusion. Many herb gardens could provide this. It is the design that is singular here—composed of the rectangle, the square, the circle, the arc—and patterned with only a few kinds of herbs. Dwarf box outlines the paths and emphasizes the forms drawn. A woven redwood screen serves two purposes—to create privacy and to provide a fitting background for the specimen *Cedrus deodara*. Six stately Italian cypress trees in planters add to the for-

mal feeling already existing. The precision of this garden is maintained with less care than might be expected. One annual pruning suffices for the winter savory in the spring, for the box after new spring growth, and for the lavender when its bloom is past. Occasional weeding of the planting beds constitutes the main chore. The bench among the cypress trees was placed where all three levels could be viewed best. But this herb garden of blue-gray and blue-green tones prevailing throughout most of the year can also be enjoyed from the living room windows, the upper deck, and the front porch of the house.

California

Designed by Owner

The number in each planting area is the key number.

1. *Chamaemelum nobile*, chamomile
2. *Viola cornuta* 'Blue Perfection', viola
3. *Satureja montana*, winter savory
4. *Lavandula angustifolia* subsp. *angustifolia*, lavender
5. *Myrtus communis* 'Microphylla', dwarf myrtle
6. *Buxus sempervirens* 'Suffruticosa', dwarf edging box
7. *Citrus limon* 'Ponderosa', lemon
8. *Cupressus sempervirens*, Italian cypress
9. *Cedrus deodara*, deodar

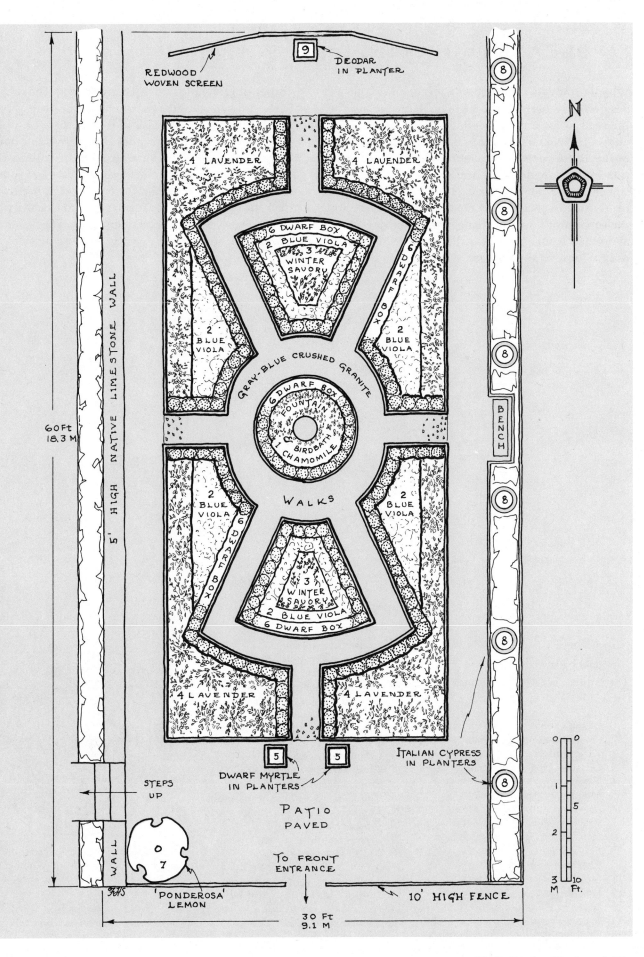

REDWOOD
WOVEN SCREEN

DEODAR
IN PLANTER

N

5' HIGH NATIVE LIMESTONE WALL

60 Ft
18.3 M

4 LAVENDER

4 LAVENDER

6 DWARF BOX

2 BLUE VIOLA

3 WINTER SAVORY

6 DWARF BOX

2 BLUE VIOLA

2 BLUE VIOLA

GRAY-BLUE CRUSHED GRANITE

6 DWARF BOX

FOUNTAIN

BIRDBATH

1 CHAMOMILE

WALKS

2 BLUE VIOLA

2 BLUE VIOLA

6 DWARF BOX

3 WINTER SAVORY

2 BLUE VIOLA

6 DWARF BOX

4 LAVENDER

4 LAVENDER

BENCH

STEPS UP

WALL

5

5

DWARF MYRTLE
IN PLANTERS

ITALIAN CYPRESS
IN PLANTERS

PATIO
PAVED

TO FRONT
ENTRANCE

'PONDEROSA'
LEMON

10' HIGH FENCE

30 Ft
9.1 M

0
0

1

5

2

3
M

10
Ft.

Herb Garden Design / 71

TO PLEASE A SHAKESPEARE SCHOLAR

Where or how is inspiration found for an original design for an herb garden? A special interest may be the catalyst, as it was with this plan. A scholarly devotion to Shakespeare led to the use of an adaptation of the Tudor rose in creating this design. The illustration of this rose depicts it as it was originally designed. It is double with white and red for the houses of York and Lancaster. Its modification for use within the squares of this plan changed the number of petals and sepals from five to four. Each square has a topiary of box for a focal point, and wild thyme at the central corner of each holds the square together. The other herbs used are as authentically Shakespearean as possible. It was not an easy task to find a source of supply for all mentioned by this poet and playwright, but it was an interesting one for a Shakespeare enthusiast. Brick edgings maintain the design winter and summer. Paths are gravel, and the crosswalk is narrower than the "forthright," as it was referred to chiefly after Shakespeare. This imaginatively created design is appropriately and pleasingly enclosed with box and is a delight in any season.

North Carolina

Designed by Owner

The number in each planting area is the key number.

1. *Hyssopus officinalis*, blue hyssop
2. *Origanum majorana*, sweet marjoram
3. *Chamaemelum nobile*, chamomile
4. *Thymus serpyllum*, wild thyme
5. *Malva sylvestris*, mallow
6. *Eryngium maritimum*, sea holly
7. *Artemisia absinthium*, absinthe
8. *Dianthus caryophyllus*, clove pink
9. *Foeniculum vulgare*, fennel
10. *Crithmum maritimum*, samphire
11. *Lilium candidum*, Madonna lily
12. *Fumaria officinalis*, earth smoke
13. *Anemone pulsatilla*, pasqueflower
14. *Iris pseudacorus*, yellow flag
15. *Aconitum napellus*, monkshood
16. *Lactuca sativa*, lettuce
17. *Petroselinum crispum*, parsley
18. *Mentha spicata*, spearmint
19. *Melissa officinalis*, lemon balm
20. *Satureja montana*, winter savory
21. *Ruta graveolens*, rue
22. *Lavandula angustifolia*, English lavender
23. *Carum carvi*, caraway
24. *Bellis perennis*, English daisy
25. *Primula vulgaris*, English primrose
26. *Calendula officinalis*, pot marigold
27. *Rosmarinus officinalis*, rosemary
28. *Primula elatior*, oxlip
29. *Myrtus communis*, classic myrtle
30. *Viola odorata*, sweet violet
31. *Mentha × piperita*, peppermint
32. *Viola tricolor*, Johnny-jump-up
33. *Poterium sanguisorba*, salad burnet
34. *Fragaria vesca*, woodland strawberry

Coin with Tudor rose design, from Peter Coats, *Roses, Pleasures and Treasures* (New York: G. P. Putnam's Sons, 1962)

35. *Crocus sativus*, saffron crocus
36. *Buxus sempervirens*, box

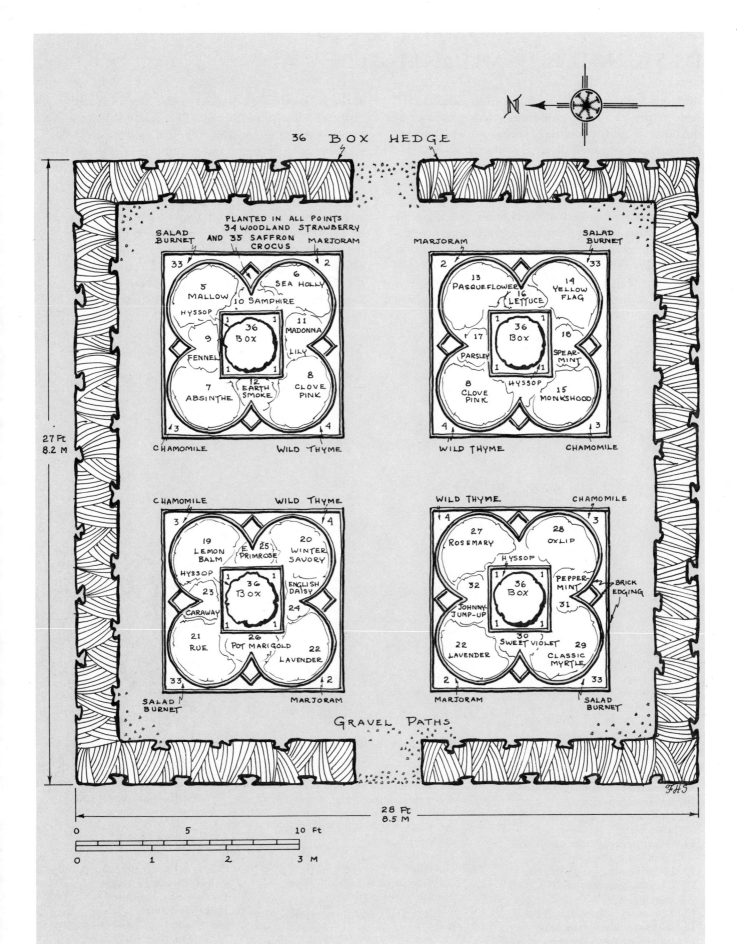

N

36 BOX HEDGE

PLANTED IN ALL POINTS
34 WOODLAND STRAWBERRY
AND 35 SAFFRON CROCUS

SALAD
BURNET
MARJORAM   MARJORAM   SALAD
BURNET

33   2   2   33

5 MALLOW   6 SEA HOLLY   13 PASQUEFLOWER   14 YELLOW FLAG
10 SAMPHIRE   16 LETTUCE
HYSSOP   1   1   1   1
9   36 BOX   11 MADONNA   17   36 BOX   18
FENNEL   LILY   PARSLEY   SPEAR-MINT
1   1   1   1
7 ABSINTHE 12 EARTH 8 CLOVE   HYSSOP
SMOKE   PINK   8 CLOVE   15 MONKSHOOD
PINK
3   4   4   3

CHAMOMILE   WILD THYME   WILD THYME   CHAMOMILE

CHAMOMILE   WILD THYME   WILD THYME   CHAMOMILE

3   4   4   3

19 LEMON 25 E.   20 WINTER   27 ROSEMARY   28 OXLIP
BALM   PRIMROSE SAVORY
HYSSOP   1   1   HYSSOP
23   36 BOX   ENGLISH   32   36 BOX   PEPPER- BRICK
DAISY   MINT   EDGING
CARAWAY   24   1   1
1   1   JOHNNY-   31
21 RUE 26 POT   22 LAVENDER   JUMP-UP 30 SWEET 29 CLASSIC
MARIGOLD   22   VIOLET   MYRTLE
LAVENDER
33   2   2   33

SALAD
BURNET   MARJORAM   MARJORAM   SALAD
BURNET

27 Ft
8.2 M

GRAVEL PATHS

28 Ft
8.5 M

0   5   10 Ft

0   1   2   3 M

Herb Garden Design / 73

DESIGNED FOR MOONLIGHT

Intended for viewing from above, this moonlight herb garden can be enjoyed from a deck-overhang of the house from the middle of spring to early autumn. Careful planning with plant selection results in a delightful succession of bloom and fragrance. A mulch of cocoa bean hulls increases contrast so that white blooms on a night flooded with moonlight reach a startling peak of reflective illumination. In a departure from the usual that is most fitting for this garden, a moondial rather than a sundial is used. It bears a motto taken from Alice Morse Earle's *Sundials and Old Roses*: "Light and Darkness by Turn, but Always Love." Concrete blocks, required for a retaining wall at the back of the garden, serve also as planters for *Artemisia schmidtiana* 'Nana', silver mound. In addition to providing containers for growing herbs, concrete blocks help create an optimum pH for nourishing them. Although this is called a "moonlight" herb garden, its tufted, spurred, plumed, white blooms and woolly, white, silvery-gray foliage are almost equally showy by day, along with a measure of fragrance. However, like the moonflowers that bedeck the elegant wrought-iron plant hoop, most of the blooms are night-scented. Selected for this reason, they further ensure this herb garden is to be most savored during the evening and nighttime hours.

New York
Designed by Owner
The number in each planting area is the key number.

1. *Dianthus* 'White Lace', pink
2. *Thymus* 'Argenteus', silver thyme
3. *Santolina chamaecyparissus*, gray santolina
4. *Rosmarinus officinalis* 'Albus', rosemary
5. *Stachys byzantina*, lamb's-ears
6. *Viola odorata*, sweet violet
7. *Yucca filamentosa*, Adam's-needle
8. *Artemisia lactiflora*, white mugwort
9. *Artemisia absinthium*, absinthe
10. *Salvia sclarea*, clary
11. *Nicotiana alata* 'Daylight', nicotiana
12. *Artemisia ludoviciana* var. *albula*, silver-king artemisia
13. *Lunaria annua*, white honesty
14. *Chrysanthemum parthenium*, feverfew
15. *Marrubiam vulgare*, horehound
16. *Dictamnus albus*, fraxinella
17. *Galium odoratum*, sweet woodruff
18. *Primula sieboldii* 'Alba', white primrose
19. *Achillea millefolium* 'The Pearl', yarrow
20. *Artemisia ludoviciana*, western mugwort
21. *Iris* × *germanica* var. *florentina*, orris
22. *Artemisia stellerana*, beach wormwood
23. *Matthiola incana*, white stock
24. *Convallaria majalis*, lily-of-the-valley
25. *Lavandula angustifolia* subsp. *angustifolia* 'Alba', lavender
26. *Aquilegia alpina* 'Alba', columbine
27. *Hesperis matronalis*, dame's rocket
28. *Digitalis purpurea* 'Alba', foxglove
29. *Petunia* 'White Cascade', petunia
30. *Artemisia schmidtiana* 'Nana', silver mound artemisia
31. *Lilium candidum*, Madonna lily
32. *Galanthus nivalis*, snowdrop
33. *Narcissus pseudonarcissus* 'Mount Hood', white daffodil
34. *Narcissus pseudonarcissus* 'Cassata', daffodil
35. *Polianthes tuberosa*, tuberose

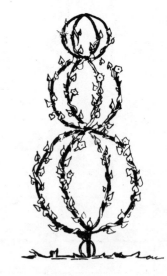

Wrought-iron plant hoop for moonflower

36. *Tulipa* 'White Triumphator', tulip
37. *Tulipa* 'Blizzard', tulip
38. *Ipomoea alba*, moonflower
39. *Rosa* 'Snowdwarf', rose
40. *Rosa* 'Cinderella', rose
41. *Malus* 'Guiding Star', crabapple

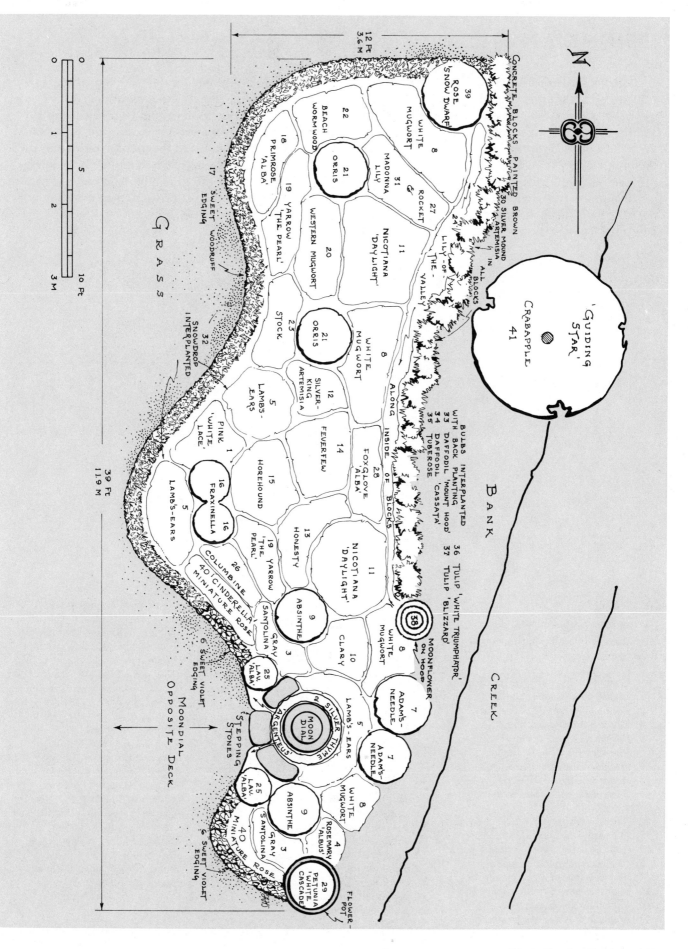

OF DYE AND TEXTILE

A specialty garden using only dye and textile-fiber plants presents another kind of challenge to a designer. Many of these herbs lack the hues, textures, and fragrances usually considered characteristic. The growth habits of some make it difficult to incorporate them into a plan. This herb garden, related to an old mill reconstruction, required their use as an educational adjunct. A design that would allow visitors to circulate easily in an area of moderate size was important, too. An existing iron fence and slope helped determine the outline for the plan. Varied shapes for the beds added interest and were arranged for ease of entrance and exit. Pattern could not be used to any extent to create interest, for most of these dye and textile herbs do not lend themselves to that sort of treatment. Rather, simplicity was the key and perhaps the factor that let this design be so in keeping with the old mill setting and yet prove so fitting for a more contemporary situation.

Rhode Island

Design from Contributor

The number in each planting area is the key number.

1. *Gossypium hirsutum*, upland cotton
2. *Linum usitatissimum*, flax
3. *Abutilon theophrasti*, China jute
4. *Hibiscus cannabinus*, kenaf
5. *Boehmeria nivea*, ramie
6. *Musa textilis*, Manila hemp
7. *Agave fourcroydes*, henequen
8. *Agave sisalana*, sisal hemp
9. *Sansevieria trifasciata*, bowstring hemp
10. *Furcraea hexapetala*, Cuban hemp
11. *Dipsacus sativus*, fuller's teasel
12. *Isatis tinctoria*, dyer's woad
13. *Chelidonium majus*, celandine
14. *Tagetes patula*, French marigold
15. *Solidago species*, goldenrod
16. *Phytolacca americana*, poke
17. *Monarda didyma*, bee balm
18. *Pteridium aquilinum*, bracken
19. *Convallaria majalis*, lily-of-the-valley
20. *Sanguinaria canadensis*, bloodroot
21. *Anthemis tinctoria*, golden marguerite
22. *Coptis trifolia*, goldthread
23. *Rumex obtusifolius*, broad dock
24. *Carthamus tinctorius*, safflower
25. *Urtica dioica*, stinging nettle
26. *Tagetes erecta*, African marigold
27. *Hypericum perforatum*, St.-John's-wort
28. *Coreopsis tinctoria*, calliopsis
29. *Polygonum hydropiperoides*, knotweed
30. *Galium odoratum*, sweet woodruff
31. *Rudbeckia hirta*, black-eyed Susan
32. *Filipendula ulmaria*, queen-of-the-meadow
33. *Anchusa officinalis*, alkanet
34. *Agrimonia eupatoria*, agrimony
35. *Rubia tinctorum*, madder
36. *Galium verum*, yellow bedstraw
37. *Rumex acetosa*, garden sorrel
38. *Reseda luteola*, weld
39. *Hydrastis canadensis*, goldenseal
40. *Crocus sativus*, saffron crocus
41. *Allium cepa*, onion
42. *Viburnum acerifolium*, dockmackie
43. *Genista tinctoria*, dyer's broom
44. *Cytisus scoparius*, Scotch broom
45. *Arctostaphylos uva-ursi*, bearberry
46. *Indigofera tinctoria*, indigo
47. *Genista germanica*, broom
48. *Mahonia aquifolium*, Oregon grape
49. *Berberis vulgaris*, barberry
50. *Vaccinium angustifolium* var. *laevifolium*, blueberry
51. *Cotinus coggygria*, smoke tree
52. *Ligustrum vulgare*, privet
53. *Cladrastis lutea*, yellowwood
54. *Rhus typhina*, sumac
55. *Morus rubra* or *alba*, mulberry
56. *Prunus persica*, peach
57. *Parmelia conspersa*, lichen

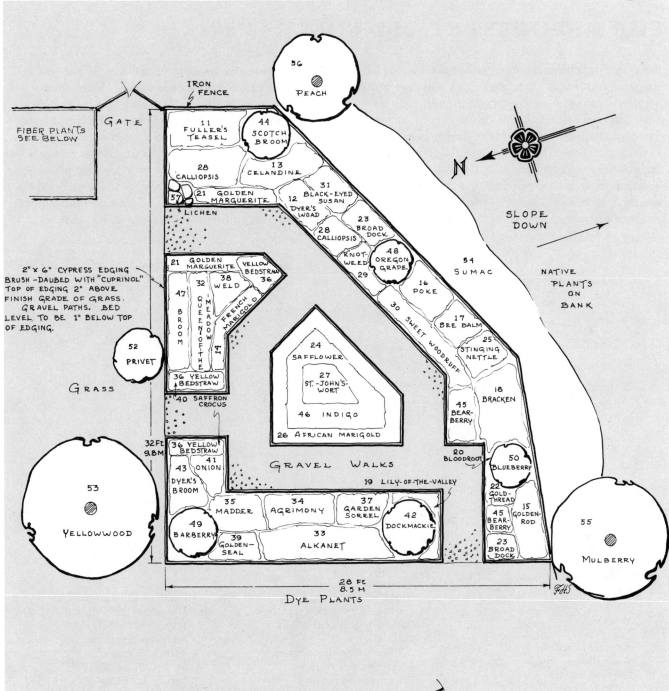

FIBER PLANTS
SEE BELOW

GATE

IRON FENCE

11 FULLER'S TEASEL
44 SCOTCH BROOM
56 PEACH

28 CALLIOPSIS
13 CELANDINE

57
21 GOLDEN MARGUERITE
31 BLACK-EYED SUSAN
12 DYER'S WOAD

LICHEN
28 CALLIOPSIS
23 BROAD DOCK
54 SUMAC

SLOPE DOWN

N

NATIVE PLANTS ON BANK

2" x 6" CYPRESS EDGING BRUSH-DAUBED WITH "CUPRINOL" TOP OF EDGING 2" ABOVE FINISH GRADE OF GRASS. GRAVEL PATHS. BED LEVEL TO BE 1" BELOW TOP OF EDGING.

21 GOLDEN MARGUERITE
47 BROOM
32 QUEEN OF THE MEADOW
38 WELD
14 FRENCH MARIGOLD
YELLOW BEDSTRAW 36

KNOTWEED 29
48 OREGON GRAPE
16 POKE

30 SWEET WOODRUFF
17 BEE BALM
25 STINGING NETTLE

52 PRIVET

GRASS

36 YELLOW BEDSTRAW
40 SAFFRON CROCUS

24 SAFFLOWER
27 ST.-JOHN'S-WORT
46 INDIGO
26 AFRICAN MARIGOLD

18 BRACKEN

45 BEAR-BERRY

32 Ft 9.8 M

36 YELLOW BEDSTRAW
41 ONION
43 DYER'S BROOM

GRAVEL WALKS

19 LILY-OF-THE-VALLEY

20 BLOODROOT

50 BLUEBERRY

53 YELLOWWOOD

35 MADDER
34 AGRIMONY
37 GARDEN SORREL
42 DOCKMACKIE

22 GOLD-THREAD
15 GOLDEN-ROD

49 BARBERRY
39 GOLDEN-SEAL
33 ALKANET

45 BEAR-BERRY
23 BROAD DOCK

55 MULBERRY

28 Ft 8.5 M

DYE PLANTS

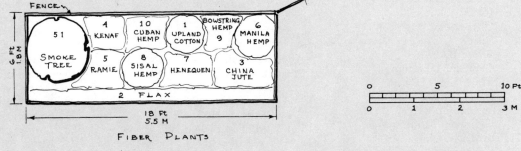

FENCE

51 SMOKE TREE
4 KENAF
10 CUBAN HEMP
1 UPLAND COTTON
BOWSTRING HEMP 9
6 MANILA HEMP

5 RAMIE
8 SISAL HEMP
7 HENEQUEN
3 CHINA JUTE

2 FLAX

6 Ft 1.8 M

18 Ft 5.5 M

FIBER PLANTS

0   5   10 Pt
0 1 2 3 M

FOR DEVOTEES OF OLD ROSES

This rectangle has been most pleasingly adapted for growing old roses. There are roomy corners for more vigorous growers—and many of the old roses are that. Sufficient space was made for a center of interest, a sundial surrounded by the dainty, pale-pink blooms of 'Cecile Brunner', by setting back the corners of the four adjacent beds. This same arc form is repeated in each long side bed. Symmetry was one of the goals in this design and is furthered with placement of three roses at each of these arcs. Elsewhere, at each end of the garden and at each entrance, balance is gained by meticulous planning of the rose selections. A totally appealing edging, *Epimedium* × *youngianum* 'Niveum', is used that blooms in late spring followed by its incomparable foliage. It needs only one clipping yearly in very early spring before the delicate white blossoms appear. Brick paving adds its air of formality and its warm tones complement the edging, as well as the roses. A white picket fence to enclose this lovely garden of old roses and support a number of climbing cultivars is no less than ideal.

Ohio

Designed by Owner

The first number in each planting area is the key number, the second shows the number of plants to be used.

1. *Rosa* 'Harison's Yellow'
2. 'White Rose of York'
3. 'Maiden's Blush'
4. 'Mignonette'
5. 'Belle Amour'
6. 'Empress Josephine'
7. 'Marie Pavic'
8. 'The Golden Rose of China'
9. 'Cecile Brunner'
10. MOSS
    'Chapeau de Napoleon'
    'Salet'
    'White Bath'
    'Capitaine John Ingram'
    'Mme. Louis Leveque'
    'Louis Gimard'
    common moss
    'Gloire des Mousseux'
11. DAMASK
    'Celsiana'
    'Cesonie'
    'Quatre Saisons'
    'Mme. Hardy'
    rose of Castile
    'York and Lancaster'
    'Leda'
    'Marie Louise'
12. GALLICA
    'Belle des Jardins'
    'Camaieux'
    'Cardinal Richelieu'
    'Duc de Fitzjames'
    'Tuscany'
    'Rosa Mundi'
    'Desiree Parmentier'
    'Duchess de Montebello'
13. BOURBON
    'Commandant Beaurepaire'
    'Coquette des Alpes'
    'Honorine de Brabant'
    'La Reine Victoria'
    'Souvenir de la Malmaison'
    'Louise Odier'
    'Mme. Ernst Calvat'
    'Variegata di Bologna'
14. CENTIFOLIA
    'Adeline'
    'Fantan Latour'
    'Petite de Hollande'
    'Prolifera de Redoute'
    red provence
    'Rose des Peintres'
    'The Bishop'
    'Blanchefleur'
15. ALBA
    'Konigen von Danemarck'
    'Mme. Legras de St. Germain'
    'Chloris'
    'Celestial'
    'Felicite Parmentier'
16. HYBRID PERPETUAL
    'Baronne Prevost'
    'Black Prince'
    'Baroness Rothschild'
    'Clio'
    'Duke of Edinburgh'
    'Duchess de Caylus'
    'Fisher Holmes'
    'Frau Karl Druschki'
    'Mabel Morrison'
    'Merry England'
    'Mrs. John Laing'
    'Paul Neyron'
    'Reine des Violettes'
    'Triomphe de L'Exposition'
    'Xavier Olibo'
17. *Rosa* 'Zephirine Drouhin', cl.
18. 'Queen of the Prairies', rambler
19. 'Seven Sisters', rambler
20. 'Crimson Rambler'
21. 'Souvenir de la Malmaison', cl.
22. 'Sombreuil', cl.
23. 'Mme. Alfred de Rougemont', cl.
24. 'American Pillar', cl.
25. 'Stanwell Perpetual'

Edging *Epimedium* × *youngianum* 'Niveum', white epimedium

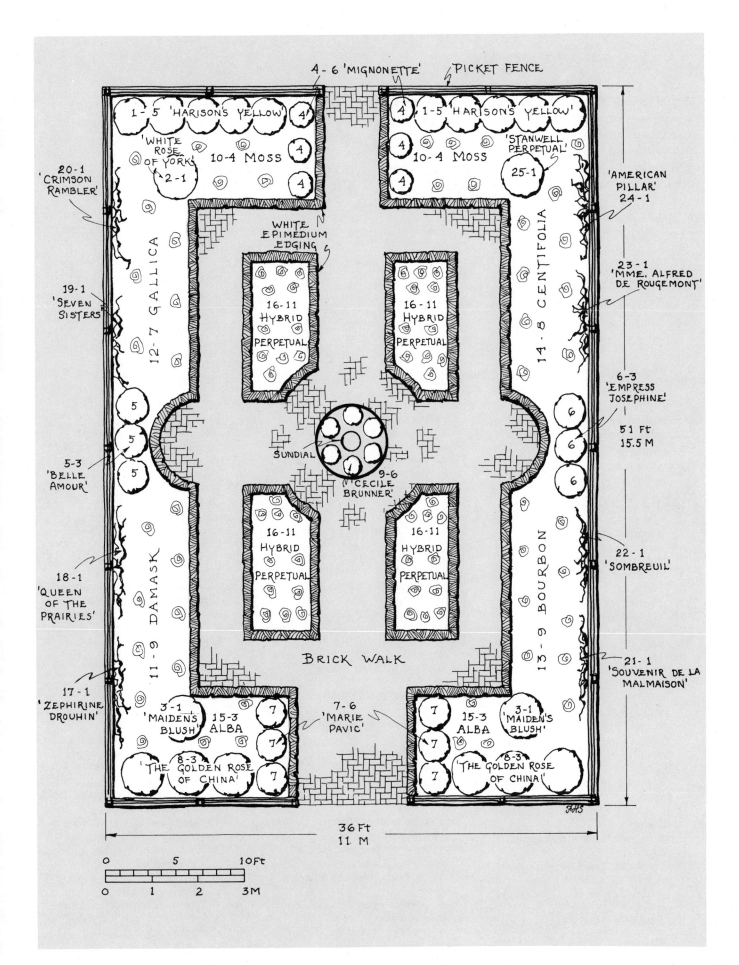

4- 6 'MIGNONETTE'
PICKET FENCE
1-5 'HARISON'S YELLOW'
4
'WHITE ROSE OF YORK' 2-1
10-4 MOSS
4
4
4
1-5 'HARISON'S YELLOW'
4
4
4
10-4 MOSS
4
4
'STANWELL PERPETUAL' 25-1
20-1 'CRIMSON RAMBLER'
'AMERICAN PILLAR' 24-1
12-7 GALLICA
WHITE EPIMEDIUM EDGING
14-8 CENTIFOLIA
23-1 'MME. ALFRED DE ROUGEMONT'
19-1 'SEVEN SISTERS'
16-11 HYBRID PERPETUAL
16-11 HYBRID PERPETUAL
6-3 'EMPRESS JOSEPHINE'
5
5
5
SUNDIAL
9-6 'CECILE BRUNNER'
6
6
6
51 Ft 15.5 M
5-3 'BELLE AMOUR'
DAMASK 11-9
16-11 HYBRID PERPETUAL
16-11 HYBRID PERPETUAL
13-9 BOURBON
22-1 'SOMBREUIL'
18-1 'QUEEN OF THE PRAIRIES'
BRICK WALK
21-1 'SOUVENIR DE LA MALMAISON'
17-1 'ZEPHIRINE DROUHIN'
3-1 'MAIDEN'S BLUSH'
15-3 ALBA
7
7-6 'MARIE PAVIC'
7
15-3 ALBA
3-1 'MAIDEN'S BLUSH'
8-3 'THE GOLDEN ROSE OF CHINA'
7
7
7
8-3 'THE GOLDEN ROSE OF CHINA'

36 Ft
11. M

0   5   10Ft
0   1   2   3M

Herb Garden Design / 79

AS A SALAD BOWL

As the design plan indicates, this "salad bowl" garden is a portion of a large complex of botanical gardens. Circles and angles provide interest, but the contrasting colors and varied textures of the plant material add greatly to it. There could be no more appropriate edging for it than the curly parsley used here. The notch of four square feet, abruptly cut out of the corner of this salad bowl plan, is easily understood when considered in relation to the whole. It is another way to make more space where paths intersect. This is a matter of importance for public gardens in particular but should not be overlooked for private gardens.

Wisconsin

Designed under the direction of Alfred L. Boerner, Landscape Architect

The number in each planting area is the key number.

Bed | Theme
I The salad bowl (ornamental vegetables and herbs)
II Medicinal herbs
III Culinary herbs
IV American native herbs
V American native herbs
VI Herbs used in design
VII Herbs used in design
VIII Scented herbs for sachets and potpourris
IX Herbs that repel insects
X Herbs for shady situations
XI Dye plants
XII Unclassified

1. *Petroselinum crispum* var. *crispum* 'Banquet', curly parsley
2. *Capsicum annuum* (Conoides Group) 'Fiesta', ornamental pepper
3. *C. annuum* 'Nosegay', ornamental pepper
4. *C. annuum* 'Pinocchio', ornamental pepper
5. *C. annuum* 'Fips', ornamental pepper
6. *C. annuum* 'Teno', ornamental pepper
7. *C. annuum* 'Red Boy', ornamental pepper
8. *C. annuum* 'Mosaic', ornamental pepper
9. *C. annuum* 'Variegata', ornamental pepper
10. *C. annuum* 'Floral Gem', ornamental pepper
11. *C. annuum* 'Black Prince', ornamental pepper
12. *Lycopersicon lycopersicum* var. *cerasiforme* 'Tiny Tim', cherry tomato
13. *L. lycopersicum* var. *pyriforme* 'Yellow Pear', pear tomato
14. *Brassica oleracea* (Capitata Group) 'Golden Acre', cabbage
15. *B. oleracea* 'Mammoth Red Rock', red cabbage
16. *B. oleracea* 'Red Acre', red cabbage
17. *B. oleracea* 'Ruby Ball', red cabbage
18. *B. oleracea* 'Green Parade', cabbage
19. *B. oleracea* 'Red Drumhead', red cabbage
20. *Allium cepa* Aggregatum Group, shallot
21. *A. schoenoprasum*, chive
22. *A. scorodoprasum*, giant garlic
23. *A. tuberosum*, garlic chive
24. *A. cepa* Proliferum Group, Egyptian onion
25. *A. ampeloprasum* (Porrum Group) 'American Flag', leek
26. *Apium graveolens* var. *dulce* 'Summer Pascal', celery
27. *A. graveolens* 'French Dinant', celery
28. *A. graveolens* var. *dulce* 'Golden Self-blanching', celery
29. *A. graveolens* var. *dulce* 'Giant Pascal', celery
30. *A. graveolens* var. *dulce* 'Utah 52–70', celery
31. *Beta vulgaris* (Cicla Group) 'White Fordhook Giant', swiss chard
32. *B. vulgaris* 'Rhubarb', ruby swiss chard
33. *B. vulgaris* 'Ruby Red', ruby swiss chard
34. *Brassica oleracea* (Gongylodes Group) 'Early Purple Vienna', kohlrabi
35. *B. oleracea* 'Early White Vienna', kohlrabi
36. *B. oleracea* 'Prima', kohlrabi
37. *Capsicum annuum* (Grossum Group) 'Whopper', sweet pepper
38. *C. annuum* 'Golden Bell', sweet pepper
39. *C. annuum* 'Sweet Chocolate', sweet pepper
40. *C. annuum* 'Sweet Cream', sweet pepper
41. *C. annuum* 'Wisconsin Lakes', sweet pepper
42. *Solanum melongena* var. *esculentum* 'Chinese Long Sword', eggplant
43. *S. melongena* var. *esculentum* 'Long Black', eggplant
44. *S. melongena* var. *esculentum* 'Black Beauty', eggplant
45. *Lactuca sativa* 'Oak Leaf', lettuce
46. *L. sativa* 'Ruby', lettuce
47. *Brassica oleracea* Acephala Group, red-flowered kale
48. *B. oleracea* Acephala Group, white-flowered kale
49. *B. oleracea* (Gemmifera Group) 'Jade Cross', brussels sprouts
50. *Cichorium intybus*, chicory

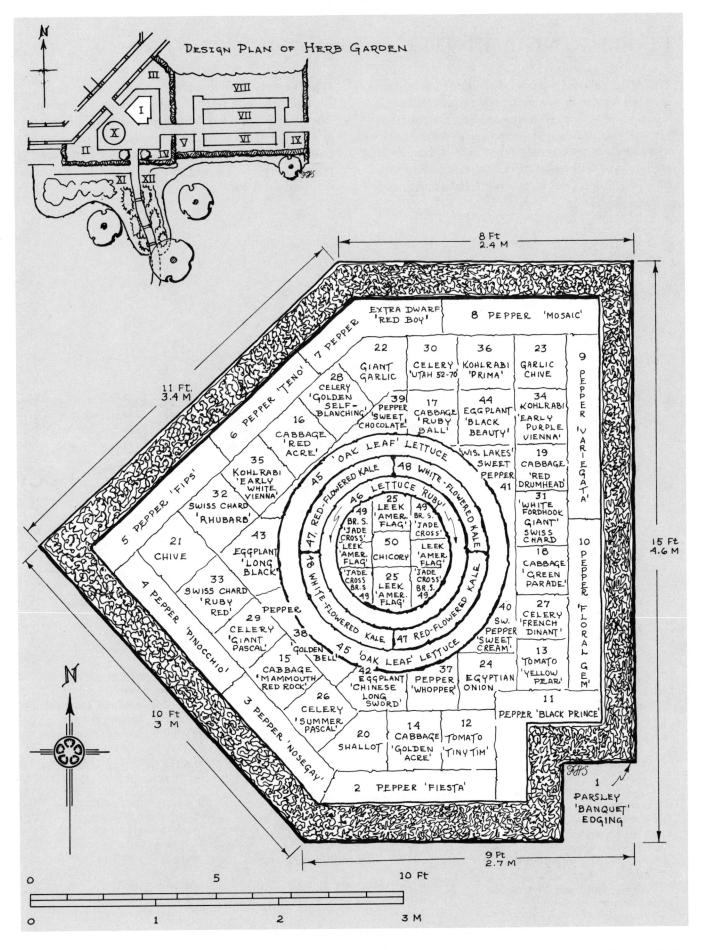

DESIGN PLAN OF HERB GARDEN

N

N

8 Ft
2.4 M

11 Ft
3.4 M

15 Ft
4.6 M

10 Ft
3 M

9 Ft
2.7 M

10 Ft

0   5

0   1   2   3 M

7 PEPPER
EXTRA DWARF 'RED BOY'   8 PEPPER 'MOSAIC'

6 PEPPER 'TENO'
5 PEPPER 'FIPS'
4 PEPPER 'PINOCCHIO'
3 PEPPER 'NOSEGAY'

9 PEPPER 'VARIEGATA'
10 PEPPER 'FLORAL GEM'

22 GIANT GARLIC
30 CELERY 'UTAH 52-70'
36 KOHLRABI 'PRIMA'
23 GARLIC CHIVE

28 CELERY 'GOLDEN SELF-BLANCHING'
39 PEPPER 'SWEET CHOCOLATE'
17 CABBAGE 'RUBY BALL'
44 EGGPLANT 'BLACK BEAUTY'
34 KOHLRABI 'EARLY PURPLE VIENNA'

16 CABBAGE 'RED ACRE'
41 WIS. LAKES' SWEET PEPPER
19 CABBAGE 'RED DRUMHEAD'

35 KOHLRABI 'EARLY WHITE VIENNA'
31 'WHITE FORDHOOK GIANT' SWISS CHARD

32 SWISS CHARD 'RHUBARB'
18 CABBAGE 'GREEN PARADE'

21 CHIVE
43 EGGPLANT 'LONG BLACK'

33 SWISS CHARD 'RUBY RED'

29 CELERY 'GIANT PASCAL'
PEPPER 'GOLDEN BELL' 38

15 CABBAGE 'MAMMOUTH RED ROCK'
26 CELERY 'SUMMER PASCAL'

45 'OAK LEAF' LETTUCE
48 WHITE-FLOWERED KALE
47 RED-FLOWERED KALE
46 LETTUCE 'RUBY'

49 BR. S. 'JADE CROSS'
25 LEEK 'AMER. FLAG'
49 BR. S. 'JADE CROSS'

LEEK 'AMER. FLAG'
50 CHICORY
LEEK 'AMER. FLAG'

'JADE CROSS BR. S. 49
25 LEEK 'AMER. FLAG'
'JADE CROSS BR. S. 49

48 WHITE-FLOWERED KALE
47 RED-FLOWERED KALE
45 'OAK LEAF' LETTUCE

40 SW. PEPPER 'SWEET CREAM'
27 CELERY 'FRENCH DINANT'
13 TOMATO 'YELLOW PEAR'

42 EGGPLANT 'CHINESE LONG SWORD'
37 PEPPER 'WHOPPER'
24 EGYPTIAN ONION

11 PEPPER 'BLACK PRINCE'

20 SHALLOT
14 CABBAGE 'GOLDEN ACRE'
12 TOMATO 'TINY TIM'

2 PEPPER 'FIESTA'

1 PARSLEY 'BANQUET' EDGING

Design Plan of Herb Garden

Herb Garden Design / 81

FEATURING A KNOT

This featured knot is the focal point for a group of herb gardens as shown in the design plan below. When viewed from the terrace above, the appeal of the whole is most apparent and the pleasing knot even more obvious. All of the circles, arcs, and angles are well defined with appropriate and varied plant material. The closed knot pattern is created using gray and green santolina, winter savory, and golden thyme. Germander edges the beds of scented-leaf geraniums. The inkberry and bayberry hedges make a fine background for them and continue as hedges, relating the knot to the rest of the gardens. Any one of the appealing herb gardens in this complex could be used separately, for each is a complete entity.

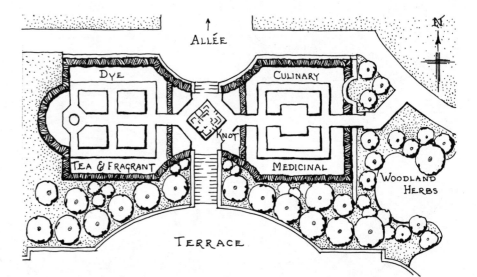

Design plan of herb garden

Ohio

Melissa R. Marshall, Landscape Architect, A.S.L.A., Assoc.

The number in each planting area is the key number.

1. *Thymus* 'Clear Gold', golden thyme
2. *Santolina chamaecyparissus*, gray santolina
3. *Satureja montana*, winter savory
4. *Santolina virens*, green santolina
5. *Teucrium chamaedrys*, germander
6. *Pelargonium denticulatum* 'Filicifolium', fern-leaf geranium
7. *P. graveolens* 'Lady Plymouth', rose geranium
8. *P. acerifolium*, maple-leaved geranium
9. *P. crispum* 'Prince Rupert', lemon geranium
10. *P. graveolens* 'Rober's Lemon Rose', rose geranium
11. *P. × nervosum* 'Toronto', ginger-scented geranium
12. *P. odoratissimum*, apple geranium
13. *P. capitatum* 'Logee's Snowflake', rose-scented geranium
14. *P. × limoneum* 'Lady Mary', English finger-bowl geranium
15. *P. radens* 'Dr. Livingston', crowfoot geranium
16. *P. tomentosum*, peppermint geranium
17. *P. graveolens*, rose geranium
18. *P. scabrum*, apricot geranium
19. *P. × fragrans* 'Variegatum', nutmeg geranium
20. *P. × nervosum*, lime geranium
21. *P. crispum*, lemon geranium
22. *P. crispum* 'French Lace,' lemon geranium
23. *P. grossularioides*, gooseberry geranium
24. *P. fulgidum* 'Scarlet Unique', pungent-scented geranium
25. *P. quercifolium* 'Village Hill Oak', oak-leaved geranium
26. *P. × domesticum* 'Clorinda', eucalyptus-scented geranium
27. *P. × citrosum* 'Prince of Orange', orange geranium
28. *Ilex glabra*, inkberry
29. *Myrica pensylvanica*, bayberry

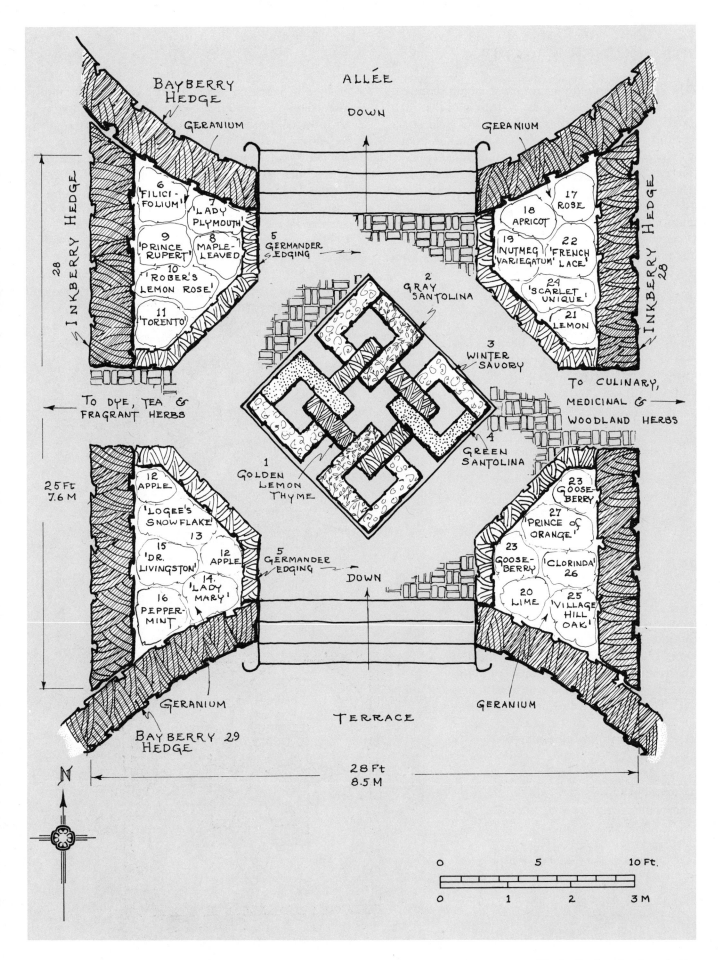

BAYBERRY HEDGE

GERANIUM

ALLÉE
DOWN

GERANIUM

INKBERRY HEDGE

28

6 'FILICI-FOLIUM'
7 'LADY PLYMOUTH'
9 'PRINCE RUPERT'
8 MAPLE-LEAVED
10 'ROBER'S LEMON ROSE'
11 'TORENTO'

5 GERMANDER EDGING

2 GRAY SANTOLINA

3 WINTER SAVORY

1 GOLDEN LEMON THYME

4 GREEN SANTOLINA

17 ROSE
18 APRICOT
19 NUTMEG 'VARIEGATUM'
22 'FRENCH LACE'
24 'SCARLET UNIQUE'
21 LEMON

INKBERRY HEDGE
28

TO CULINARY, MEDICINAL & WOODLAND HERBS

TO DYE, TEA & FRAGRANT HERBS

25 Ft 7.6 M

12 APPLE
'LOGEE'S SNOWFLAKE' 13
15 'DR. LIVINGSTON'
12 APPLE
14 'LADY MARY'
16 PEPPERMINT

5 GERMANDER EDGING

DOWN

23 GOOSEBERRY
27 'PRINCE of ORANGE'
23 GOOSEBERRY
'CLORINDA' 26
20 LIME
25 'VILLAGE HILL OAK'

GERANIUM

GERANIUM

TERRACE

BAYBERRY 29 HEDGE

N

28 Ft 8.5 M

0   5   10 Ft.

0   1   2   3 M

ON MORE KNOTS

The knot garden with its history spanning centuries has obviously appealed to many. It follows that such favor would spawn experimentation and yield a variety of treatments with a variety of designs. A knot can be as intricate or as simple as individual taste dictates. Its interspaces can be mulched, filled with plants that have contrasting color, texture, and growth to the plants of the knot design, or simply filled with inert material such as gravel, sand, or marble chips. Maintenance is high for a knot. Clipping is required on a routine basis to sustain the design. For the knot to look its best at all times, extra plants of each kind used should be grown elsewhere to fill in should one or more fail to thrive. Sometimes a knot is referred to as "closed," when bands of contrasting colors pass over and under each other in the design. One referred to as "open" is a patterned design without this interlacing. To ease the care for a more complicated design, slower-growing plant material needs to be used, such as a dwarf edging box. A few pleasing knot designs are included here and their plant material is listed.

For ease of maintenance this same knot design, on page 37, was planted using edging box only. A totally different effect —that of a closed knot—is created here using much interlacing with three varieties of herbs.

1. *Lavandula angustifolia*, English lavender
2. *Hyssopus officinalis*, blue hyssop
3. *Santolina virens*, green santolina

1 LAVENDER

2 HYSSOP

3 GREEN SANTOLINA

FHS

9½ Ft
2.9 M

Four circles and a square are used to create an unusual, closed knot design. The selection of herbs for their contrasting textures and colors emphasizes the intricacy of the pattern, which is framed with a brick edging. The background carpet of crimson creeping thyme creates a pleasing contrast, especially when it is blooming.

Texas

Designed by Owner

The number in each planting area is the key number.

1. *Santolina virens*, green santolina
2. *Santolina chamaecyparissus*, gray santolina
3. *Buxus sempervirens* 'Suffruticosa', dwarf edging box
4. *Thymus praecox* subsp. *arcticus* 'Coccineus', crimson creeping thyme

BRICK EDGING

1 GREEN SANTOLINA

2 GRAY SANTOLINA

10 FT
3.05 M
SQUARE

3 DWARF BOX

4 CRIMSON CREEPING THYME

FHS

This is unusual placement for a knot, which is found more often out in the open. It is situated in a corner formed by two walls of the house and is a part of the terrace. A brick edging raises the knot to the same level as the floor in the house. The knot material is maintained at six inches, the height of the edging. Located to provide more hours of enjoyment from the much-used terrace and the floor-length window of the house, the knot has the effect of being a part of the room. In another departure from the usual, 'Crimson Pigmy' barberry is combined with germander—often used—to create this closed knot. A dwarf box ties it together at the center. The four interspaces are planted with as many varieties of very low-growing, creeping thymes, which are confined to that area. The four corners are accented with specimens of preference, and the espaliered 'Brown Turkey' fig adds interest to and softens the brick wall. Some maintenance is required for clipping, but weeding is minimal since a mulch is used of pecan shells, a pleasing cinnamon-brown color and nice background for the herbs.

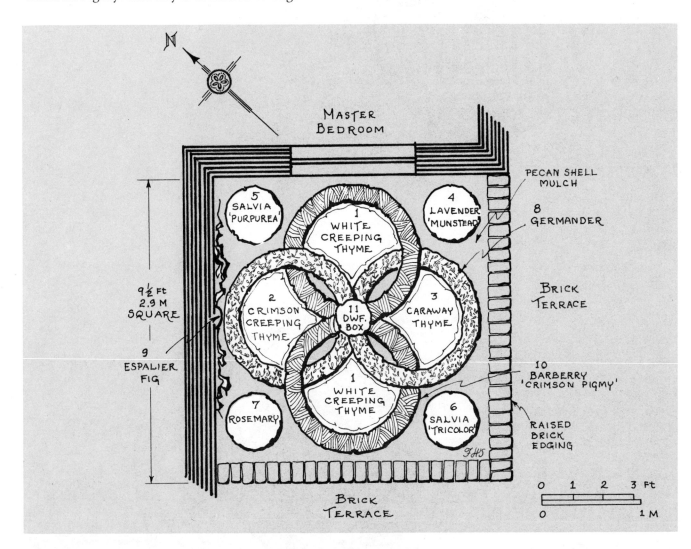

Tennessee

Designed by Owner

The number in each planting area is the key number.

1. *Thymus praecox* subsp. *arcticus* 'Albus', white creeping thyme
2. *T. praecox* subsp. *arcticus* 'Coccineus', crimson creeping thyme
3. *T. herba-barona*, caraway thyme
4. *Lavandula angustifolia* subsp. *angustifolia* 'Munstead', lavender
5. *Salvia officinalis* 'Purpurea', purple variegated garden sage
6. *S. officinalis* 'Tricolor', variegated garden sage
7. *Rosmarinus officinalis*, rosemary
8. *Teucrium chamaedrys*, germander
9. *Ficus* 'Brown Turkey', fig
10. *Berberis thunbergii* 'Crimson Pigmy', Japanese barberry
11. *Buxus sempervirens* 'Suffruticosa', dwarf edging box

The design plan shows how this knot garden serves as the center of interest and relates to the rest of the herb garden. Inert material of red and white stones makes the design even more apparent than would foliage contrast alone. The knot is most suitably framed with concentric circles of brick paving.

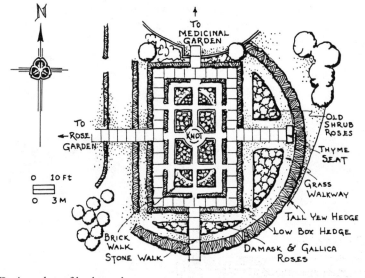

Design plan of herb garden

Michigan

Designed by Contributor

1. *Santolina chamaecyparissus*, gray santolina
2. *Teucrium canadense*, American germander
3. *Lavandula angustifolia* subsp. *angustifolia* 'Hidcote', lavender

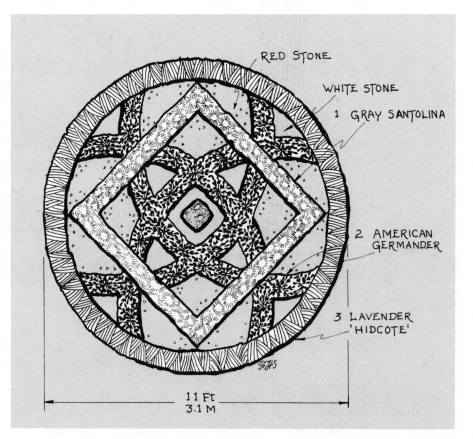

This knot garden is patterned after the square knot. Its simplicity creates a contemporary feeling. The design plan illustrates the use of this knot as a focal point for the herb garden. Marble chips are used in the unplanted portion of the knot, setting it off admirably.

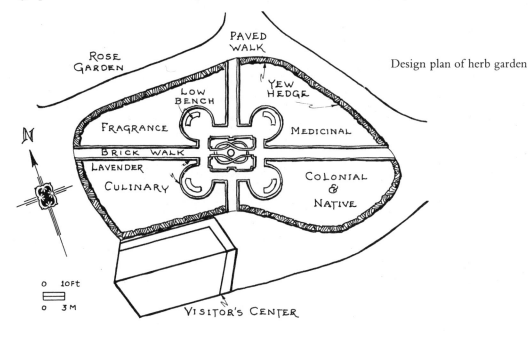

Design plan of herb garden

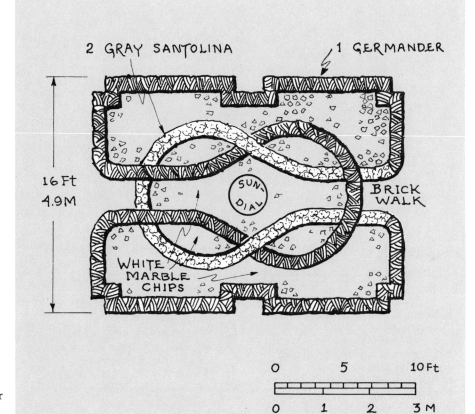

Michigan

Designed by Contributor

1. *Teucrium chamaedrys*, germander
2. *Santolina chamaecyparissus*, gray santolina

ALL GRAY AND SILVER

Only gray and silver herbs are used for this plan created with three circles of brick for its circumference. The inner circle of brick is laid on edge and ties in with the work paths, which are also laid on edge. The result is a different look and more firmly defined beds, each one a quarter-circle. Concentric plantings emphasize the octagon where the paths meet—a nice spot to display a specimen plant or a strawberry jar, for it is a low-growing *Allium* circling it. The center is further set apart from the remainder of the plant-ings by brick, again laid on edge, a device that may discourage roots from intermingling. Santolinas are a fine choice to frame this herb garden. They take clipping well and keep the exterior path clear for walking. The choice of brick for paths provides a warm, pleasing color, a complement for the colors of the plant material. The foliage of a number of these gray and silver herbs brings their strongly textural quality to this plan, adding another facet to an appealing design.

Ohio

Designed by Owner

The number in each planting area is the key number.

1. *Santolina chamaecyparissus*, gray santolina
2. *Santolina neapolitana*
3. *Dianthus* × *caryophyllus*, dwarf grenadin pink
4. *Salvia clevelandii*, blue sage
5. *Crithmum maritimum*, samphire
6. *Salvia argentea*, silver sage
7. *Lavandula angustifolia* subsp. *angustifolia* 'Hidcote', lavender
8. *Lavandula angustifolia* subsp. *angustifolia* 'Munstead', lavender
9. *Leontopodium alpinum*, edelweiss
10. *Marrubium incanum*, silver horehound
11. *Lavandula dentata* var. *candicans*, French lavender
12. *Anthemis marschalliana*, chamomile
13. *Lavandula angustifolia* subsp. *angustifolia* 'Rosea', lavender
14. *Thymus* 'Argenteus', silver thyme
15. *Helichrysum angustifolium*, curry plant
16. *Stachys byzantina*, lamb's-ears
17. *Artemisia frigida*, fringed wormwood
18. *Lavandula angustifolia* subsp. *angustifolia* 'Gray Lady', lavender
19. *Santolina chamaecyparissus* 'Nana', dwarf gray santolina
20. *Ruta graveolens* 'Blue Mound', rue
21. *Teucrium fruticans*, tree germander
22. *Achillea tomentosa* 'King Edward', woolly yarrow
23. *Perovskia atriplicifolia*, Russian sage
24. *Anthemis tinctoria*, golden marguerite
25. *Artemisia arborescens*, tree artemisia
26. *Achillea filipendulina* 'Moonshine', fern-leaf yarrow
27. *Allium senescens* var. *glaucum*

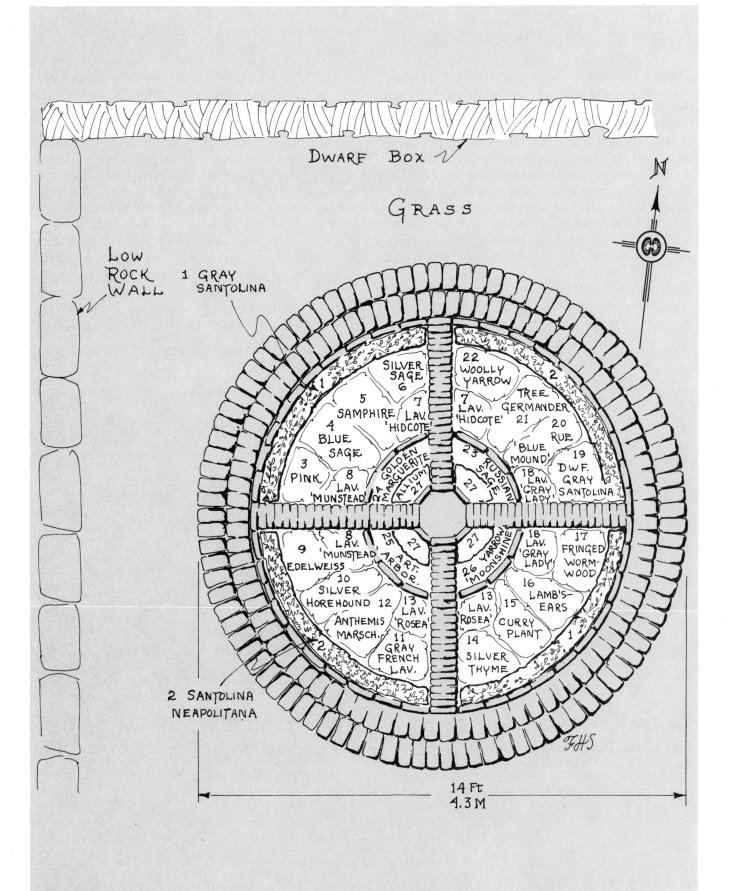

DWARF BOX

GRASS

N

LOW
ROCK
WALL

1 GRAY
SANTOLINA

1

SILVER
SAGE
6

22
WOOLLY
YARROW

2

5

7

7
LAV.
'HIDCOTE'

TREE
GERMANDER
21

SAMPHIRE

LAV.
'HIDCOTE'

20
RUE

4
BLUE
SAGE

'BLUE
MOUND'

3
PINK

8
LAV.
'MUNSTEAD'

A GOLDEN
MARGUERITE
ALLIUM
27

23
RUSSIAN
SAGE

18
LAV.
'GRAY
LADY'

19
DWF.
GRAY
SANTOLINA

27

27

8
LAV.
'MUNSTEAD'

9
EDELWEISS

25
ART.
ARBOR.

27

26
YARROW
'MOONSHINE'

27

18
LAV.
'GRAY
LADY'

17
FRINGED
WORM-
WOOD

10
SILVER
HOREHOUND 12

13
LAV.
'ROSEA'

13
LAV.
'ROSEA'

15

16
LAMB'S-
EARS

ANTHEMIS
MARSCH.

11
GRAY
FRENCH
LAV.

14
SILVER
THYME

CURRY
PLANT

1

2

2 SANTOLINA
NEAPOLITANA

FHS

14 Ft
4.3 M

USING CONTAINERS

Container gardening can be a satisfying way to grow herbs, either as an adjunct to an established herb garden or as a sole means of growing them. Many herbs lend themselves to being cultivated in containers. If one is familiar with herbs, it is easy to visualize those more suitable for this purpose. Some are rosemary, thyme, sweet marjoram, oregano, lady's-mantle, basil, and the savories. Styles of containers, which include hanging baskets, are without number. If the container is compatible with the general aspect of the area to be used, only its size and relative proportion are of real concern. The color of the container plays a lesser role, but it should set off the herbs and not overpower their subtle tones. For some locales growing herbs in containers may mean the difference between having an herb garden or not having one.

Areas in Florida and desert areas in the southwestern United States are hostile environments for herbs. Their extremes of heat and humidity or aridity make it more difficult to grow herbs than do the extremes of northern cold. Apartment and condominium dwellers have the same need to cultivate herbs in containers if fresh herbs are to be on hand at all. The advantages of container herb gardening are worth noting: mobile, the herb garden "design" is flexible—ready to be altered when the season or artistic fancy dictates—and the growing conditions are more easily controlled. As with other plant material, the culture of herbs in containers is sufficiently different from their culture in the open ground to warrant the use of one of the references currently available on this subject, a number of which are listed in the bibliography.

A condominium terrace might be an attractive site for a half-barrel that accommodates an assortment of herbs.

Often, the only sunny spot in a city lot is the space between the driveway and house, as with this container herb garden. It has endured for twenty years and has proved thoroughly satisfying, providing herbs in abundance.

A balcony garden, visually pleasing against the backdrop of a great metropolitan skyline. Herbs have flourished in this growing arrangement for nearly twenty years.

GARDENS FOR CIVIC
OR EDUCATIONAL PURPOSES

STRICTLY FOR CHILDREN

These gardens were designed strictly for children, and so they are strictly uncomplicated. They need to be planned in this manner so that children can learn as much as possible on their own. Of course supervision is necessary, and an obvious interest in how the garden fares is in order for the overseer. Seeds are used for the most part—for the fun of growing things from seed and for the knowledge to be gained. Enclosure is not recommended for these three plans since an enclosure usually represents substantial time and expenditure. If children's interest is not sustained, such an outlay would be unwarranted. However, good soil and a well-drained location in full sun are needed to ensure the success necessary to encourage a continuing interest. Simple plans like these provide ample opportunity for younger children to experiment with the world of plants.

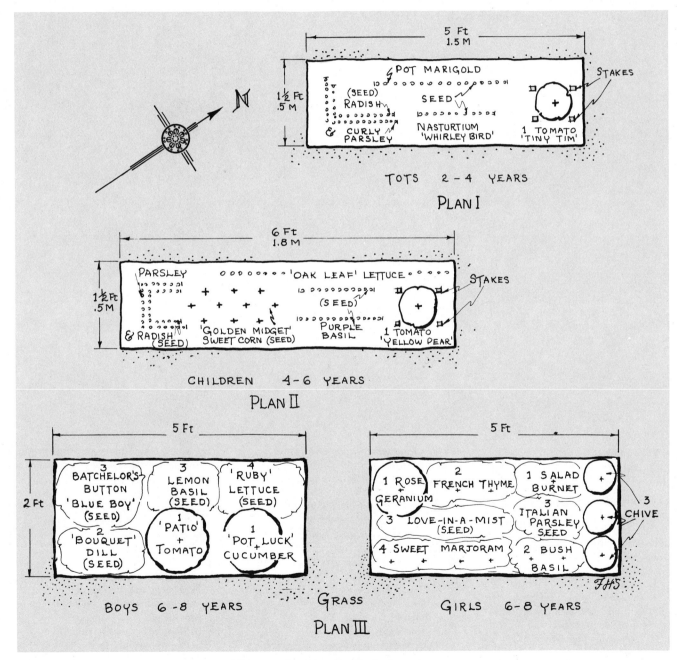

Connecticut

Margaret Osborn Holt, Landscape Architect, A.S.L.A.

The number in each planting area is the quantity of plants to be used.

By eight to twelve years of age it may be clear that children's interest justifies expanding the garden area, using simple means for raising the beds and including a small rest area or private patio. Children in this age group can help with the construction, too. There is a feeling of enclosure here with the layout of the outer beds and the roses. These are "old roses," selected for their greater fragrance, and perhaps just as much because they demand less care than hybrid tea roses. Ordinarily no sprays or dusts are essential for their survival and many are recurrent bloomers. If Japanese beetles are a nuisance, they are easily handpicked. A sundial can be fun and also educational. Instead of benches on the patio, an experiment with turf seats could be tried. It is an ambitious project but likely to be successful with the proper plant material; woolly thyme and mother-of-thyme are two. Just keep a garden design for children simple, with room for a project or two to rouse the curiosity and to impart the idea that learning is fun. It can foster an interest in gardening with herbs.

Connecticut

Margaret Osborn Holt, Landscape Architect, A.S.L.A.

The number in each planting area is the key number.

1. *Levisticum officinale*, lovage
2. *Ocimum basilicum* 'Purpurascens', purple basil
3. *Nigella damascena*, love-in-a-mist
4. *Borago officinalis*, borage
5. *Ocimum basilicum* 'Minimum', purple form bush basil
6. *Lavandula angustifolia* subsp. *angustifolia* 'Munstead', English lavender
7. *Dianthus plumarius*, cottage pink
8. *Ocimum basilicum* 'Minimum', bush basil
9. *Petroselinum crispum* var. *crispum*, curly parsley
10. *Hedeoma pulegioides*, American pennyroyal
11. *Satureja hortensis*, summer savory
12. *Chenopodium botrys*, ambrosia
13. *Fragaria* 'Fraises des Bois', alpine strawberry
14. *Lavandula angustifolia*, English lavender
15. *Artemisia abrotanum*, southernwood
16. *Artemisia camphorata*, camphor-scented wormwood
17. *Tropaeolum minus*, dwarf nasturtium
18. *Calendula officinalis*, pot marigold
19. *Isatis tinctoria*, dyer's woad
20. *Origanum majorana*, sweet marjoram
21. *Anethum graveolens*, dill
22. *Petroselinum crispum* var. *neapolitanum*, Italian parsley
23. *Salvia officinalis*, garden sage
24. *Salvia sclarea*, clary
25. *Marrubium vulgare*, horehound
26. *Nepeta cataria*, catnip
27. *Allium sativum* var. *ophioscorodon*, rocambole
28. *Allium tuberosum*, garlic chive
29. *Allium moly*, lily leek
30. *Allium senescens* var. *glaucum*
31. *Rosa damascena*, damask rose
32. *Rosa gallica*, French rose

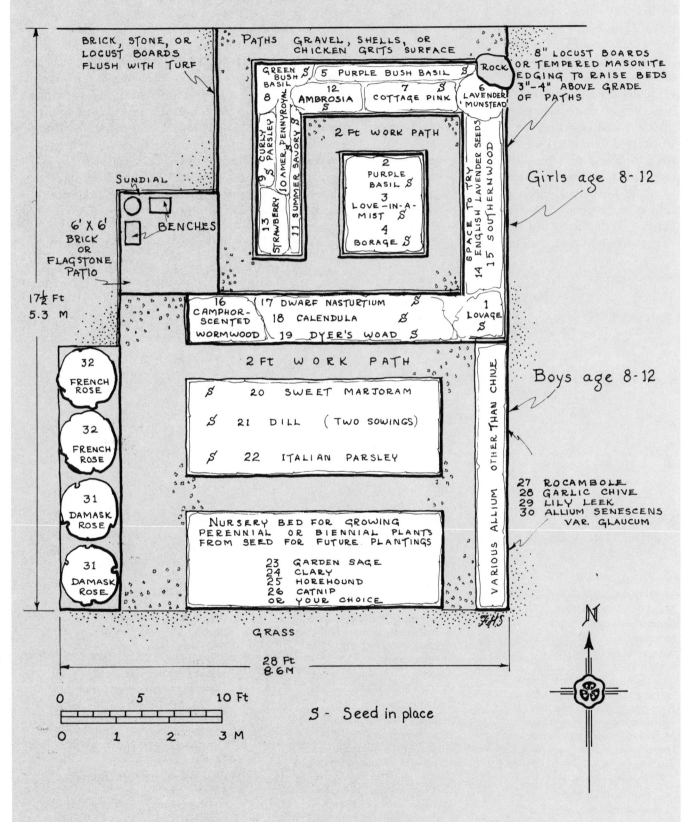

WALK

BRICK, STONE, OR LOCUST BOARDS FLUSH WITH TURF

Paths GRAVEL, SHELLS, OR CHICKEN GRITS SURFACE

8" LOCUST BOARDS OR TEMPERED MASONITE EDGING TO RAISE BEDS 3"-4" ABOVE GRADE OF PATHS

GREEN BUSH BASIL

8

5 PURPLE BUSH BASIL

Rock

12 AMBROSIA

7 COTTAGE PINK

6 LAVENDER MUNSTEAD

9 CURLY PARSLEY

10 AMER. PENNYROYAL

11 SUMMER SAVORY

13 STRAWBERRY

2 FT WORK PATH

2 PURPLE BASIL

3 LOVE-IN-A-MIST

4 BORAGE

14 SPACE TO TRY ENGLISH LAVENDER SEEDS

15 SOUTHERNWOOD

Girls age 8-12

SUNDIAL

BENCHES

6' X 6' BRICK OR FLAGSTONE PATIO

17½ Ft 5.3 M

16 CAMPHOR-SCENTED WORMWOOD

17 DWARF NASTURTIUM

18 CALENDULA

19 DYER'S WOAD

1 LOVAGE

32 FRENCH ROSE

32 FRENCH ROSE

31 DAMASK ROSE

31 DAMASK ROSE

2 FT WORK PATH

20 SWEET MARJORAM

21 DILL (TWO SOWINGS)

22 ITALIAN PARSLEY

NURSERY BED FOR GROWING PERENNIAL OR BIENNIAL PLANTS FROM SEED FOR FUTURE PLANTINGS

23 GARDEN SAGE
24 CLARY
25 HOREHOUND
26 CATNIP
OR YOUR CHOICE

Boys age 8-12

VARIOUS ALLIUM OTHER THAN CHIVE

27 ROCAMBOLE
28 GARLIC CHIVE
29 LILY LEEK
30 ALLIUM SENESCENS VAR. GLAUCUM

GRASS

28 Ft 8.6 M

0   5   10 Ft

0   1   2   3 M

S - Seed in place

N

OF EXPLORATION

A special plan to meet a special need, this herb garden enclosed by a deutzia hedge has fourteen planting boxes. The oval, previously used as a skating rink, was excavated and the boxes constructed at a height of eighteen inches—a good height for use by children or by an adult in a wheelchair. The design is a medley of shapes and textures, for this is an herb garden for those whose vision is impaired or absent. Tailored for their exploration with other senses in every manner, from the different fragrances and textures of herbs to the sculptures, it is a product of extraordinary imagination in planning. The sculptures, not noted on the plan, are a seal and a turtle, plus a lead squirrel artfully placed on the edge of one of the beds. All are inviting to the touch. An uncommonly designed walk of concrete bordered with brick facilitates the progress of the explorer from one box to another. The three circles resulting from the design are used for a central fish pond—complete with water lilies and a fine-spray fountain—flanked by a star magnolia specimen on each side. Varied shapes of the planting boxes and varied textures underfoot help orient the investigator. Giving each box a different name and planting it with herbs that fit its category makes the learning process not simply painless but a true joy. The list of plants is seemingly endless and necessarily abridged. A few from some groups are listed and show that imagination was not limited to design alone but was used in the complete concept of the herb garden, making it a total delight not only to the disadvantaged but to all.

Arkansas
Neil Hamill Park, Landscape Architect, F.A.A.R.

Bee Garden

Trifolium pratense, red clover
Myrrhis odorata, sweet cicely
Foeniculum vulgare, fennel
Origanum majorana, sweet marjoram
Borago officinalis, borage
Monarda didyma, bee balm
Satureja montana, winter savory
Salvia officinalis, garden sage
Hyssopus officinalis, blue hyssop
Teucrium chamaedrys, germander
Melissa officinalis, lemon balm
Origanum heracleoticum, Greek oregano
Thymus vulgaris 'Narrow-leaf French' French thyme

Pest Repellent Garden

Ocimum basilicum, sweet basil
Nepeta cataria, catnip
Chamaemelum nobile, chamomile
Allium schoenoprasum, chive
Allium sativum, garlic
Lavandula angustifolia, English lavender
Hedeoma pulegioides, American pennyroyal
Santolina chamaecyparissus, gray santolina
Rosmarinus officinalis, rosemary
Artemisia abrotanum, southernwood
Tanacetum vulgare, tansy
Mentha, mint
Tagetes, marigold
Achillea millefolium, yarrow

Zoo Garden

Stachys byzantina, lamb's-ears
Nepeta cataria, catnip
Armoracia rusticana, horseradish
Marrubium vulgare, horehound
Taraxacum officinale, dandelion
Tussilago farfara, coltsfoot
Mimulus, monkey flower
Chenopodium bonus-henricus, fat-hen
Primula veris, cowslip
Linaria, toadflax
Chrysanthemum leucanthemum, oxeye daisy
Ophrys apifera, bee orchid
Erigeron, fleabane
Stellaria, chickweed
Pedicularis canadensis, lousewort
Viola canina, dog violet
Lemna, duckweed
Antennaria, pussy-toes
Celosia cristata, cockscomb
Sedum morganianum, donkey's tail
Monarda punctata, horsemint
Justicia brandegeana, shrimp plant
Lychnis flos-cuculi, cuckoo flower
Tragopogon pratensis, goatsbeard
Campanula divaricata, harebell

Tea Garden

Chamaemelum nobile, chamomile
Mentha, mint
Galium odoratum, sweet woodruff
Gaultheria procumbens, wintergreen
Aloysia triphylla, lemon verbena

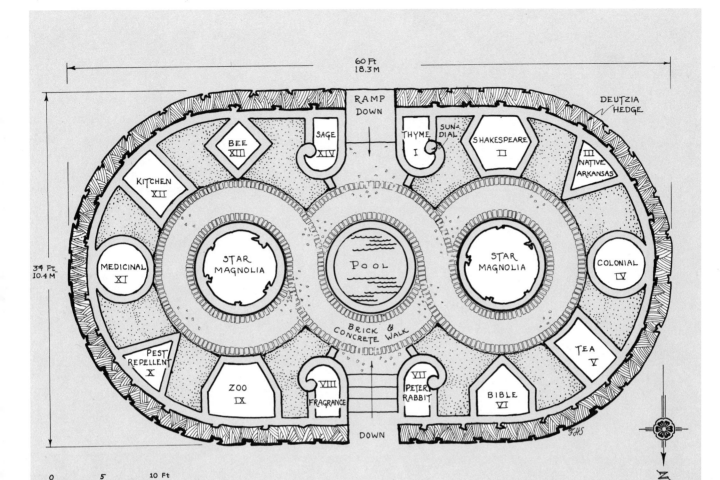

60 Ft
18.3 M

RAMP
DOWN

DEUTZIA
HEDGE

BEE
XIII

SAGE
XIV

THYME
I

SUN-
DIAL

SHAKESPEARE
II

III
NATIVE
ARKANSAS

KITCHEN
XII

34 Ft.
10.4 M

MEDICINAL
XI

STAR
MAGNOLIA

POOL

STAR
MAGNOLIA

COLONIAL
IV

BRICK &
CONCRETE WALK

PEST
REPELLENT
X

TEA
V

ZOO
IX

VIII
FRAGRANCE

VII
PETER
RABBIT

BIBLE
VI

DOWN

FHS

N

0   5   10 Ft

0   1   2   3 M

FOR SCHOLARLY PURSUIT

No need to construct an enclosure here, for an old barn foundation of stone, its wooden structure long gone, makes a site well protected from excesses of weather. An herb garden exposure is important in any location; in a climate like this it can be of critical import. A longer growing season is highly desirable for this garden of herbs, developed particularly for study. Its plant list, an exceedingly long one, reflects its purpose and explains the absence of drifts of color for effect. Instead, it is more important to add another single species or variety needed to satisfy intellectual curiosity. An existing concrete wall eighteen inches high formed one long bed, and old barn beams another about the same height. Their height eases the task of weeding. A smaller bed so constructed completes the growing area—except for a variety of thymes, a mint, feverfew, and plantain that grow casually on the basket-weave-patterned brick floor. A number of wooden window frames, minus the lintel but still in place at the top of the stone foundation, are superb for displaying potted herbs. The subtle gray of weathered wood frames them most suitably. Some herbs were relegated to a bed outside the foundation and near the entrance. Here, their invasiveness could not crowd out the individual specimens. There is no intricate pattern to demand hours for grooming, hours that are desired for the scholarly pursuit of herbs. Still, it is a most satisfying growing situation, and there is no doubt that its nicely sheltered location does much to make it so.

Ontario

Designed by Owner

The number in each planting area is the key number.

1. *Viola odorata*, sweet violet
2. *Galium odoratum*, sweet woodruff
3. *Achillea millefolium*, yarrow
4. *Angelica archangelica*, angelica
5. *Agastache foeniculum*, anise hyssop
6. *Artemisia dracunculus* var. *sativa*, French tarragon
7. *A. pontica*, Roman wormwood
8. *A. stellerana*, beach wormwood
9. *A. abrotanum*, southernwood
10. *A. camphorata*, camphor-scented wormwood
11. *A. abrotanum* 'Tangerine', southernwood
12. *A. absinthium*, absinthe
13. *Melissa officinalis*, lemon balm
14. *Ocimum basilicum*, sweet basil
15. *O. basilicum* 'Citriodorum', lemon basil
16. *O. basilicum* 'Minimum', bush basil
17. *O. basilicum* 'Purpurascens', purple basil
18. *Monarda didyma*, bee balm
19. *M. didyma* 'Rosea', pink bee balm
20. *Digitalis lanata*, Grecian foxglove
21. *Poterium sanguisorba*, salad burnet
22. *Chrysanthemum balsamita*, costmary
23. *Calamintha grandiflora*, calamint
24. *Nepeta mussinii*, catmint
25. *Campanula persicifolia*, peach-bells
26. *Echium vulgare*, viper's bugloss
27. *Chelidonium majus*, celandine
28. *Ranunculus ficaria*, lesser celandine
29. *Chamaemelum nobile*, chamomile
30. *Anthriscus cerefolium*, chervil
31. *Cichorium intybus*, chicory
32. *Symphytum officinale*, comfrey
33. *Primula veris*, cowslip
34. *Helichrysum angustifolium*, curry plant
35. *Chrysanthemum leucanthemum*, ox-eye daisy
36. *Dianthus plumarius* 'Nanus', cottage pink

37. *Origanum dictamnus*, dittany-of-Crete
38. *Oenothera biennis*, evening primrose
39. *Chrysanthemum parthenium*, feverfew
40. *Digitalis purpurea*, foxglove
41. *Genista tinctoria*, dyer's broom
42. *Geranium robertianum*, herb Robert
43. *Pelargonium crispum*, lemon geranium
44. *P. tomentosum*, peppermint geranium
45. *P. graveolens*, rose geranium
46. *P. odoratissimum*, apple geranium
47. *Teucrium chamaedrys*, germander
48. *Physalis heterophylla*, ground cherry
49. *Viola tricolor*, Johnny-jump-up
50. *Sempervivum tectorum*, houseleek
51. *Althaea officinalis*, marsh mallow
52. *Marrubium vulgare*, horehound
53. *Hyssopus officinalis*, blue hyssop
54. *Asarum canadense*, wild ginger
55. *Alchemilla vulgaris*, lady's-mantle
56. *Lavandula angustifolia*, English lavender
57. *Agastache cana*, mosquito plant
58. *Levisticum officinale*, lovage
59. *Euphorbia cyparissias*, cypress spurge
60. *Pulmonaria officinalis*, blue lungwort
61. *Lychnis coronaria*, rose campion
62. *Valeriana officinalis*, valerian
63. *Calendula officinalis*, pot marigold
64. *Origanum vulgare* 'Aureum', golden marjoram
65. *O. onites*, pot marjoram
66. *O. majorana*, sweet marjoram
67. *Rubia tinctorum*, madder
68. *Mentha suaveolens*, apple mint
69. *M. suaveolens* 'Variegata', pineapple mint
70. *M. × piperita* var. *citrata*, orange mint
71. *M. × gentilis*, red mint
72. *M. spicata*, spearmint
73. *Verbascum thapsus*, mullein
74. *V. blattaria*, moth mullein
75. *Lysimachia vulgaris*, garden loosestrife
76. *Atriplex hortensis*, orach
77. *Origanum vulgare*, wild marjoram

78. *Chrysanthemum cinerariifolium*, pyrethrum
79. *Plantago major*, plantain
80. *Campanula rapunculus*, rampion
81. *Rosmarinus officinalis*, rosemary
82. *Ruta graveolens*, rue
83. *Salvia officinalis*, garden sage
84. *S. officinalis* 'Purpurea', purple variegated garden sage
85. *S. officinalis* 'Aurea', golden variegated garden sage
86. *S. officinalis* 'Tricolor', variegated garden sage
87. *Satureja montana*, winter savory
88. *Acinos alpinus*, alpine savory
89. *Sium sisarum*, skirret
90. *Hypericum perforatum*, St.-John's-wort
91. *Stachys officinalis*, betony
92. *Stachys grandiflora*
93. *Myrrhis odorata*, sweet cicely
94. *Tanacetum vulgare* var. *crispum*, fern-leaf tansy
95. *Thymus praecox* subsp. *arcticus* 'Coccineus', crimson creeping thyme
96. *T. praecox* subsp. *arcticus* 'Albus', white creeping thyme
97. *T.* 'Clear Gold', golden thyme
98. *T. × citriodorus* 'Aureus', golden lemon thyme
99. *T. × citriodorus*, lemon thyme
100. *T. praecox* subsp. *arcticus* 'Lanuginosus', woolly thyme
101. *T. richardii* subsp. *nitidus*, thyme
102. *T. herba-barona*, caraway thyme
103. *T. pallasianus*, odorous thyme
104. *T.* 'Argenteus', silver thyme
105. *Aloysia triphylla*, lemon verbena
106. *Veronica serpyllifolia*, creeping veronica
107. *Veronica officinalis*, veronica
108. *Yucca filamentosa*, yucca
109. *Isatis tinctoria*, dyer's woad
110. *Allium sativum*, garlic
111. *A. cepa*, Proliferum Group, tree onion
112. *A. ostrowskianum*
113. *Lilium candidum*, Madonna lily
114. *Myrtus communis*, classic myrtle
115. *Laurus nobilis*, bay
116. *Sorbaria sorbifolia*, false spiraea
117. *Prunus pensylvanica*, pin cherry

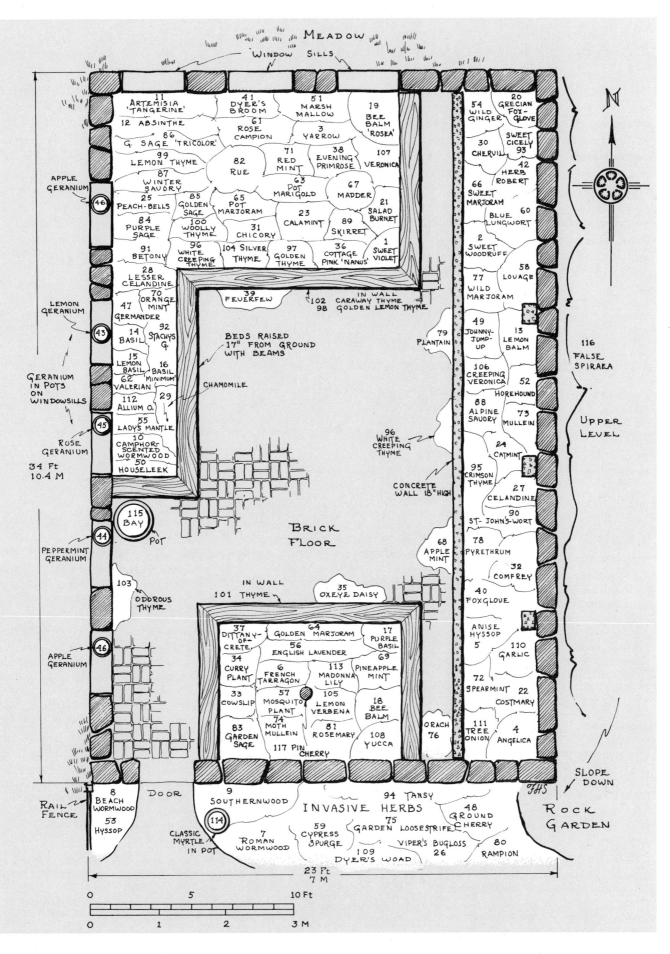

MEADOW

WINDOW SILLS

11 ARTEMISIA 'TANGERINE'
41 DYER'S BROOM
51 MARSH MALLOW
19 BEE BALM 'ROSEA'
54 WILD GINGER
20 GRECIAN FOX-GLOVE
12 ABSINTHE
61 ROSE CAMPION
3 YARROW
30 CHERVIL
SWEET CICELY 93
86 G. SAGE 'TRICOLOR'
71 RED MINT
38 EVENING PRIMROSE
107 VERONICA
42 HERB ROBERT
99 LEMON THYME
82 RUE
66 SWEET MARJORAM
87 WINTER SAVORY
63 POT MARIGOLD
67 MADDER
BLUE 60 LUNGWORT
25 PEACH-BELLS
85 GOLDEN SAGE
65 POT MARJORAM
21 SALAD BURNET
2 SWEET WOODRUFF
84 PURPLE SAGE
100 WOOLLY THYME
23 CALAMINT
89 SKIRRET
77 WILD MARJORAM
58 LOUAGE
91 BETONY
96 WHITE CREEPING THYME
104 SILVER THYME
97 GOLDEN THYME
36 COTTAGE PINK 'NANUS'
1 SWEET VIOLET
28 LESSER CELANDINE
39 FEVERFEW
IN WALL
102 CARAWAY THYME
98 GOLDEN LEMON THYME
79 PLANTAIN
49 JOHNNY-JUMP-UP
13 LEMON BALM
116 FALSE SPIRAEA
70 ORANGE MINT
47 GERMANDER
BEDS RAISED 17" FROM GROUND WITH BEAMS
106 CREEPING VERONICA
52 HOREHOUND
14 BASIL
92 STACHYS G.
CHAMOMILE
88 ALPINE SAVORY
73 MULLEIN
15 LEMON BASIL
16 BASIL 'MINIMUM'
62 VALERIAN
96 WHITE CREEPING THYME
24 CATMINT
UPPER LEVEL
112 ALLIUM O.
29
95 CRIMSON THYME
55 LADY'S MANTLE
27 CELANDINE
10 CAMPHOR-SCENTED WORMWOOD
CONCRETE WALL 18" HIGH
90 ST. JOHN'S-WORT
50 HOUSELEEK
68 APPLE MINT
78 PYRETHRUM
115 BAY
POT
BRICK FLOOR
32 COMFREY
40 FOXGLOVE
APPLE GERANIUM 46
LEMON GERANIUM 43
GERANIUM IN POTS ON WINDOWSILLS
ROSE GERANIUM
34 Ft 10.4 M
44
PEPPERMINT GERANIUM
103 ODOROUS THYME
IN WALL
101 THYME
35 OXEYE DAISY
ANISE HYSSOP
5
110 GARLIC
46
37 DITTANY-OF-CRETE
64 GOLDEN MARJORAM
17 PURPLE BASIL
56 ENGLISH LAVENDER
69
72 SPEARMINT
22 COSTMARY
APPLE GERANIUM
34 CURRY PLANT
6 FRENCH TARRAGON
113 MADONNA LILY
PINEAPPLE MINT
33 COWSLIP
57 MOSQUITO PLANT
105 LEMON VERBENA
18 BEE BALM
111 TREE ONION
4 ANGELICA
83 GARDEN SAGE
74 MOTH MULLEIN
81 ROSEMARY
108 YUCCA
76 ORACH
117 PIN CHERRY

RAIL FENCE
8 BEACH WORMWOOD
DOOR
9 SOUTHERNWOOD
94 TANSY
48 GROUND CHERRY
JHS
ROCK GARDEN
53 HYSSOP
CLASSIC MYRTLE IN POT
114
7 ROMAN WORMWOOD
59 CYPRESS SPURGE
75 GARDEN LOOSESTRIFE
INVASIVE HERBS
109 DYER'S WOAD
VIPER'S BUGLOSS 26
80 RAMPION
SLOPE DOWN

45

23 Ft 7 M

0   5   10 Ft
0 1   2   3 M

AS AN HERB COLLECTOR'S

An herb collector's garden uses every inch of planting space. Its many random beds are served appropriately by random flagstone paths edged with brick. A wheel-shaped bed, its outline constructed of brick, creates eight planting beds and is a center of interest. This bed is set off by a flagstone path with a variety of creeping thymes planted in its crevices. Many gardeners are faced with a utility pole or some "necessary evil" that detracts from the garden. The grape stake fence camouflages such a pole cleverly here, not just hiding it; there is a circular opening cut in the fence and a niche is created. A statue of St. Francis, of good proportion for the size of the opening, is featured in it with interesting foliage for the background. Sometimes a hanging basket of herbs is displayed here. With an herb garden containing hundreds of different herbs, a lathhouse is very useful and a greenhouse helpful. The lathhouse work area is conveniently located, but not obvious, and is well situated for starting cuttings or growing seedlings or potting. This herb collector's garden is readily viewed and enjoyed from the windows of the house or from the patio, where a selection of planters increases the planting area.

California

Designed by Owner

The plants in this garden number in the hundreds; only those not found on other lists are noted here.

AREA I
Potentilla nepalensis, Nepal cinquefoil
Campanula carpatica, tussock bellflower
Eschscholzia californica, California poppy

AREA II
Trachelospermum jasminoides, star jasmine
Osmanthus fragrans, sweet olive
Solanum jasminoides, potato vine
Lychnis coronaria 'Alba', white campion
Gardenia jasminoides, gardenia
Eucalyptus torquata, coral gum
Eriobotrya japonica, loquat

AREA III
Ceanothus 'Julia Phelps', California lilac
Leonotis leonurus, lion's-ear
Anemone hupehensis var. *japonica*, Japanese anemone
Cestrum nocturnum, night jessamine
Watsonia rosea, bugle lily

Jasminum officinale, poet's jessamine
Nandina domestica, heavenly bamboo
Salvia microphylla, baby sage
Oxalis crassipes, pink sorrel
Pinus strobus 'Nana', pine

AREA IV
Ixia maculata, corn lily
Acacia longifolia, Sidney golden wattle
Eleocharis dulcis, Chinese water chestnut
Montia perfoliata, miner's lettuce
Hibiscus rosa-sinensis, Chinese hibiscus
Justicia carnea, Brazilian-plume

AREA V
Barbarea vulgaris, upland cress
Pogostemon cablin, patchouli
Agastache breviflora, licorice mint

AREA VI
Hedychium flavescens, yellow ginger
Teucrium marum, cat thyme
Solidago californica, California goldenrod

AREA VII
Atriplex halimus, sea orach
Verbascum olympicum, mullein
Convolvulus cneorum, silverbush

AREA VIII
Nigella sativa, black cumin
Lilium chalcedonicum, scarlet Turk's-cap
Agrostemma githago, corn cockle
Cistus ladanifer, labdanum
Cistus crispus, myrrh

AREA IX
Chenopodium ambrosioides, Mexican tea
Trichostema lanatum, woolly blue-curls
Doronicum pardalianches, leopard's-bane
Ephedra viridis, ephedra
Ferula assafoetida, asafetida
Anacyclus officinarum, pellitory-of-the-wall
Lycopus europaeus, gypsywort

AREA X
Brassica eruca, wall rocket
Cymbopogon citratus, lemongrass
Vetiveria zizanioides, vetiver
Ocimum sanctum, sacred basil

AREA XI
Cichorium intybus, red-leaved chicory
Monarda fistulosa var. *menthifolia*, oregano de la Sierra
Origanum vulgare var. *prismaticum*, oregano

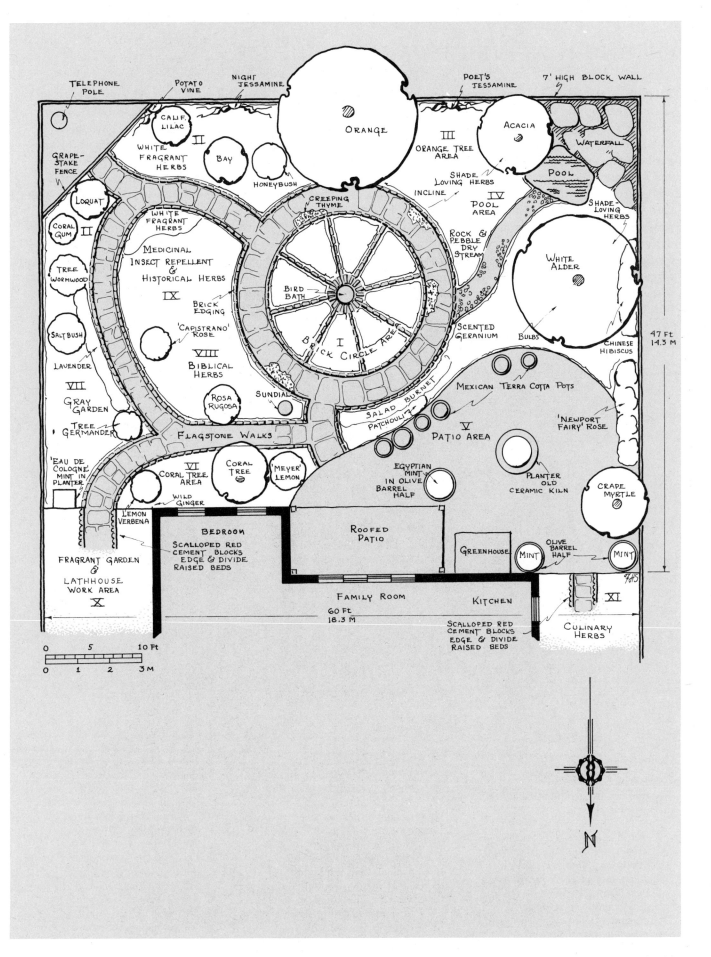

TELEPHONE POLE

POTATO VINE

NIGHT JESSAMINE

POET'S JESSAMINE

7' HIGH BLOCK WALL

ORANGE

ACACIA

WATERFALL

CALIF. LILAC

II

WHITE FRAGRANT HERBS

BAY

ORANGE TREE AREA

III

POOL

GRAPE-STAKE FENCE

HONEYBUSH

SHADE LOVING HERBS

SHADE-LOVING HERBS

LOQUAT

CREEPING THYME

INCLINE

IV

POOL AREA

CORAL GUM

II

WHITE FRAGRANT HERBS

ROCK & PEBBLE DRY STREAM

TREE WORMWOOD

Medicinal INSECT REPELLENT & HISTORICAL HERBS

IX

BRICK EDGING

BIRD BATH

WHITE ALDER

SALT BUSH

'CAPISTRANO' ROSE

I

BRICK CIRCLE AREA

SCENTED GERANIUM

BULBS

CHINESE HIBISCUS

LAVENDER

VIII

BIBLICAL HERBS

VII

GRAY GARDEN

ROSA RUGOSA

SUNDIAL

SALAD BURNET

MEXICAN TERRA COTTA POTS

'NEWPORT FAIRY' ROSE

TREE GERMANDER

FLAGSTONE WALKS

PATCHOULI?

V

PATIO AREA

'EAU DE COLOGNE' MINT IN PLANTER

VI

CORAL TREE AREA

CORAL TREE

'MEYER' LEMON

EGYPTIAN MINT IN OLIVE BARREL HALF

PLANTER OLD CERAMIC KILN

CRAPE MYRTLE

WILD GINGER

LEMON VERBENA

BEDROOM

SCALLOPED RED CEMENT BLOCKS EDGE & DIVIDE RAISED BEDS

ROOFED PATIO

GREENHOUSE

MINT

OLIVE BARREL HALF

MINT

FRAGRANT GARDEN & LATHHOUSE WORK AREA

X

FAMILY ROOM

60 Ft
18.3 M

KITCHEN

SCALLOPED RED CEMENT BLOCKS EDGE & DIVIDE RAISED BEDS

XI

CULINARY HERBS

47 Ft
14.3 M

0   5   10 Ft
0   1   2   3 M

N

OF BIBLICAL HERBS, A LESSER ONE

An elementary geometric design—an equilateral triangle placed within a circle—produces three planting beds for as many purposes. One is a garden of legends, another a Mary garden, and a third a culinary garden. The damask rose 'Celsiana', an "old rose" and fragrant, is a center of interest. Rue and chive are used as accents within the triangle. The exterior brick path, its pattern bordered in correct proportion, emphasizes the circle. Another dimension is added to this design by the one-foot-high brick wall enclosing the triangle. The foliage of absinthe is fine color and texture contrast inside the wall, the deep green ivy reinforcing the triangle design on the outside. All of the borders of ivy must be routinely clipped to restrain the ivy and keep the paths clear. The use of ivy requires careful selection to secure the proper cultivar, not only for hardiness where needed, but also for proper leaf size, which is as wide-ranging as the leaf shape of ivies. A smaller garden requires a smaller leaf to observe good proportion. Maintenance for this garden of symbolical biblical herbs demands constant trimming for the entire garden if the design is to be kept intact. In situations other than around a church structure one might substitute specialty herbs such as lemon-scented, scented-leaf geraniums, or potpourri, to name a few. The same maintenance demands would prevail and for the same reasons.

Connecticut

Designed by Contributor

The number in each planting area is the key number.

1. *Angelica archangelica*, angelica
2. *Chamaemelum nobile*, chamomile
3. *Artemisia absinthium*, absinthe
4. *Chrysanthemum cinerariifolium*, pyrethrum
5. *Chrysanthemum balsamita*, costmary
6. *Anethum graveolens*, dill
7. *Linum usitatissimum*, flax
8. *Hyssopus officinalis*, blue hyssop
9. *Viola tricolor*, Johnny-jump-up
10. *Alchemilla vulgaris*, lady's-mantle
11. *Origanum majorana*, sweet marjoram
12. *Mentha spicata*, spearmint
13. *Brassica nigra*, black mustard
14. *Lamium album*, white dead nettle
15. *Galium verum*, yellow bedstraw
16. *Calendula officinalis*, pot marigold
17. *Rosmarinus officinalis*, rosemary
18. *Ruta graveolens*, rue
19. *Salvia officinalis*, garden sage
20. *Santolina chamaecyparissus*, gray santolina
21. *Ocimum basilicum*, sweet basil
22. *Thymus* 'Broad-leaf English', English thyme
23. *Narcissus*
24. *Ornithogalum umbellatum*, star-of-Bethlehem
25. *Allium schoenoprasum*, chive
26. *Crocus sativus*, saffron crocus
27. *Hedera helix*, English ivy
28. *Rosa damascena* 'Celsiana', rose

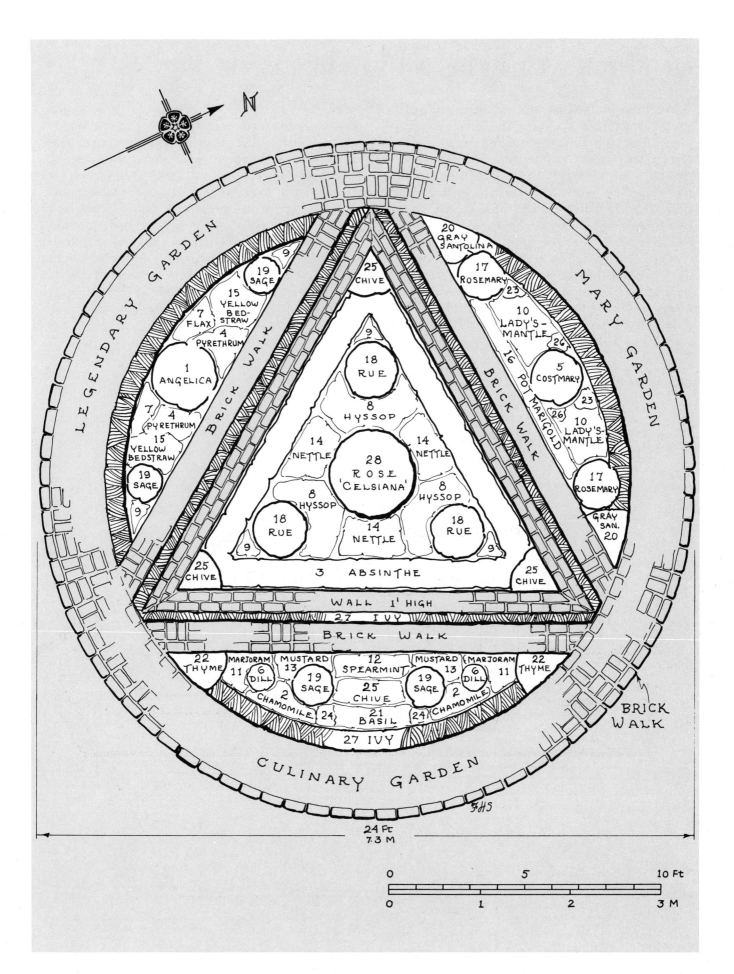

N

LEGENDARY GARDEN

MARY GARDEN

9
19 SAGE
25 CHIVE
20 GRAY SANTOLINA
17 ROSEMARY
23
15 YELLOW BEDSTRAW
7 FLAX
4 PYRETHRUM
BRICK WALK
9
18 RUE
10 LADY'S-MANTLE
26
1 ANGELICA
8 HYSSOP
16 POT MARIGOLD
5 COSTMARY
BRICK WALK
23
7 PYRETHRUM
4
14 NETTLE
28 ROSE 'CELSIANA'
14 NETTLE
10 LADY'S-MANTLE
15 YELLOW BEDSTRAW
8 HYSSOP
8 HYSSOP
19 SAGE
9
18 RUE
14 NETTLE
18 RUE
17 ROSEMARY
9
9
GRAY SAN. 20
25 CHIVE
3 ABSINTHE
25 CHIVE

WALL 1' HIGH
27 IVY
BRICK WALK

22 THYME
MARJORAM 11
6 DILL
MUSTARD 13
12 SPEARMINT
MUSTARD 13
19 SAGE
6 DILL
MARJORAM 11
22 THYME
19 SAGE
25 CHIVE
2 CHAMOMILE 24
21 BASIL
24 CHAMOMILE 2
27 IVY

CULINARY GARDEN

BRICK WALK

FHS

24 Ft
7.3 M

0   5   10 Ft
0   1   2   3 M

OF BIBLICAL HERBS, A GREATER ONE

In keeping with the contemporary architecture of a church structure, this asymmetrical design is boldly modernistic. It has a number of interesting angles in unexpected places. On either side of the entrance court there are excellent ideas to adapt for use with odd-shaped lots not uncommon in residential situations. The bed with a fountain for its center of interest could be used alone as an herb garden in another location. Adequate seating for this large area is unobtrusively and skillfully gained by recessing most of the benches within the planting beds. The reflection pool adds a pleasing note and creates interest for the large area outside the vestibule doors and is wisely placed outside their path. Long beds lend themselves to the long sweeps of color a large area permits, and the colors and textures of their foliage are made more obvious by the warm tones of the brick paving. Trees have been used to advantage as accents and sweet woodruff allowed to run its course—as it loves to—for a ground cover. No maintenance for mowing of grass or fretting over snow mold damage is required. This herb garden's southern exposure is ideal for the northwest, and its enclosure by a cedar fence four feet high produces an enviable spot for this purpose in this climate. It is admirably suited to the needs of this garden composed of symbolic, biblical herbs representative of the faith of those who established it.

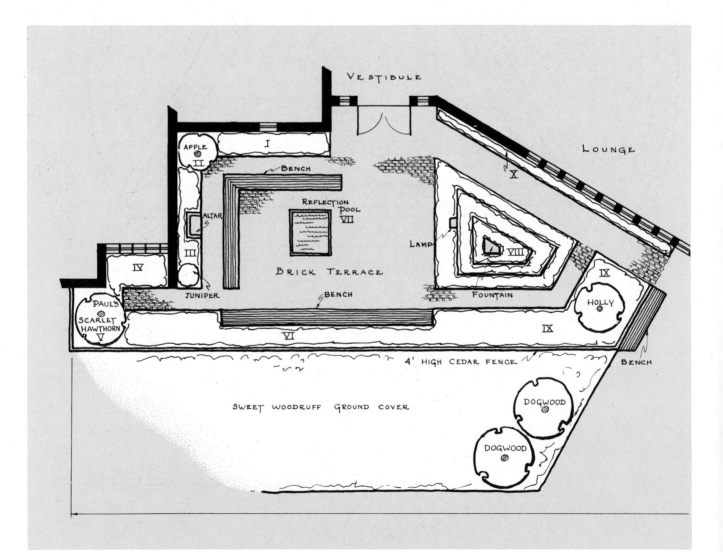

Washington

Designed by Milton Stricker, Architect

BED I

Lythrum virgatum 'Dropmore Purple', loosestrife
Lobularia maritima, white sweet alyssum

BED II

Malus 'Red Spy', dwarf apple

BED III

Galium odoratum, sweet woodruff
Juniperus chinensis var. *chinensis* 'Pyramidalis', juniper

BED IV

Ruta graveolens, rue
Malva alcea var. *fastigiata*, mallow
Artemisia gmelinii, Russian wormwood

BED V

Hyssopus officinalis, blue hyssop
Marrubium vulgare, horehound
Crataegus laevigata 'Paulii', Paul's scarlet hawthorn

BED VI

Melissa officinalis, lemon balm
Mentha spicata, spearmint
Mentha × piperita, peppermint
Laurus nobilis, bay

BED VII

Reflection Pool

BED VIII

Lavandula angustifolia subsp. *angustifolia* 'Hidcote', lavender
Thymus vulgaris, thyme
Cnicus benedictus, blessed thistle
Lamium maculatum, spotted dead nettle
Linum perenne, perennial flax
Myrtus communis, myrtle

BED IX

Alchemilla vulgaris, lady's-mantle
Fragaria chiloensis, beach strawberry
Artemisia absinthium, absinthe
Rosmarinus officinalis 'Prostratus', prostrate rosemary
Myrrhis odorata, sweet cicely
Rosa damascena 'Bifera', autumn damask

BED X

Dianthus caryophyllus, clove pink

BED XI

Echeveria × imbricata, hen-and-chickens
Angelica archangelica, angelica
Chrysanthemum balsamita, costmary
Rosa rugosa 'Blanc Double de Coubert', Turkestan rose
Rosa moschata 'Bishop Darlington', musk rose

BED XII

Passiflora caerulea, blue passionflower

BED XIII

Lilium candidum, Madonna lily
Cotinus coggygria, smoke tree

BED XIV

Monarda didyma, bee balm

BED XV

Coriandrum sativum, coriander
Vitis aestivalis 'Fredonia', grape
Ilex wilsonii, holly

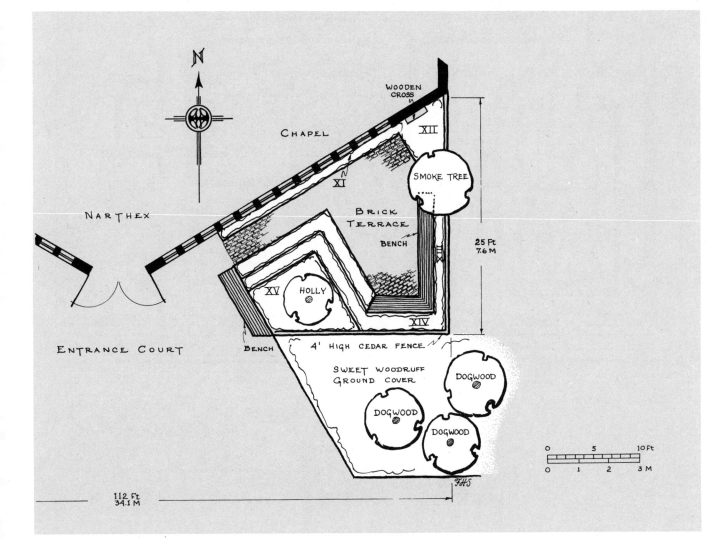

AT A METROPOLITAN GARDEN CENTER

This large garden, fittingly related to the structure of a metropolitan garden center, features a closed knot of superior design. Viewed from the terrace garden, the relationship of its specialty gardens is obvious and the stately quality of the design can be appreciated as a whole. At the terminus the paths that intersect are expanded to accommodate the armillary. This is a general rule observed, too, where paths enter an area or take a different direction. An air of spaciousness within enclosures is gained in this manner. The listed shrubs and trees are possibilities for smaller gardens, simply on a smaller scale. Appropriately used as accents, they help the design to be clearly seen in all seasons. The generous use of edgings, millstones, and huge, old foundation stones for walls within this garden contributes in even greater degree to this visibility throughout the year. There is much to be noted about the beauty of this garden, but it has been the aim here to point out again some principles of design so carefully observed in the planning of this totally pleasing and functional garden of herbs.

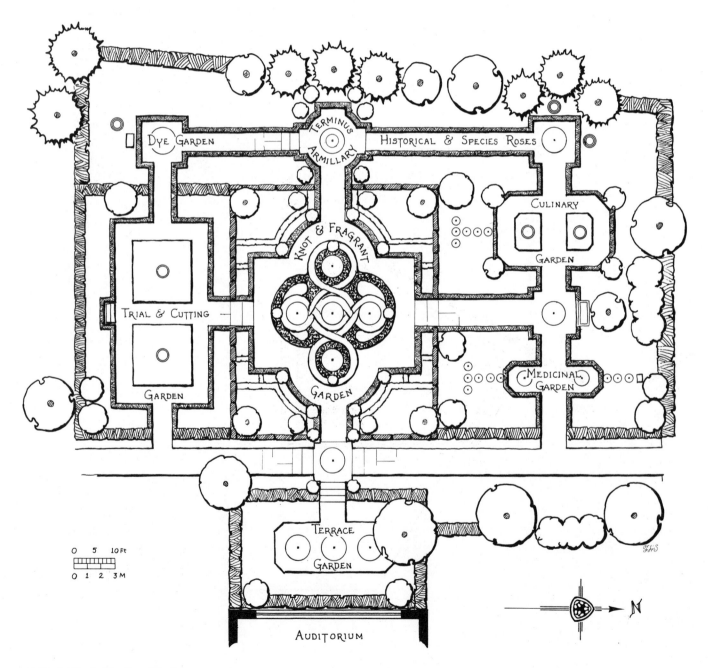

This knot, of greater size than is commonly found, has its size dictated by a rule of design, that of good proportion. The beauty of its design is heightened by the contrasting colors and textures of the plant material and of the five millstones, six feet in diameter, and the mulch. Routine clipping is required, and the choice of plant material has been adjusted on occasion when necessary. This exceptional knot design is most suitably framed by the warm tones of the brick walk encircling it. Its unusual pattern is reminiscent of that used in Spanish gardens.

Ohio

Elsetta Gilchrist Barnes, Landscape Architect, A.S.L.A.

The number in each planting area is the key number.

Design plan of herb garden

1. *Teucrium chamaedrys*, germander
2. *Hyssopus officinalis*, blue hyssop
3. *Dianthus gratianopolitanus*, 'Tiny Rubies', cheddar pink
4. *Lavandula angustifolia* subsp. *angustifolia* 'Munstead', lavender
5. *Santolina virens*, green santolina
6. *Santolina chamaecyparissus*, gray santolina
7. *Buxus microphylla* 'Green Pillow', dwarf box

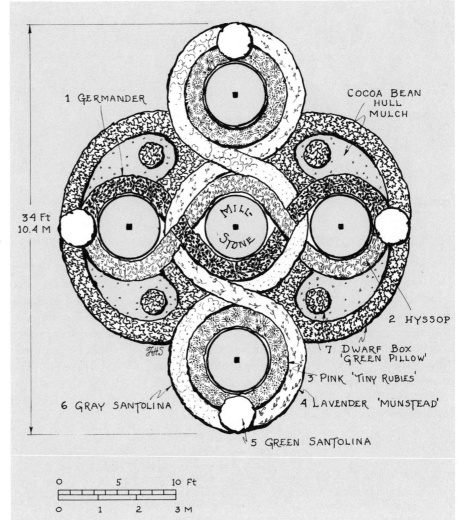

SHRUBS
Euonymus fortunei 'Erecta'
Eunoymus fortunei 'Colorata'
Buxus microphylla 'Green Pillow', box
Calycanthus floridus, sweet shrub
Mahonia aquifolium, Oregon grape
Lindera benzoin, spicebush
Chionanthus virginicus, fringe tree
Syringa reticulata var. *japonica*, Japanese lilac tree
Deutzia gracilis
Viburnum prunifolium, black haw
Prunus americana, plum

Prunus maritima, beach plum
Corylus avellana, European hazelnut
Hamamelis vernalis, witch hazel
Cydonia oblonga 'Lusitanica', quince
Magnolia virginiana, sweet bay
Buxus sempervirens, box
Myrica pensylvanica, bayberry
Viburnum carlesii
Taxus × media 'Hicksii', columnar yew
Paxistima canbyi, cliff-green
Cotoneaster apiculatus, cranberry cotoneaster

TREES
Tsuga canadensis, Canada hemlock
Crataegus phaenopyrum, Washington hawthorn
Amelanchier canadensis, shadbush
Salix caprea, goat willow
Sassafras albidum, sassafras
Gleditsia tricanthos, honey locust
Cornus florida, dogwood
Pinus nigra, Austrian pine

Among the features of this herb garden, the wrought-iron plant hoop is quite appealing. It could easily be used as a focal point in smaller herb gardens, its plant material varied.

Wrought-iron plant hoop

TRIAL GARDEN FOR A METROPOLITAN GARDEN CENTER

The trial garden is a relatively small portion of the splendid garden on the preceding pages. However, it makes a substantial contribution to the garden's continuing success. This area thirteen feet by thirteen feet is devoted to trying new plants for potential use in the herb garden complex. Currently, there are a number of specimens from the genera *Thymus, Salvia, Lavandula, Rosmarinus,* and a miscellany of others. As a rule, a two-year trial is afforded each prospect. The thymes were selected to border three sides of this area, and brick pavers were used to segregate each species or cultivar. This maneuver and routine pruning have proved successful. A trial garden is an idea that could be put into effect on a smaller scale in a home environment. The benefits reaped from experimenting with new plants are substantial and ensure a place for the trial garden in the herb garden's future.

Thymes

Thymus 'Longwood'
T. doerfleri
T. herba-barona, caraway thyme
T. 'Argenteus', silver thyme
T. 'Annie Hall'
T. 'Woolly-stemmed Sweet'
T. 'Long-leaf Gray'
T. 'Woolly-stemmed Sharp'
T. vulgaris 'Miniature'
T. praecox subsp. *arcticus*
T. praecox subsp. *arcticus* 'Rosea'
T. leucotrichus
T. 'Doone Valley'
T. praecox subsp. *arcticus* 'Lanuginosus', woolly thyme
T. praecox subsp. *arcticus* 'Coccineus', crimson creeping thyme
T. 'Clear Gold', golden thyme
T. vulgaris 'Albus'
T. nummularius

Lavenders

Lavandula 'Mitchum Blue'
L. angustifolia subsp. *angustifolia* 'Hidcote'
L. angustifolia subsp. *angustifolia* 'Gray Lady'
L. heterophylla, sweet lavender
L. angustifolia subsp. *angustifolia* 'Munstead'
L. angustifolia, English lavender
L. angustifolia subsp. *angustifolia* 'Rosea'
L. dentata, French lavender

Sages

Salvia clevelandii, blue sage
S. guaranitica, anise sage
S. greggii, autumn sage
S. officinalis 'Purpurea', purple variegated garden sage
S. officinalis 'Aurea', golden variegated sage
S. leucantha, Mexican bush sage
S. involucrata, rosy leaf sage

Rosemaries

Rosmarinus officinalis 'Blue Spears'
R. officinalis 'Lockwood de Forest'
R. angustissimus, pine-scented rosemary
R. officinalis 'Prostratus'
R. officinalis 'Prostratus', golden rosemary
R. officinalis 'Beneden Blue'
R. officinalis 'Tuscan Blue'

Miscellaneous Genera

Alchemilla alpina, alpine lady's-mantle
Helichrysum petiolatum, false licorice
Hydrocotyle asiatica, gotu kola
Teucrium fruticans, tree germander
Boehmaria nivea, ramie
Cedronella canariensis, balm-of-Gilead
Tagetes lucida, sweet-scented Mexican marigold
Leontopodium alpinum, edelweiss
Greek artemisia

HISTORICAL GARDENS

FOR A COLONIAL HOUSEWIFE

For a 1730 housewife, family needs—medicinal, culinary, and household—dictated the selection of plants for an herb garden. Utility and convenience required the garden to be near the house. Circumstances determined these priorities, and access to the resulting specialty beds was gained by ample grass paths. Balance was achieved by devoting the same area to the three herb beds and the scatter seed plot. Fruit trees and a rose shrub created a quincunx pattern in each area, a design device also used in the apple orchard to save space. The apple trees, selected for their authenticity in this restoration, are still good varieties and remain available at some commercial nurseries today. The gardens were enclosed with a fence that supported roses and grapes and banished some wayward animals. The effect of the thought given to design is an orderly plan that allows the grounds to look appealing. The house, constructed of brick made on the property, was built in the interesting Flemish-bond pattern and was situated on a knoll overlooking the gardens, which were located between the water supply, a well beside the house, and a tidal stream at the foot of a long slope.

Some herbaceous plants found in the early eighteenth-century housewife's garden not commonly used today are skirret, *Sium sisarum*, used in salads or boiled; the following used for medicinal purposes: heal-all, *Prunella vulgaris*; balmony, *Chelone glabra*; rupturewort, *Herniaria glabra*; and the following for varied household uses: dame's violet, *Hesperis matronalis*, to sweeten the air; horsetail, *Equisetum arvense*, for scrubbing pots; obedient plant, *Physostegia virginiana*, to lure bees. Primarily, this was a garden planned for self-sufficiency.

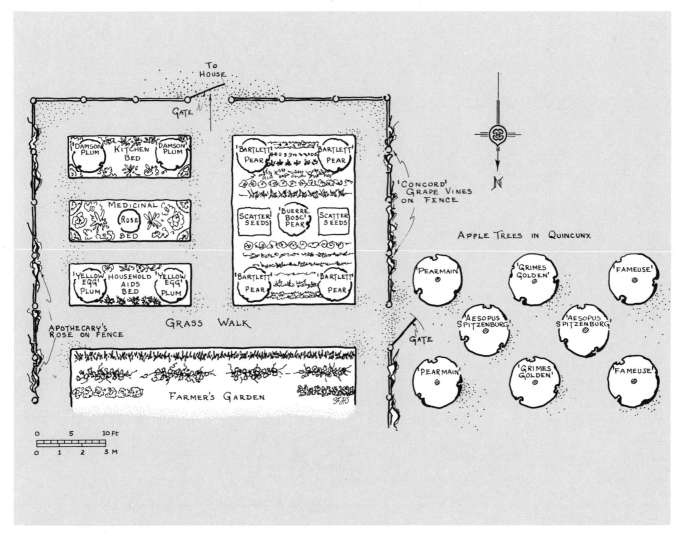

New Hampshire   Designed by Isadore L. L. Smith, Landscape Architect

OF PLANTATION PLAIN

Restored with great respect for authenticity, this is a fine example of gardens that would have been in existence around 1835, as a part of the grounds around a plantation plain-style house. At that time flower beds were situated in the front yard area and herb beds in the back. Then herbs were grown in almost every corner with herb beds all around the periphery of the yard at the side and the rear of the house. The planting beds were laid out with fieldstones or sapling trees placed on the ground. This retained the soil and raised the beds from the level of the yard. Paths between the beds and the yard areas were swept clean with brush brooms. Today, the concept of a swept yard is still considered practical by some, for a few are in use now. The square flower bed with a grindstone center of interest reflects thought for design, and the herb beds in the side yard indicate a feeling for it, too. The picket fence enclosing these yards is constructed of palings that are replicas of those in an 1847 heart-pine fence extant nearby. Picket fences were used universally in the area then and, while functional, were not without a decorative aspect and were compatible with the architecture of the structures. The familiar well house makes an appealing contribution to the overall layout of the back yard and serves also as a support for a climbing rose or a vine. These faithful reconstructions are to be greatly appreciated for many reasons. Not the least of these is the thought given to making an herb growing area not only functional but appealing, too, in an era when leisure time to do so was more limited than it is today.

Georgia

Design from Contributor

The number in each planting area is the key number.

1. *Rosmarinus officinalis*, rosemary
2. *Allium sativum*, garlic
3. *Lonicera sempervirens*, trumpet honeysuckle
4. *Lonicera flava*, yellow honeysuckle
5. *Wisteria frutescens*, wisteria
6. *Rosa banksiae*, Banksia rose
7. *Sambucus canadensis*, American elderberry
8. *Syringa* × *persica* var. *laciniata*, Persian lilac
9. *Gardenia jasminoides*, Cape jasmine
10. *Punica granatum*, pomegranate
11. *Lagerstroemia indica*, crape myrtle
12. *Prunus angustifolia*, chickasaw plum
13. *Ficus carica*, fig
14. *Laurus nobilis*, bay
15. *Pinus taeda*, loblolly pine
16. *Malus angustifolia*, southern wild crab apple

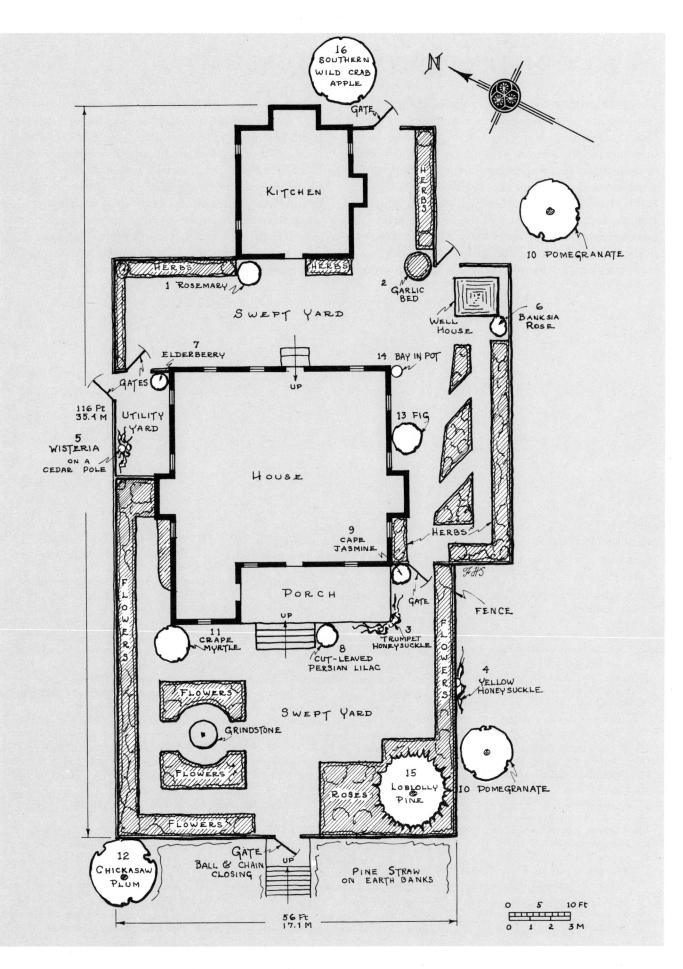

16
SOUTHERN
WILD CRAB
APPLE

GATE

N

Kitchen

HERBS

10 POMEGRANATE

HERBS

HERBS

1 ROSEMARY

SWEPT YARD

2
GARLIC
BED

WELL
HOUSE

6
BANKSIA
ROSE

7
ELDERBERRY

14 BAY IN POT

UP

GATES

116 Ft
35.1 M

Utility
Yard

13 FIG

5
WISTERIA
ON A
CEDAR POLE

HOUSE

9
CAPE
JASMINE

HERBS

F L O W E R S

F H S

PORCH

UP

GATE

FENCE

11
CRAPE
MYRTLE

UP

8
CUT-LEAVED
PERSIAN LILAC

3
TRUMPET
HONEYSUCKLE

F L O W E R S

4
YELLOW
HONEYSUCKLE

FLOWERS

Grindstone

SWEPT YARD

FLOWERS

15
LOBLOLLY
PINE

10 POMEGRANATE

FLOWERS

ROSES

12
CHICKASAW
PLUM

GATE
BALL & CHAIN
CLOSING

UP

PINE STRAW
ON EARTH BANKS

56 Ft
17.1 M

0   5   10 Ft

0 1 2 3 M

Herb Garden Design / 117

AT A COUNTRY DOCTOR'S MUSEUM

This medicinal herb garden is more than a fitting complement for a country doctor museum. At the time it was dedicated in December 1968 it was the only medical museum in our country dedicated solely to family doctors. Appropriately, the landscape architect patterned the design after the Botanic Garden at Padua, Italy, one of the oldest medicinal gardens in Europe. It is a fine example of the timeless quality of some designs. The plantings make their contribution to the historical value of this garden, too. They include many herbs that were used for healing purposes in ancient times. All walkways and paths are constructed with nineteenth-century handmade brick. It is interesting to note the course of the bricks crossing the paths to complete the circumference of the outer circle in the design. The effect would be quite different without them. Peripheral beds initiate enclosure of this herb garden and its grassy plot with bench. The white picket fence completes the enclosure from the carriagehouse to the doctor's office. Trumpet honeysuckle vine softens the primness of the fence and leads the eye to the meadow beyond.

North Carolina

Elizabeth Lawrence, Landscape Architect

The number in each planting area is the key number.

1. *Melissa officinalis*, lemon balm
2. *Ocimum basilicum*, sweet basil
3. *Monarda didyma*, bee balm
4. *Cimicifuga racemosa*, black cohosh
5. *Eupatorium perfoliatum*, boneset
6. *Borago officinalis*, borage
7. *Asclepias tuberosa*, butterfly weed
8. *Chamaemelum nobile*, chamomile
9. *Nepeta cataria*, catnip
10. *Levisticum officinale*, lovage
11. *Dianthus caryophyllus*, clove pink
12. *Catharanthus roseus* 'Albus', white periwinkle
13. *Symphytum officinale*, comfrey
14. *Anethum graveolens*, dill
15. *Foeniculum vulgare*, fennel
16. *Digitalis purpurea*, foxglove
17. *Marrubium vulgare*, horehound
18. *Armoracia rusticana*, horseradish
19. *Hyssopus officinalis*, blue hyssop
20. *Lavandula angustifolia*, lavender
21. *Pulmonaria officinalis*, blue lungwort
22. *Lobelia siphilitica*, great lobelia
23. *Calendula officinalis*, pot marigold
24. *Verbascum thapsus*, mullein
25. *Mentha pulegium*, pennyroyal
26. *Paeonia officinalis*, peony
27. *Mentha × piperita*, peppermint
28. *Vinca minor*, myrtle
29. *Chimaphila umbellata*, pipsissewa
30. *Rosmarinus officinalis*, rosemary
31. *Ruta graveolens*, rue
32. *Hypericum perforatum*, St.-John's-wort
33. *Agrimonia eupatoria*, agrimony
34. *Salvia officinalis*, garden sage
35. *Santolina chamaecyparissus*, gray santolina
36. *Artemisia abrotanum*, southernwood
37. *Mentha spicata*, spearmint
38. *Teucrium chamaedrys*, germander
39. *Galium odoratum*, sweet woodruff
40. *Tanacetum vulgare*, tansy
41. *Artemisia dracunculus* var. *sativa*, French tarragon
42. *Dipsacus sativus*, fuller's teasel
43. *Thymus* 'Broad-leaf English', English thyme
44. *Asarum virginicum*, wild ginger
45. *Gaultheria procumbens*, wintergreen
46. *Achillea millefolium*, yarrow
47. *Monarda punctata*, horsemint
48. *Acorus calamus*, sweet flag
49. *Crocus sativus*, saffron crocus
50. *Lilium candidum*, Madonna lily
51. *Colchicum autumnale*, autumn crocus
52. *Allium schoenoprasum*, chive
53. *Lonicera sempervirens*, trumpet honeysuckle
54. *Rosa laevigata*, Cherokee rose
55. *Rosa gallica* 'Officinalis', apothecary's rose
56. *Xanthoriza simplicissima*, yellowroot
57. *Rubus alleghteniensis*, blackberry
58. *Buxus sempervirens*, box
59. *Calycanthus floridus*, sweet shrub
60. *Hamamelis virginiana*, witch hazel
61. *Ilex vomitoria*, yaupon
62. *Lindera benzoin*, spicebush
63. *Punica granatum*, pomegranate
64. *Cassia marilandica*, senna
65. *Ilex opaca*, American holly
66. *Populus balsamifera*, balm-of-Gilead
67. *Cornus florida*, dogwood
68. *Pinckneya pubens*, fever tree
69. *Sassafras albidum*, sassafras
70. *Laurus nobilis*, bay

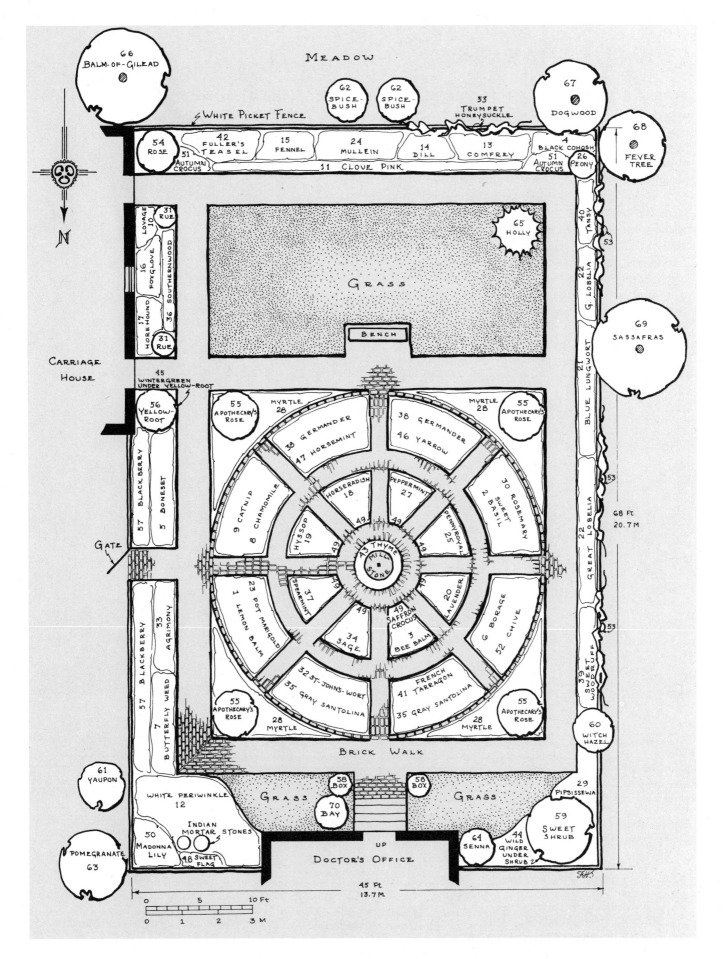

FOR THE SHAKERS

The Shakers were industrious and serious herb gardeners. Their herb gardens are one manner in which to grow herbs when easier harvest and greater quantities are paramount. It is well known that the Shaker philosophy did not allow treatment of material for ornamentation. Perhaps this left more time and energy for creating products from herbs and collecting seeds for commercial purposes. In any event, the Shakers are generally credited with being the first in the United States to sell seeds locally and abroad. Theirs was no small contribution to the perpetuity and even progress of herb gardening. Natural fibers were processed and dyed by them using their herbaceous plants, thereby gaining knowledge for future generations by reason of their excellent recordkeeping. This is true for the remedies, preventives, and fragrances they developed, too—whether for their own use or to sell to others. Commercial growers today could use a plan such as this, for it is functional but still observes rules of balance. The result is a well-designed garden that is a credit to the Shakers' industry and inventiveness with herbs.

Shaker Herbs
2 parts sage
2 parts marjoram
1 part summer savory
1 part tarragon
1 part thyme
1 part lovage
1 part basil
1 part rosemary
1 part dillweed
1 T. of herbs for one loaf of bread.
1 T. of herbs per pound for meat loaf.

This recipe using dried culinary herbs is a long-time universal favorite developed by the Shakers. Many have found this to be a good all-purpose seasoning.

Massachusetts

Designed by Contributor

The number in each planting area is the key number.

1. *Artemisia absinthium*, absinthe
2. *Lavandula angustifolia*, English lavender
3. *Tanacetum vulgare*, tansy
4. *Digitalis purpurea*, foxglove
5. *Ocimum basilicum*, sweet basil
6. *Thymus* 'Broad-leaf English', English thyme
7. *Marrubium vulgare*, horehound
8. *Nepeta cataria*, catnip
9. *Calendula officinalis*, pot marigold
10. *Levisticum officinale*, lovage
11. *Satureja montana*, winter savory
12. *Papaver somniferum*, opium poppy
13. *Origanum majorana*, sweet marjoram
14. *Rosmarinus officinalis*, rosemary
15. *Salvia officinalis*, garden sage
16. *Mentha spicata*, spearmint
17. *Mentha × piperita*, peppermint
18. *Carum carvi*, caraway
19. *Monarda punctata*, horsemint
20. *Hyssopus officinalis*, blue hyssop
21. *Rosa gallica* 'Officinalis', apothecary's rose
22. *Viburnum prunifolium*, black haw
23. *Cydonia oblonga*, quince
24. *Pyrus communis*, pear

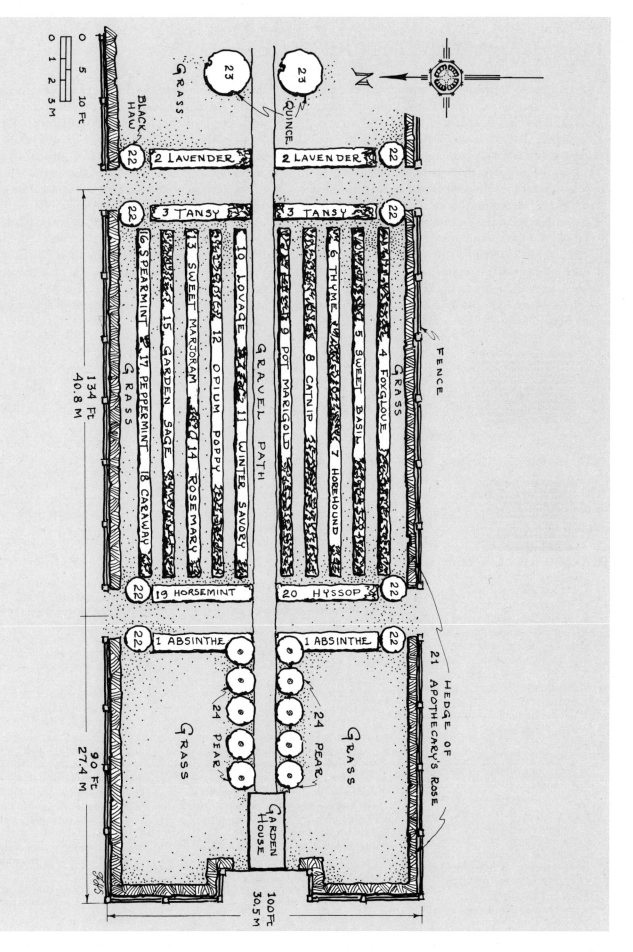

FROM A MORAVIAN SETTLEMENT

Still another restoration is a reminder that the past has contributed much to herb gardens and their design, and if the best has not always survived, often it is reconstructed. Thus it was for this garden, for its plan was based on the only extant garden plans, one dated 1759, the other 1761, from early Moravian settlements. The Moravian philosophy seemed not to discourage artistic approaches to gardens that initially had a utilitarian purpose. Allowed such freedom of expression, a planner used work paths to create designs: diagonal paths in a rectangular bed, and curved paths that meet in the middle of larger beds of the same shape. A single work path cut diagonally across a smaller square is the simplest, and the treatment of the bed about thirteen feet square, centrally located, makes it something of a focal point. The beds are used to achieve balance, and their tanbark paths are good contrast for the colors and textures of herbal foliage. Shaded by hop vines, a garden house is a seemly place to sit and enjoy this garden, to study it, and to see that one or more of the beds could be used to create a complex of beds. Some could be used singly, for example the large square bed with circular path. The main paths of brick unify the garden, and bricks raise the beds. A variety of vines use the picket fence for support while adding their practical and aesthetic qualities. The fence and the manufactory nearly enclose this herb garden, its design so enhanced by skillful planning in the placement of functional work paths.

North Carolina

Robert G. Campbell, Landscape Architect, A.S.L.A.

The number in each planting area is the key number.

1. *Thymus* 'Broad-leaf English', English thyme
2. *Salvia viridis*, annual clary
3. *Achillea millefolium*, yarrow
4. *Borago officinalis*, borage
5. *Tanacetum vulgare*, tansy
6. *Althaea officinalis*, marsh mallow
7. *Cnicus benedictus*, blessed thistle
8. *Levisticum officinale*, lovage
9. *Rheum rhabarbarum*, rhubarb
10. *Inula helenium*, elecampane
11. *Tropaeolum majus*, garden nasturtium
12. *Tropaeolum minus*, dwarf nasturtium
13. *Ruta graveolens*, rue
14. *Salvia officinalis*, garden sage
15. *Aquilegia vulgaris*, columbine
16. *Chamaemelum nobile*, chamomile
17. *Artemisia absinthium*, absinthe
18. *Nigella sativa*, black cumin
19. *Celosia cristata*, cockscomb
20. *Lavandula angustifolia* subsp. *angustifolia*, lavender
21. *Rosmarinus officinalis*, rosemary
22. *Matthiola incana*, stock
23. *Alcea rosea*, hollyhock
24. *Armoracia rusticana*, horseradish
25. *Dianthus caryophyllus*, clove pink
26. *Chrysanthemum parthenium*, feverfew
27. *Origanum majorana*, sweet marjoram
28. *Marrubium vulgare*, horehound
29. *Salvia sclarea*, clary
30. *Asparagus officinalis*, asparagus
31. *Petroselinum crispum*, parsley
32. *Symphytum officinale*, comfrey
33. *Mentha spicata*, spearmint
34. *Mentha* × *piperita*, peppermint
35. *Pulmonaria officinalis*, blue lungwort
36. *Melissa officinalis*, lemon balm
37. *Rumex acetosa*, sorrel
38. *Artemisia abrotanum*, southernwood
39. *Artemisia vulgaris*, mugwort
40. *Consolida ambigua*, larkspur
41. *Hyssopus officinalis*, blue hyssop
42. *Nepeta cataria*, catnip
43. *Ocimum basilicum*, sweet basil
44. *Carum carvi*, caraway
45. *Anethum graveolens*, dill
46. *Coriandrum sativum*, coriander
47. *Capsicum annuum* Longum Group, red pepper
48. *Atriplex hortensis*, orach
49. *Amaranthus caudatus*, love-lies-bleeding
50. *Bellis perennis*, English daisy
51. *Papaver rhoeas*, corn poppy
52. *Scabiosa atropurpurea*, sweet scabious
53. *Saponaria officinalis*, bouncing Bet
54. *Stachys officinalis*, betony
55. *Foeniculum vulgare*, fennel
56. *Silybum marianum*, holy thistle
57. *Rubia tinctorum*, madder
58. *Lilium candidum*, Madonna lily
59. *Narcissus tazetta*, polyanthus narcissus
60. *Narcissus poeticus*, poet's narcissus
61. *Colchicum autumnale*, autumn crocus
62. *Crocus sativus*, saffron crocus
63. *Allium sativum*, garlic
64. *Allium schoenoprasum*, chive
65. *Gelsemium sempervirens*, Carolina jessamine
66. *Humulus lupulus*, hop
67. *Clematis virginiana*, virgin's bower
68. *Vitis*, grape
69. *Passiflora incarnata*, maypop
70. *Rosa roxburghii*, chestnut rose
71. *Rosa centifolia* 'Muscosa', moss rose
72. *Rosa moschata*, musk rose
73. *Rosa gallica*, French rose
74. *Rosa damascena*, damask rose
75. *Rosa eglanteria*, eglantine
76. *Rosa centifolia*, cabbage rose
77. *Hydrangea quercifolia*, oakleaf hydrangea
78. *Lagerstroemia indica*, crape myrtle
79. *Cercis canadensis*, redbud
80. *Ficus*, fig
81. *Cornus florida*, dogwood
82. *Magnolia grandiflora*, southern magnolia

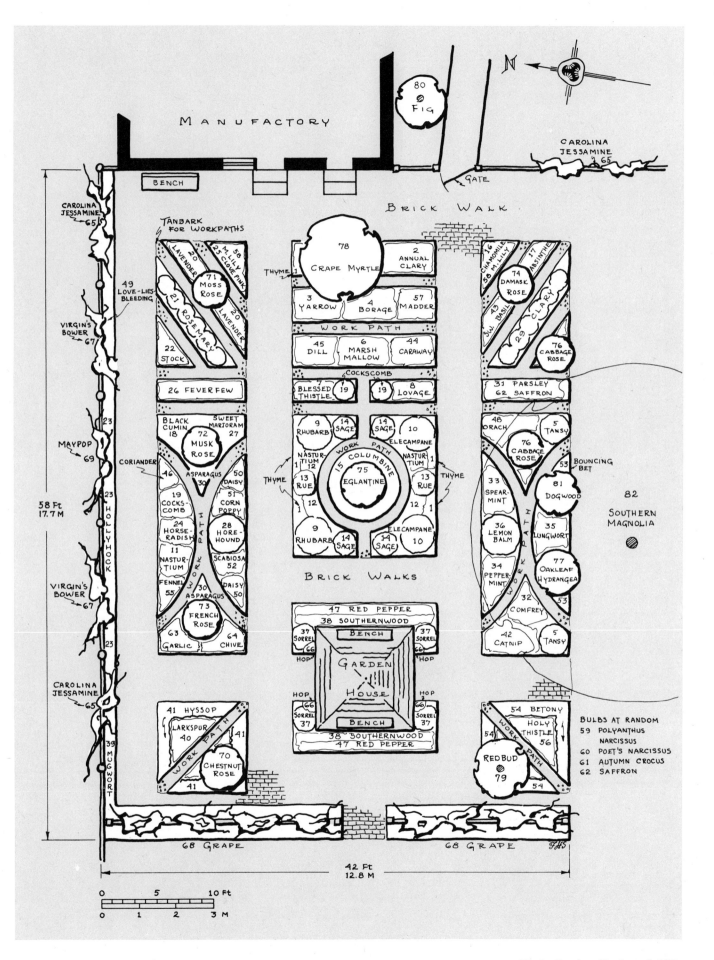

MANUFACTORY

BENCH

N

80
FIG

CAROLINA
JESSAMINE
65

GATE

BRICK WALK

CAROLINA
JESSAMINE
65

TANBARK
FOR WORKPATHS

58 M. LILY
23 CLOVE PINK
20 LAVENDER
71 MOSS ROSE
21 ROSEMARY
20 LAVENDER
22 STOCK

26 FEVERFEW

BLACK CUMIN 18
72 MUSK ROSE
SWEET MARJORAM 27
46
ASPARAGUS 30
50 DAISY
19 COCKS-COMB
51 CORN POPPY
24 HORSE-RADISH
28 HORE-HOUND
11 NASTURTIUM
SCABIOSA 52
FENNEL 55
30 ASPARAGUS
DAISY 50
73 FRENCH ROSE
63 GARLIC
64 CHIVE

CORIANDER

78
CRAPE MYRTLE

THYME 1

2 ANNUAL CLARY

3 YARROW
4 BORAGE
57 MADDER

WORK PATH

45 DILL
6 MARSH MALLOW
44 CARAWAY

COCKSCOMB

7 BLESSED THISTLE
19
19
8 LOVAGE

9 RHUBARB
14 SAGE
14 SAGE
10 ELECAMPANE

NASTURTIUM 12 1
WORK PATH
15 COLUMBINE
NASTURTIUM 1

THYME
13 RUE
75 EGLANTINE
13 RUE
THYME

12
1
1
12

9 RHUBARB
14 SAGE
14 SAGE
10 ELECAMPANE

BRICK WALKS

47 RED PEPPER
38 SOUTHERNWOOD
37 SORREL
BENCH
37 SORREL
HOP
HOP

GARDEN HOUSE

HOP
66 SORREL 37
BENCH
HOP
66 SORREL 37

38 SOUTHERNWOOD
47 RED PEPPER

16
58 M. LILY
17 ABSINTHE
CHAMOMILE
74 DAMASK ROSE
43 S.W. BASIL
29 CLARY
76 CABBAGE ROSE

31 PARSLEY
62 SAFFRON

48 ORACH
5 TANSY
76 CABBAGE ROSE
53 BOUNCING BET
33 SPEARMINT
81 DOGWOOD
36 LEMON BALM
35 LUNGWORT
34 PEPPERMINT
77 OAKLEAF HYDRANGEA
32 COMFREY
53
42 CATNIP
5 TANSY

82
SOUTHERN MAGNOLIA

54 BETONY
HOLY THISTLE 56
54
54
RED BUD 79
54

BULBS AT RANDOM
59 POLYANTHUS NARCISSUS
60 POET'S NARCISSUS
61 AUTUMN CROCUS
62 SAFFRON

41 HYSSOP
LARKSPUR 40
41
70 CHESTNUT ROSE
41

39 MUGWORT

CAROLINA JESSAMINE 65

VIRGIN'S BOWER 67

MAYPOP 69

23 HOLLYHOCK

23

VIRGIN'S BOWER 67

23

49 LOVE-LIES-BLEEDING

58 Ft
17.7 M

68 GRAPE
68 GRAPE

42 Ft
12.8 M

0   5   10 Ft
0   1   2   3 M

PART III SELECTING AND ADAPTING AN HERB GARDEN DESIGN

A TRIAL RUN

When proposing a plan of action, it is proper to make a trial run. Thus, all of the procedures detailed on the following pages were undertaken step-by-step. This is a true account of the design of an herb garden. Although some observations may seem obvious, they are noted as the overall plan is studied and a design is developed.

First, an overall plan of the property was made as suggested in Part I. The scale is one-eighth inch equals six feet, and the north point is established. Pertinent information was gained from a survey map and the deed description of the property.

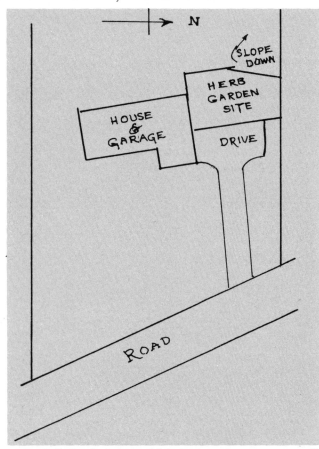

Overall plan for location of the herb garden on a very small scale. The lesser the scale, the easier it is to visualize the relationship between structures and the area for the site of the herb garden

The usually desirable southern exposure is impossible in this situation. A ravine and existing, mature evergreens wanted for privacy make it impossible to locate an herb garden on the south side of the house, and it would be nice to have the garden as near the kitchen as possible. The eastern exposure is at the front of the house and heavily wooded. The next most desirable exposure, the western, has been in use for growing herbs edging the terraces. This space was

never adequate. Its inadequacy was worsened by a slope that drops rather sharply to another brook. All that remains near the house is a northern exposure. There is a vegetable garden in a clearing in the back woods, far from the house; and herbs have been grown there in quantities—but not conveniently so.

What about sunny areas adjacent to the brook? Those areas are wet, even boggy. They are home to water rodents and have defied drainage by tile. Only the slopes are reasonably well drained, but these slopes would not make a good site for an herb garden since the soil is by nature too acidic. Although these sunny slopes make excellent beds for the *Erica* (heath), *Calluna* (heather), and *Arctostaphylos uva-ursi* (bearberry) planted there, to neutralize the soil and to level the slopes would be nearly impossible. The only area remaining to be considered is a northern exposure. Usually this is least desirable, but the house-garage structure is low and thus casts no appreciable shade to the north except in midwinter. Adjacent to the existing workshop-drying room for herbs is an area formerly used as a driveway turnaround. This area is ideal in several respects—it is on higher ground where drainage is better, the stone provides a good base of the proper pH for growing herbs, and it is near the herb drying area and near the kitchen. Only two existing trees need to be felled to create a day-long, sunny exposure in the spring and summer growing season. The new herb garden has been located.

The next step is to see if the general outline of the herb garden is predetermined by any existing structure. Indeed, all four sides are so determined, if a garden as large as desired is to be established. There is the house-garage structure on one side, a natural slope not to be tampered with on another, a driveway on still another, and the property line on the last. The outline is fixed, as the drawing on p. 127 indicates. Then, all the designs in this book were thoroughly studied to determine if a portion of one of them could be used. It was a pleasurable assignment, and the search did not take long. The Dye and Textile Herb Garden on p. 77 provided the needed inspiration. The general outline is similar, certainly not precisely the same, but it need not be identical. The similarity is sufficient to inspire any planner in tailoring an herb garden to individual needs. Culinary herbs will fill a large, single bed. Herbs for wreaths and teas and tussie-mussies will grow in the L-shaped bed. Potpourri and sweet bag herbs will thrive in a medium-size bed. The smallest bed will be home for a few select dye and medicinal herbs.

Especially helpful are the three gateways into the garden. One is conveniently at the door to the drying room, another is close to the rear of the house. The

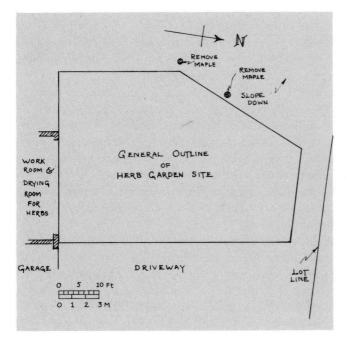

General outline of herb garden site

third is a ramp that provides easy access to the driveway. A service path four feet wide between the drying room and garden sets the beds away from the structure far enough to allow full sun in the growing season. This service path continues around the west and north boundaries of the beds to the ramp entering the driveway.

Two drawings were required to work out problems. The first drawing made it quite apparent that paths of three feet—thought to be adequate within the herb garden—looked skimpy. A staked-out plan on the spot proved the same thing. In addition, use of the garden cart would have to be limited to the external service paths, which would add countless steps to weeding or filling the beds. So it was necessary to go back to the drawing board for a second drawing allowing the inches needed to widen the inner paths to four feet. With the herb beds placed near the drying room, a desired picnic and sitting area would be situated farther north nearer the property line. Privacy for this area can be provided by shrubs and the existing native dogwood and spicebush. This zone is to be tied into the garden area with a low stone wall of the same native stone used at the foot of the drive in the wall that forms the back of the long herb bed on the east side. In fact, this low wall will enclose the garden area. It begins at the back corner of the house and continues west, then north, forming the outer boundary of the service path, and around three sides of the picnic-sitting area.

One of the more helpful steps of the "test" thus far was staking out the proposed design on the site. This

sort of mock-up of the design will make any flaws apparent. It is much better to learn of problems such as ours with the garden cart in the planning stage before construction begins. If all is well, the planner is reassured and can proceed with confidence. If, as in this case, something is amiss, it is comforting to know it was discovered at a point when correcting it took little effort.

With the plan established, a decision regarding edgings for the beds had to be made. There was no

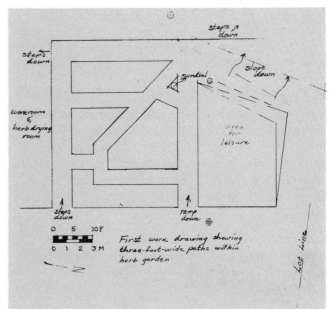

First working drawing showing three-foot-wide paths within the herb garden

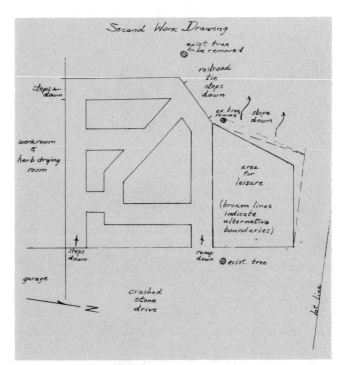

Second working drawing showing improved design with width of inner paths increased to four feet

Paths and beds staked out with twine

treated timbers (four by four inches by six, eight, or ten feet) are generally available and relatively inexpensive, and they can be tailored to the size and shape of each bed. In this case, the eight-foot length was more practical. Two layers of timbers were used to make the beds the desired depth. Joints were preferred for the added strength they would provide. At corners, even those other than a ninety-degree-angle, a lapped joint was fashioned. To secure each joint and at the same time anchor the timbers to the ground, a three-eighths-inch rod fifteen inches long was driven through a previously drilled hole in the joint and then into the ground. This left the rod flush with the top of the timber edging. In the earlier stage of planning, it was thought best to have only the joints at corners coincide. However, at the beginning of construction it became clear that this was not practical. To construct the joints of each timber layer so that they coincide would be more efficient, and the finished edging would be effective. Construction of this edging could not be considered easy, but it was a do-it-yourself project. However, this was, admittedly, not one completed in a weekend.

question that the beds would be raised. The old turn-around stone made it necessary. A structural edging was in order. Before edgings could be put in place, however, the site required some leveling. A slight fall of approximately one-fourth inch per foot was needed to make sure surface water would drain away from the structure toward the slope. In this area, pressure-

Method of joint construction used in preparing the structural edgings

Edgings partially constructed, with some rods not yet driven into the ground at joints

With edgings in place, filling the beds with soil was next. Aged compost, sand, leaves, and sheep manure were at hand to make a good soil mix. The crushed stone base would encourage root growth. Weeds, which in the past had grown vigorously on the stone base, had been proof of that. Unfortunately, this same base underlies all the paths, which will become filled with weeds unless some method is discovered to make this impossible. Heavy black plastic, topped by smaller crushed stone or bark, could serve this purpose. These inner paths need not be of the same material as the outer service paths. The latter need to be more substantially paved, for they will likely have more traffic. Bricks or river stones are good possibilities for the service paths, although the angles could make it more difficult to establish a pattern in brick.

There are no steps within the herb garden itself, but there are exits to different levels. One is the ramp to the driveway. Another is an existing set of steps that cannot be removed but must be altered to make their use easier and safer. Five steps with a tread of fourteen inches and risers of six inches lead from the southwest corner of the herb garden to a terrace three feet lower. These steps are of railroad ties and river gravel. Wide risers of railroad ties and a deep tread of river gravel create steps down the slope on the west side. These will be used often for cart traffic and offer a direct avenue to a bridge and the path through the woods to a clearing and the vegetable garden. A wrought-iron railing of simple design used at the back of the stone wall on the east side will continue as a hand railing down the steps by the garage. The same railing will be used from the northwest corner of the house and at the steps to the lower terrace.

The only artifact to be used is a terra-cotta sundial. It will be located in the center of the large bed of culinary herbs.

Paving for the terraced area is brick. A choice of five colors was available, and "woodland" paver was selected for its muted tones that blend with this wooded environment. The pattern is running bond, selected for its simplicity, so it does not compete with the design of the herb garden. This pattern is more readily laid than some of the more complicated patterns and uses less brick. A good base of crushed stone was in place from the old turnaround, but it was necessary to loosen the stone with tilling so that it could be leveled properly and well tamped. Then construction of the outline of the area to be paved was completed, using two-by-six-inch pressure-treated timbers. This method of treatment now guarantees

All structural edgings completed

wood life for thirty years, worth the added cost. A level was used during this construction to ensure a gentle slope for the area. The placement of timbers was calculated so a minimum cutting of brick would be needed. However, on a trial run of one course of brick, it was found that the slight variance of size in the bricks over the sixteen feet resulted in a gap between the last brick and the retaining timber. At this point the timber was easily moved to accommodate this variance of the brick. A two-inch layer of sand topped the crushed stone base and was watered and tamped to make a firm, even bed for the pavers. Sand brushed over the finished surface and watered well helps the bricks to become well-seated.

Paths are of river gravel of medium size to be topped later by smaller gravel of the same kind, for the colors of the gravel blend with the edging timbers and the "woodland" pavers. It is the consideration for details that enables the herb garden to take on a unified look. Some preparation was required to ready the paths for the stone. French drains, learned about decades earlier, came to mind as a practical means of improving drainage during heavier rains. Sometimes called "rubble drains," their construction can be somewhat varied. In this instance, they were made by cutting a channel four to five inches deep in the center of each path and pitched toward the slope, converging where it was logical to do so. These channels drain into perforated plastic pipes that empty into unperforated pipes down the slope and into the brook. The service path running the length of the south side of the garden was also fitted with perforated drain pipe, since that path borders the house. No black plastic was used under the river gravel to discourage weeds, for it would interfere with the drainage system.

It is possible to make some assessment of the trial now. The structural edgings have come through two winters without any sign of strain. Herbs have flourished in the beds. With the completion of the paths, the terraced area, and the steps to other levels, a practical and pleasing herb garden has been created using the recommendations prescribed.

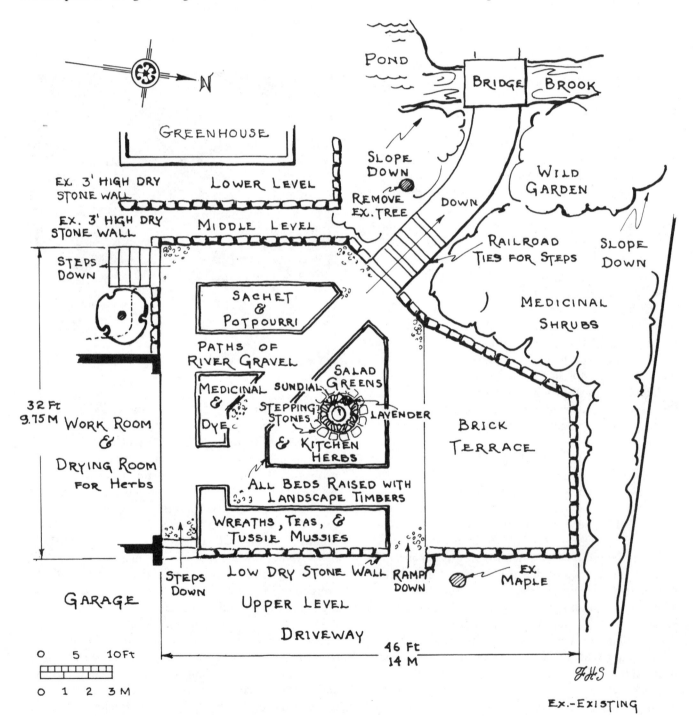

GLOSSARY

Allée. A walk or path between two rows of formally planted trees or shrubs that are at least two times as high as the width of the walk or path.

Arbor. A bower of vines or branches or of latticework covered with climbing shrubs or vines.

Architects' scale. Usually a triangular section made of box-wood, having a variety of gradations, in inches, sixteenths of an inch, twelfths of an inch, and so on.

Armillary sphere. An old astronomical instrument composed of rings representing the positions of important circles of the celestial sphere.

Asymmetry. Exists when elements on either side of an axis are unlike, but balance is maintained by equal quantity or weight.

Axis. A line actually drawn and used as the basis of measurements in an architectural or other working drawing; a straight line with respect to which a body or figure, for example, a garden plan, is symmetrical.

Cold frame. A usually glass-covered frame without artificial heat used to protect plants and seedlings.

Cordon. An espalier trained to a single horizontal shoot or to two opposed shoots so as to form one line.

Cultivar. A term derived from *cultivated variety*; a horticultural variety or race that has originated and persisted under cultivation, not necessarily referable to botanical species, and of botanical or horticultural importance requiring a name. Cultivars are denoted by single quotation marks, for example: *Rosmarinus officinalis* 'Prostratus'.

Cutting garden. Where plants are grown primarily for cut flowers or foliage rather than for their artistic landscape appearance.

Dipping bowl. A device for holding water so as to water plants conveniently by dipping or setting plants into it. In Old World gardens water was exposed in "wells" to open air and sun to improve it for use with plants.

Ellipse. An oval.

Engineer's scale. Usually a triangular section having a variety of gradations, in tenths of an inch, hundredths of an inch, and so on.

Epithet. A word following the name of a genus and not denoting rank; for example, in *Artemisia ludoviciana* var. *albula*, *ludoviciana* is a specific epithet and *albula* is a varietal epithet.

Equatorial sundial. A sundial with its hour lines on a curved metal strip representing the equator. Its arrow points north and, being perpendicular to the symbolic equator, casts the shadow for the hour.

Espalier. A plant—often a fruit tree—trained to grow flat against a support, often a wall or trellis.

Flemish bond. A pattern of brickwork consisting of alternate headers (ends of brick) and stretchers (lengths of brick) in the same course. Preferred by those who strive for neatness.

Flue liners. Sections of tile used to channel flame and smoke safely through a chimney.

Forthright. A straight course or path. Chiefly after Shakespeare: "Here's a maze trod indeede Through fourth rights and meanders" (*Tempest* 3.3.3).

French drain. A drain consisting of an underground passage made by filling a trench with loose stone, sometimes covered with earth or more stones, also called *rubble drain*.

Gazebo. A freestanding, roofed structure usually open on the sides.

Genus. The taxonomic category ranking between the family and the species.

Grindstone. Millstone; a flat, circular stone of sandstone used for grinding tools or shaping or smoothing objects.

Ground cover. Low-growing plants used to form a mat over the surface of the ground.

Heart-pine. *Pinus palustris*, a long-leaf pine called also Georgia pine and southern pine.

Hotbeds. A bed of soil enclosed in glass, heated especially by fermenting manure, and used for forcing or for raising seedlings. Electric cables are more commonly used today to provide heat.

Interplant. To plant a variety of compatible plants within the same bed; sometimes used to produce a succession of blooms.

Knot garden. An elaborately designed garden especially of flowers or herbs.

Lathhouse. A structure made chiefly of laths or slats spaced to reduce excessive sunlight while permitting moderate air circulation and used for growing plants that require some shade and protection from strong winds.

Manufactory. A factory.

Maypole. A tall flower-wreathed pole forming a center for May Day sports and dances.

Millstone. Either of two circular stones often built up of several pieces and used for grinding grain or another substance fed through a center hole in the upper stone.

Moondial. A dial for nocturnal use showing time by the moon's shadow.

Mulch. Material used to cover exposed soil around plants. Usually a few inches thick, sometimes inert but more often organic material such as leaves or peat is used for this purpose.

Paling. A pale or a picket for a fence.

Parterre. An ornamental garden with paths between the beds; a patterned garden, its design often worked in low-growing evergreens, its compartments filled with flowers, turf, or colored earths.

Pea gravel. Small, loose, rounded fragments of rock.

Pergola. A structure usually consisting of parallel colonnades supporting an open roof of girders and cross rafters; an open-work arch or covering for a walk or passageway over which climbing plants are trained.

Quincunx. An arrangement of five things with one at each corner and one in the middle of a square or rectangle; a manner of growing plants to save space and provide the maximum amount of room for their maturity.

Rose, Tudor. A double rose with white and red for the houses of York and Lancaster.

Shrub. A woody plant that remains relatively low and produces shoots or trunks from the base, not treelike or with a single trunk.

Sill cock. A water faucet at about sill height on the outside of a building and usually threaded for attaching a hose; called also a hose cock.

Species. This word serves as both singular and plural. It is the basic unit in classification of plants.

Standard. A shrub or herb grown with an erect main stem so that it forms or resembles a tree.

Stone, dressed. Stone cut cleanly for a more precise, snug fit for walks, walls, or steps.

Subspecies. A major subdivision of a species, ranking between species and variety. The subspecies name often implies a distinct geographic distribution.

Swept yard. Bare-ground yards and walks between beds that are clean-swept with brush brooms.

Symmetry. The arrangement of elements equally and identically on either side of a central axis.

Synonym. A taxonomic name (as of a species or genus) rejected as being incorrectly applied or incorrect in form or spelling or rejected in favor of another because of evidence of the priority of that other or evidence establishing a more natural genetic classification.

Topiary. The practice or art of training, cutting, and trimming plant material into odd or ornamental shapes.

Treillage. Latticework for vines.

Turf seat. Banked-up earth, turfed and planted with uncultivated flowers; often planted with aromatic herbs. Turfed seats were sometimes supported by wattle fences or brick walls.

Variety. A category below species.

Wall, dry stone. An enclosure or a retainer made of stones or rocks and laid without mortar.

Wattle fence. An enclosure made of sapling trees laced in a latticework manner.

BIBLIOGRAPHY

Arber, Agnes. *Herbals, Their Origin and Evolution: A Chapter in the History of Botany, 1470–1670*. Cambridge: Cambridge University Press, 1938.

Bailey, L. H. *How Plants Get Their Names*. New York: Dover, 1963.

Bailey Hortorium, Liberty Hyde, Staff of. *Hortus Third*. London: Macmillan, 1976.

Bardswell, Frances A. *The Herb Garden*. London: Adam and Charles Black, 1911.

Baumgardt, John Philip. *Hanging Plants for Home, Terrace, and Garden*. New York: Simon and Schuster, 1972.

Behme, Robert Lee. *The Outdoor How-to-Build-It Book*. New York: Hawthorne Books, 1971.

Berrall, Julia S. *The Garden (An Illustrated History)*. New York: Viking Press, 1966.

Beston, Henry. *Herbs and the Earth*. Garden City: Doubleday, Doran & Co., 1935.

Brookes, John. *Room Outside*. New York: Viking Press, 1970.

———. *The Small Garden*. London: Marshall Cavendish, 1977.

Brownlow, Margaret E. *Herbs and the Fragrant Garden*. Seal, Sevenoaks, Kent: The Herb Farm, 1957.

Carpenter, Prof. Jot, ed. *Handbook of Landscape Architectural Construction*. American Society of Landscape Architects and Associated Landscape Contractors of America.

Clarkson, Rosetta E. *Green Enchantment*. New York: Macmillan, 1944, 1961.

———. *Herbs: Their Culture and Uses*. New York: Macmillan, 1942, 1971.

Coats, Peter. *Roses*. New York: G. P. Putnam's Sons, 1962.

Cross, John E. *Book of the Geranium*. London: Saturn Press, 1951.

Crowe, Sylvia. *Garden Design*. London: Country Life, 1958.

Darrah, Helen H. *The Cultivated Basils*. Independence, Mo.: Buckeye Printing Co., 1980.

Earle, Alice Morse. *Sun-Dials and Roses of Yesterday*. New York: Macmillan, 1902.

Edlin, H. L. *British Plants*. London, New York, Toronto, Sydney: B. T. Batsford, 1951.

Erichsen-Brown, Charlotte. *Use of Plants for the Past Five Hundred Years*. Aurora, Ontario: Breezy Creeks Press, 1979.

Flannery, Harriet Ballard. *A Study of the Taxa of* Thymus L. *(Labiatae) Cultivated in the United States*. Ann Arbor: University Microfilms, 1982.

Foley, Daniel J. *The Complete Book of Garden Ornaments, Complements, and Accessories*. New York: Crown Publishers, 1972.

Foster, Gertrude B. *Herbs for Every Garden*. New York: E. P. Dutton & Co., 1966, 1973.

Foster, Gertrude B., and Louden, Rosemary F. *Park's Success with Herbs*. Greenwood, S.C.: Geo. W. Park Seed Co., 1980.

Fox, Helen Morgenthau. *Gardening with Herbs for Flavor and Fragrance*. New York: Macmillan, 1933.

Garland, Sarah. *The Complete Book of Herbs and Spices*. New York: Viking Press, 1979.

Grieve, Mrs. M. *Modern Herbal*. New York: Dover, 1971.

Hamel, Paul B., and Chiltoskey, Mary U. *Cherokee Plants*. Sylva, N.C.: Herald Publishing Co., 1975.

Hay, Roy, and Synge, Patrick M. *The Color Dictionary of Flowers and Plants*. New York: Crown Publishers, 1974.

Hendrickson, Robert. *The Berry Book*. New York: Doubleday, 1981.

Howard, Frances. *Landscaping with Vines*. New York: Macmillan, 1959.

Ireys, Alice Recknagel. *How to Plan and Plant Your Own Property*. New York: William Morrow & Co., 1975.

Johns, Rev. C. A. *Flowers of the Field*. Edited by Clarence Elliott. London: George Routledge & Sons, 1911.

Johnson, Loyal R. *How to Landscape Your Grounds*. New York: De La Mare, 1946.

Jones, Dorothy Bovee. *The Herb Garden*. 2d ed. Philadelphia: Dorance & Co., 1972.

Kiaer, Eigel. *The Concise Handbook of Roses*. New York: E. P. Dutton & Co., 1966.

Krauss, Helen K. *Geraniums for Home and Garden*. New York: Macmillan, 1964.

Lathrop, Norma Jean. *Herbs, How to Select, Grow and Enjoy*. Tucson: H. P. Books, 1981.

Lawrence, Elizabeth. *Gardens in Winter*. New York: Harper & Bros., 1961.

Lawrence, George H. M. *Taxonomy of Vascular Plants*. New York: Macmillan, 1951.

Leighton, Ann. *American Gardens in the Eighteenth Century*. Boston: Houghton Mifflin, 1976.

———. *Early American Gardens*. Boston: Houghton Mifflin, 1970.

Lerner, Carol. *A Biblical Garden*. New York: William Morrow and Co., 1982.

Lesch, Alma. *Vegetable Dyeing*. New York: Watson-Guptill Publications, Division Billboard Publications, 1970.

Loewenfeld, Claire. *Herb Gardening: Why and How to Grow Herbs*. London: Faber and Faber, 1971.

Loewenfeld, Claire, and Back, Philippa. *Complete Book of Herbs and Spices*. Boston, Toronto: Little, Brown & Co., 1974.

McFarland, J. Horace. *Roses of the World in Color*. Boston, New York: Houghton Mifflin Co., 1938.

Miller, Amy Bess. *Shaker Herbs*. New York: Clarkson N. Potter, 1976.

Moldenke, Harold N. and Alma L. *Plants of the Bible*. Waltham, Mass.: Chronica Botanica Co., 1952.

Muenscher, Walter, and Rice, Myron. *Garden Spice and Wild Pot Herbs*. Ithaca: Cornell University Press, 1978.

Pozza, Neri, ed., and Brunello, Franco, chemist. *The Art of Dyeing*. Vicenza, Italy, 1973. (1st American edition trans. Bernard Hickey.)

Rohde, Eleanour Sinclair. *A Garden of Herbs*. New York: Dover, 1983.

Rosengarten, Frederic, Jr. *The Book of Spices*. Wynnewood, Pa.: Livingston Pub. Co., 1969.

Simmons, Adelma G. *Herb Gardening in Five Seasons*. New York: Van Nostrand, 1969.

Simonds, John Ormsbee. *Landscape Architecture*. New York: McGraw-Hill, 1961.

Singleton, Esther. *The Shakespeare Garden*. New York: William Farquhar Payson, 1931.

Smith, A. W. *A Gardener's Dictionary of Plant Names*. Revised by Dr. W. T. Stearn. New York: St. Martin's Press, 1972.

Stearn, William T. *Botanical Latin*. New York: Hafner, 1966.

Stuart, Malcolm, ed. *The Encyclopedia of Herbs and Herbalism*. Los Angeles: Crescent Books, 1979.

Taloumis, George. *Container Gardening Outdoors*. New York: Simon & Schuster, 1972.

Tarantino, Rhoda Specht. *Small Gardens Are More Fun*. New York: Simon & Schuster, 1972.

Taylor, Norman. *Fragrance in the Garden*. New York, Toronto: Van Nostrand, 1953.

———. *Herbs in the Garden*. New York, Toronto: Van Nostrand, 1953.

Thacker, Christopher. *The History of Gardens*. Berkeley and Los Angeles: University of California Press, 1979.

Thomas, Graham Stuart. *Climbing Roses Old and New*. New York: St. Martin's, 1965.

———. *The Old Shrub Roses*. Rev. ed. London: Phoenix House, 1957.

———. *Shrub Roses of Today*. London: Phoenix House, 1962.

Vivian, John. *Building Stone Walls*. Charlotte, Vt.: Garden Way, 1976.

Weber, Nelva M. *How to Plan Your Own Home Landscape*. Indianapolis, New York: Bobbs-Merrill, 1976.

Webster, Helen Noyes. *Herbs: How to Grow Them and How to Use Them*. New ed. Boston: Ralph T. Hale & Co., 1942.

White, Katherine S. *Onward and Upward in the Garden*. New York: Farrar, Straus, Giroux, 1979.

Wilder, Louise Beebe. *The Fragrant Garden*. New York: Dover, 1974.

Wilson, Helen Van Pelt, and Bell, Leonie. *The Fragrant Year*. New York: William Morrow & Co., 1967.

Yang, Linda. *The Terrace Gardener's Handbook*. New York: Doubleday, 1975.

Zohary, Michael. *Plants of the Bible*. Cambridge: Cambridge University Press, 1982.

CONTRIBUTORS

The following have contributed garden designs used in this book:
Florence B. Baker, L.A.; Elsetta Gilchrist Barnes, L.A., A.S.L.A.; Mrs. Philip Batchelder; Marion E. Bates; Mrs. Winthrop G. Bleecker; Alfred L. Boerner, L.A.; Mrs. George T. Bradner; Mrs. Berkeley Brandt; Vera Breed, L.A.; Mrs. Austin R. Bush; Mrs. Z. T. Bynam, Jr.; Robert G. Campbell, L.A.; Barbara Capen, L.D.; Mrs. A. C. Cozart; Mrs. Hammond Crawford; Martha Dahlen; Mrs. Maxton Davies; Mrs. William Y. Dear, Jr.; Mrs. Leonard Dreyfuss; Charlotte Erichsen-Brown; Mrs. Charles L. Gannaway; Mrs. Jack Emil Geist; James D. Graham, L.A.; Mrs. William W. Griffin; Mrs. Henry Gund; Sandy Hicks; Madalene Hill; Mr. and Mrs. Benjamin McF. Hines; Margaret Osborn Holt, L.A.; Mrs. Raymond V. Ingersoll; Dorothy Bovee and Jonathan Jones; Mrs. James C. Keebler; Lucile Teeter Kissack, L.A., A.S.L.A.; Mrs. William T. Lamm, Jr.; Elizabeth Lawrence, L.A.; Jo Lohmolder; Frank M. McGarry; Melissa R. Marshall, L.A., A.S.L.A., Associate; Diane C. Martin; Mrs. Herbert G. Meyer; Amy Bess Miller; Mrs. Peter M. Moffit; Elisabeth W. Morss; Neil Hamill Park, L.A., F.A.A.R.; Mrs. Charles Patch; Mrs. H. Donald Paxton; William C. Paxton, L.A.; Sherry D. Pees; Susan W. Plimpton, L.A.; Mrs. John Poinier; Mrs. Robert K. Price; William Radler; Virginia B. and Robert B. Rady; Eloise and Jo Ray, L.A.; Mrs. Walter Rebmann; Frederick E. Roberts; Mrs. Milton C. Rose; Jean Ruh; Timothy Procter Ruh; Mrs. Nathan Sameth; Mrs. G. Lawrence Schetky; Mrs. Eric Duke Scott; Joan E. Semple, L.A.; Mrs. John A. Skinner; Isadore L. L. Smith (Ann Leighton), L.A.; Mrs. Elbert Smith; Mrs. Christopher Spencer; Milton Stricker, Architect; Faith H. Swanson; Mrs. Joe H. Talbot III; Helen M. Whitman; Edmund G. Wilcox, L.A.; Mr. and Mrs. Booker Worthen; Linda Yang.

The following provided historical, civic, and educational gardens:
Arkansas School for the Blind, Little Rock, Ark.; Boerner Botanical Gardens, Milwaukee County Park Commission, Hales Corners, Wisc.; The Country Doctor Museum, Bailey, N.C.; The Emma Ormsby Griffith Memorial Garden, Matthew Miksch House, Old Salem, Winston-Salem, N.C.; The Garden Center of Greater Cleveland, Western Reserve Herb Society, Cleveland, Ohio; Hancock Shaker Village, Shaker Community, Inc., Hancock, Mass.; Kingwood Center, Mansfield, Ohio; Matthaei Botanical Gardens, University of Michigan, Ann Arbor, Mich.; Old Slater Mill Museum, Pawtucket, R.I.; Tullie Smith House Restoration, Atlanta Historical Society, Atlanta, Ga.; Wayne County Extension and Education Center, Michigan State University, Lansing, Mich.; Weeks Brick House, Leonard Weeks and Descendants in America, Inc., Greenland, N.H.

The following provided photographs used in this book:
Everest P. Derthick; James F. Gayle, Plain Dealer Photo; James S. Harper; Christopher Rady; Kathleen Byroads Sowers; Linda Yang.

COMMON NAME TO BOTANICAL NAME INDEX

Abaca	*Musa textilis*
Absinthe	*Artemisia absinthium*
Aconite	*Aconitum*
winter	*Eranthis, E. hyemalis*
Adam's needle	*Yucca filamentosa, Y. smalliana*
Agrimony	*Agrimonia, A. eupatoria*
Alecost	*Chrysanthemum balsamita*
Alehoof	*Glechoma hederacea*
Alexanders	*Angelica atropurpurea, Smyrnium olusatrum*
Alkanet	*Anchusa, A. officinalis, Alkanna tinctoria*
All-heal	*Prunella vulgaris*
Allspice, Carolina	*Calycanthus fertilis, C. floridus*
Aloe	*Aloe*
Barbados	*Aloe barbadensis*
Curaçao	*A. barbadensis*
medicinal	*A. barbadensis*
Alyssum, sweet	*Lobularia maritima*
purple	*L. maritima*
dwarf	*L. maritima*
Amaranth	*Amaranthus*
Ambrosia	*Chenopodium botrys*
Amsonia	*Amsonia tabernaemontana*
Anemone, Japanese	*Anemone hupehensis, A. × hybrida*
Angelica	*Angelica archangelica*
Angel's-tears	*Datura sanguinea, Narcissus triandrus, Soleirolia soleirolii*
Anise	*Foeniculum vulgare* var. *azoricum, Myrrhis odorata, Pimpinella anisum*
common	*Pimpinella anisum*
Apple	*Malus, M. sylvestris*
crab	*Malus*
gold	*Lycopersicon lycopersicum*
love	*L. lycopersicum, Solanum aculeatissimum*
mad	*S. melongena* var. *esculentum*
southern wild crab	*Malus angustifolia*
thorn	*Crataegus, Datura*
Apple-of-Peru	*Nicandra physalodes*
Arborvitae	*Thuja*
American	*Thuja occidentalis*
Archangel	*Angelica archangelica, Lamium album*
Arrowwood	*Viburnum, V. acerifolium, V. dentatum*
Artemisia	*Artemisia ludoviciana*
silver-king	*A. ludoviciana* var. *albula*
silver mound	*A. schmidtiana* 'Nana'
tree	*A. arborescens*
Arum, Italian	*Arum italicum*
Asafetida	*Ferula assafoetida, F. foetida*
Asarabacca	*Asarum*
Ash	*Fraxinus*
American mountain	*Sorbus americana*
Ashweed	*A. podagraria*
Asparagus	*Asparagus*
garden	*A. officinalis*
Aspen	*Populus, P. tremuloides*
Asp-of-Jerusalem	*Isatis tinctoria*
Aster, Stoke's	*Stokesia, S. laevis*
Azalea	*Rhododendron*
Baby's-breath, false	*Galium aristatum, G. mollugo*
Balloon flower	*Platycodon, P. grandiflorus*
Balm	*Melissa*
bee	*M. officinalis, Monarda didyma*
field	*Glechoma hederacea*
lemon	*M. officinalis*
sweet	*M. officinalis*
Balm-of-Gilead	*Cedronella canariensis, Populus balsamifera, P. gileadensis*
hoary	*Agastache cana*
Balmony	*Chelone glabra*
Balsam	*Impatiens*
Bamboo, heavenly	*Nandina domestica*
sacred	*N. domestica*
Banana	*Musa*
Barbe-de-capuchin	*Cichorium intybus*
Barberry	*Berberis*
blue	*Mahonia aquifolium*
common	*Berberis vulgaris*
holly	*B. ilicifolia, Mahonia aquifolium*
Japanese	*B. thunbergii*
Barrenwort	*Epimedium × versicolor, E. × youngianum*
Basil	*Clinopodium vulgare, Ocimum*
bush	*O. basilicum* 'Minimum'
lemon	*O. basilicum* 'Citriodorum'
purple	*O. basilicum* 'Purpurascens'
sacred	*O. sanctum*
sweet	*O. basilicum*
Bay	*Gordonia lasianthus, Laurus nobilis, Pimenta racemosa*
bull	*Magnolia grandiflora*
California	*Umbellularia californica*
sweet	*Laurus, L. nobilis, Magnolia virginiana, Persea borbonia*
Bayberry	*Myrica pensylvanica*
Bay-tree	*Laurelia, Laurus*
Bearberry	*Arctostaphylos, Rhamnus purshiana*
common	*A. uva-ursi*
Bedstraw	*Galium*
our-lady's	*G. verum*
white	*G. mollugo*
yellow	*G. verum*
Bee balm	*Monarda, M. didyma*
Beefsteak plant	*Acalypha wilkesiana, Iresine herbstii Perilla, P. frutescens* var. *crispa*
Beet	*Beta*
Begonia, winter	*Bergenia ciliata*
Bellflower	*Campanula, Wahlenbergia*
tussock	*Campanula carpatica*
willow	*C. persicifolia*
Benjamin bush	*Lindera benzoin*
Benzoin	*L. benzoin*
Bergamot	*Citrus aurantium* subsp. *bergamia, Monarda didyma*
wild	*Monarda, M. fistulosa*
Betony	*Stachys, S. officinalis*
woolly	*S. byzantina, S. olympica*
Bilberry	*Vaccinium, V. myrtillus*
Bindweed	*Convolvulus*
Bine	*Humulus lupulus*
Birch, white	*Betula papyrifera*
Bishop's weed	*Aegopodium podagraria, Ammi majus*
Bitter Indian	*Tropaeolum*

Blackberry	Rubus, R. allegheniensis
sow-teat	R. allegheniensis
Black-eyed Susan	Rudbeckia hirta
Blacking plant	Hibiscus rosa-sinensis
Bleeding heart	Dicentra spectabilis
Bloodroot	Sanguinaria, S. canadensis
Bluebell, Spanish	Endymion hispanicus
Bluebells	Mertensia, M. virginica
Virginia	M. virginica
Blueberry	Vaccinium
Blue-curls	Trichostema, Phacelia congesta
woolly	T. lanatum
Blue-devil	Echium vulgare
Bluestar	Amsonia, A. tabernaemontana
Blueweed	Echium vulgare
Boneset	Eupatorium, E. perfoliatum
	Symphytum officinale
common	Eupatorium perfoliatum
Borage	Borago officinalis
Bouncing Bet	Saponaria officinalis
Box	Buxus
common	B. sempervirens
dwarf	B. microphylla 'Green Pillow'
dwarf edging	B. sempervirens 'Suffruticosa'
Korean	B. microphylla var. koreana
mountain	Arctostaphylos uva-ursi
Boxwood	Buxus
Bracken	Pteridium, P. aquilinum
Brake	Pteridium, P. aquilinum, Pteris
canker	Polystichum acrostichoides
hog-pasture	Pteridium aquilinum
pasture	P. aquilinum
Bramble	Rubus
Brazilian-plume	Justicia carnea
Brooklime	Veronica
Broom	Cytisus, C. supinus, Genista,
	G. germanica
dyer's	Genista tinctoria
Scotch	Cytisus scoparius
Brussels sprouts	Brassica oleracea, Gemmifera Group
Buckhorn	Osmunda cinnamomea, Plantago
	lanceolata
Bugbane	Cimicifuga
Bugleweed	Ajuga, Lycopus
carpet	Ajuga reptans
Bugloss	Anchusa, A. officinalis
viper's	Echium
Burnet	Sanguisorba, Poterium sanguisorba
Canadian	Sanguisorba canadensis
garden	Poterium sanguisorba
salad	P. sanguisorba
Burning bush	Combretum microphyllum, Dictamnus
	albus, Euonymus atropurpurea, Kochia
	scoparia var. culta
Buttercup	Ranunculus
Butterfly flower	Asclepias, Bauhinia monandra,
	Schizanthus
Butterfly weed	Asclepias tuberosa
Butter-print	Abutilon theophrasti
Cabbage	Brassica oleracea, Capitata Group
wild	B. oleracea
Calamint	Calamintha, C. grandiflora
Calamus	Acorus calamus
Calico bush	Kalmia latifolia
Calliopsis	Coreopsis tinctoria
Campion	Lychnis, Silene, Lychnis coronaria
rose	L. coronaria
Candleberry	Myrica cerifera, M. pensylvanica
swamp	M. pensylvanica

Candytuft	Iberis
edging	I. sempervirens
Caraway	Carum carvi
Cardinal flower	Lobelia cardinalis, Sinningia cardinalis
blue	Lobelia siphilitica
Carnation	Dianthus caryophyllus
Cart-track plant	Plantago major
Cassena	Ilex cassine, I. vomitoria
Cassina	Ilex cassine, I. vomitoria
Cassine	Ilex cassine, I. vomitoria
Catchfly	Lychnis, Silene
Catmint	Nepeta, N. cataria, N. × faassenii
	N. mussinii
Catnip	N. cataria
Cedar	Cedrus
red	Acrocarpus fraxinifolius
	Juniperus virginiana
Celandine	Chelidonium, C. majus
greater	C. majus
lesser	Ranunculus ficaria
tree	Macleaya cordata
Celeriac	Apium graveolens var. rapaceum
Celery	Apium graveolens var. dulce
wild	A. graveolens, Vallisneria americana
Century plant	Agave, A. americana
Chamomile	Anthemis, Chamaemelum nobile
garden	C. nobile
Russian	C. nobile
Chard	Beta vulgaris, Cicla Group
Swiss	B. vulgaris, Cicla Group
Checkerberry	Gaultheria procumbens
Cherry	
clammy ground	Physalis heterophylla
ground	Physalis, P. heterophylla,
	P. peruviana, P. pubescens
Jerusalem	Solanum pseudocapsicum
pin	Prunus pensylvanica
Cherry-pie	Heliotropium arborescens
Chervil	Anthriscus cerefolium
sweet	Myrrhis odorata
Chestnut	Castanea
Chinese water	Eleocharis dulcis
Chickweed	Paronychia, Stellaria, S. media
Chicory	Cichorium
common	C. intybus
red-leaved	C. intybus
Chive	Allium schoenoprasum
Chinese	A. tuberosum
garlic	A. tuberosum
Ciboule	Allium fistulosum
Cicely	
sweet	Myrrhis odorata, Osmorhiza
Cinquefoil	Potentilla
Nepal	P. nepalensis
shrubby	P. fruticosa
three-toothed	P. tridentata
Cive	Allium schoenoprasum
Clary	Salvia sclarea
annual	S. viridis
Cleavers	Galium
Clematis	Clematis lanuginosa, C. × jouiniana
Cliff-green	Paxistima canbyi
Clover	Trifolium
red	T. pratense
Cockle	Vaccaria pyramidata
corn	Agrostemma, A. githago
purple	A. githago
Cocklebur	Agrimonia, A. eupatoria, Huernia
	pillansii

Cockscomb	*Celosia cristata*		Dandelion	*Taraxacum, T. officinale*
Cohosh	*Actaea*		Daisy	*Bellis, Chrysanthemum frutescens,*
black	*Cimicifuga racemosa*			*C. leucanthemum*
Colchicum	*Colchicum autumnale*		English	*Bellis perennis*
Cole	*Brassica, B. oleracea,* Acephala Group		oxeye	*Chrysanthemum leucanthemum*
red	*Armoracia rusticana*		painted	*C. coccineum*
Coltsfoot	*Galax urceolata, Tussilago farfara*		Paris	*C. frutescens*
Columbine	*Aquilegia*		Shasta	*C. × superbum*
garden	*A. vulgaris*		Daylily	*Hemerocallis, Hosta*
white	*A. alpina* 'Alba'		lemon	*H. lilioasphodelus*
yellow	*A. chrysantha*		yellow	*H. lilioasphodelus, H. × luteola*
Comfrey	*Symphytum*		Deodar	*Cedrus deodara*
white	*S. officinale*		Devil's-darning-	*Clematis virginiana*
Coneflower	*Dracopsis amplexicaulis, Rudbeckia*		needle	
Cool-tankard	*Borago officinalis*		Devil's-tongue	*Amorphophallus, A. rivieri, Ferocactus*
Coriander	*Coriandrum sativum*			*latispinus, Sansevieria, Tacca chantrieri*
Roman	*Nigella sativa*		Devilweed	*Osmanthus*
Cornel	*Cornus*		Deutzia	*Deutzia, D. gracilis*
Costmary	*Chrysanthemum balsamita*		Dill	*Anethum graveolens*
Cotoneaster,	*Cotoneaster apiculata*		Dittany	*Cunila, Dictamnus albus*
cranberry			Crete	*Origanum dictamnus*
Cotton	*Gossypium*		Divine flower	*Dianthus caryophyllus*
lavender	*Santolina chamaecyparissus*		Dock	*Rumex*
upland	*Gossypium hirsutum*		bitter	*R. obtusifolius*
Cottonwood	*Populus, P. deltoides*		broad	*R. crispus, R. obtusifolius*
Cow-itch	*Campsis radicans, Rhus radicans*		sorrel	*Rumex*
Cowslip	*Caltha palustris, Mertensia virginica,*		sour	*R. acetosa, R. crispus*
	Primula veris		Dockmackie	*Viburnum acerifolium*
Jerusalem	*Pulmonaria officinalis*		Dogwood	*Cornus*
Virginia	*Mertensia virginica*		flowering	*C. florida*
Crab	*Malus*		Donkey's tail	*Sedum morganianum*
American	*M. angustifolia, M. coronaria*		Dove's-dung	*Ornithogalum umbellatum*
wild	*M. angustifolia, M. coronaria,*		Dragonhead, false	*Physostegia*
	M. ioensis		Dragonroot	*Arisaema dracontium, A. triphyllum*
Cranberry	*Vaccinium, V. macrocarpon,*		Dropwort	*Filipendula vulgaris*
	V. vitis-idaea		Duckweed	*Lemna, Spirodela*
hog	*Arctostaphylos uva-ursi*		Dusty-miller	*Artemisia stellerana, Centaurea*
Cranesbill	*Geranium*			*cineraria, C. gymnocarpa, C. ragusina,*
spotted	*G. maculatum*			*Chrysanthemum ptarmiciflorum, Lychnis*
wild	*G. maculatum*			*coronaria, Senecio cineraria, S. vira-vira*
Creashak	*Arctostaphylos uva-ursi*		Earth-smoke	*Fumaria officinalis*
Creme-de-menthe	*Mentha requienii*		Edelweiss	*Leontopodium alpinum*
plant			Eggplant	*Solanum melongena* var. *esculentum*
Cress			Eglantine	*Rosa eglanteria*
garden	*Lepidium sativum*		Elaeagnus	*Elaeagnus*
Indian	*Tropaeolum majus*		thorny	*E. pungens*
upland	*Barbarea, B. verna, Lepidium sativum*		Elder, elderberry	*Sambucus*
winter	*Barbarea, B. vulgaris*		American	*S. canadensis*
Crocus	*Crocus*		sweet	*Sambucus canadensis*
autumn	*Colchicum, C. autumnale*		Elecampane	*Inula helenium*
saffron	*Crocus sativus*		Epimedium	*Epimedium*
Crowfoot	*Ranunculus*		Eryngo	*Eryngium*
European	*Aquilegia vulgaris*		sea	*E. maritimum*
Crown-imperial	*Fritillaria imperialis*		Estragon	*Artemisia dracunculus*
Crown plant	*Calotropis gigantea, Campsis*		Eucalypt	*Eucalyptus*
Cuckoo flower	*Cardamine pratensis,*		Everlasting	*Anaphalis, Antennaria, Gnaphalium,*
	Lychnis flos-cuculi			*Helichrysum, Helipterum*
Cumin	*Cuminum cyminum*		white-leaf	*Helichrysum angustifolium*
black	*Nigella sativa*		Fat-hen	*Chenopodium bonus-henricus*
Currant	*Ribes*		Fennel	*Foeniculum vulgare*
alpine	*R. alpinum*		bronze	*F. vulgare*
garden	*R. sativum*		dog	*Anthemis cotula*
mountain	*R. alpinum*		Florence	*Foeniculum vulgare* var. *azoricum*
red	*R. sativum*		wild	*Nigella, N. arvensis, N. damascena, N.*
Curry plant	*Helichrysum angustifolium*			*sativa*
Cypress, Italian	*Cupressus sempervirens*		Fennel flower	*Nigella*
Daffodil	*Narcissus, N. pseudonarcissus*		Fern	
miniature	*N. asturiensis*		Christmas	*Polystichum acrostichoides*
winter	*Sternbergia lutea*		cinnamon	*Osmunda cinnamomea*

dagger	*Polystichum acrostichoides*		lime	*P. × nervosum*
five-finger	*Adiantum pedatum*		maple-leaved	*P. acerifolium*
flowering	*Anemia, Osmunda, O. regalis*		mint	*Chrysanthemum balsamita*
maidenhair	*Adiantum, A. pedatum*		nutmeg	*Pelargonium fragrans*
northern maidenhair	*Adiantum pedatum*		oak-leaved	*P. quercifolium*
shield	*Polystichum, P. braunii*		orange	*P. × citrosum*
sweet	*Comptonia peregrina*		peppermint	*P. tomentosum*
Feverfew	*Chrysanthemum parthenium*		pheasant's-foot	*P. glutinosum, P. × jatrophifolium*
Fever tree	*Pinckneya pubens*		pine	*P. denticulatum*
Fiddleheads	*Osmunda cinnamomea*		rose	*P. graveolens*
Fig	*Ficus*		rose-scented	*P. capitatum*
common	*F. carica*		southernwood	*P. abrotanifolium*
Fig tree	*F. carica*		strawberry	*P. scabrum*
Filbert	*Corylus*		sweet-scented	*P. graveolens*
American	*C. americana*		village-oak	*P. quercifolium*
Finocchio	*Foeniculum vulgare* var. *azoricum*		wild	*Geranium maculatum*
Fir, joint	*Ephedra*		zonal	*Pelargonium × hortorum*
Fire thorn	*Pyracantha*		Germander	*Teucrium, T. chamaedrys*
Five-finger	*Potentilla*		American	*T. canadense*
Flag	*Iris, I. × germanica*		tree	*T. fruticans*
blue	*I. versicolor, I. virginica*		Gill-over-the-ground	*Glechoma hederacea*
myrtle	*Acorus calamus*		Gillyflower	*Matthiola incana*
poison	*Iris versicolor*		Ginger	*Zingiber, Z. officinale*
sweet	*Acorus calamus*		Canton	*Z. officinale*
water	*Iris pseudacorus*		European	*Asarum europaeum*
yellow	*I. pseudacorus*		true	*Zingiber officinale*
Flagroot	*Acorus calamus*		wild	*Asarum, A. canadense, A. virginicum*
Flamingo plant	*Justicia carnea*			*Costus speciosus*
Flannel plant	*Verbascum thapsus*		yellow	*Hedychium flavescens*
Flax	*Linum, L. usitatissimum*		Goatsbeard	*Aruncus, Tragopogon, T. pratensis*
perennial	*L. perenne*		Golden-buttons	*Tanacetum vulgare*
Fleabane	*Erigeron*		Goldenrod	*Solidago*
Fleece flower	*Polygonum*		California	*S. Californica*
Fleur-de-lis	*Iris, I. × germanica*		Goldenseal	*Hydrastis canadensis*
Forget-me-not	*Myosotis*		Goldthread	*Coptis, C. trifolia*
garden	*M. sylvatica*		Good-luck plant	*Cordyline terminalis, Oxalis deppei,*
Foxglove	*Digitalis*			*Sansevieria*
common	*D. purpurea*		Gooseberry	*Ribes*
Grecian	*D. lanata*		Goosefoot	*Chenopodium, C. bonus-henricus*
yellow	*D. grandiflora*		Gotu kola	*Hydrocotyle asiatica*
Fraxinella	*Dictamnus albus*		Goutweed	*Aegopodium podagraria*
Fringe tree	*Chionanthus virginicus*		Grape	*Vitis*
Fritillary	*Fritillaria*		bear's	*Arctostaphylos uva-ursi*
Fumitory	*Corydalis lutea, Fumaria*		European	*Vitis vinifera* 'Purpurea'
hedge	*C. lutea*		holly	*Mahonia*
Gardenia	*Gardenia*		mountain	*Mahonia aquifolium, Vitis monticola,*
Garlic	*Allium sativum*			*V. rupestris*
daffodil	*A. neapolitanum*		Oregon	*Mahonia aquifolium, M. nervosa*
giant	*A. scorodoprasum*		wine	*V. vinifera* 'Purpurea'
Oriental	*A. tuberosum*		Grass	
round-headed	*A. sphaerocephalum*		China	*Boehmeria nivea*
serpent	*A. sativum* var. *ophioscorodon*		fever	*Cymbopogon citratus*
society	*Tulbaghia violacea*		oil	*Cymbopogon*
Gas plant	*Dictamnus albus*		pudding	*Hedeoma pulegioides*
Geranium	*Geranium, Pelargonium, P. × hortorum*		rib: see ribgrass	*Plantago lanceolata*
almond	*P. quercifolium*		ripple: see	*Plantago lanceolata*
apple	*P. odoratissimum*		ripplegrass	
apricot	*P. scabrum*		scorpion	*Myosotis*
camphor-scented	*P. graveolens* 'Camphor Rose'		Green-dragon	*Arisaema dracontium*
coconut	*P. grossularioides*		Greenweed, dyer's	*Genista tinctoria*
crowfoot	*P. radens*		Gum	
English finger-bowl	*P. × limoneum*		Australian	*Eucalyptus*
eucalyptus-scented	*P. × domesticum* 'Clorinda'		coral	*E. torquata*
feather	*Chenopodium botrys*		lemon-scented	*E. citriodora*
fern-leaf	*Pelargonium denticulatum* 'Filicifolium'		Gum tree	*Eucalyptus*
filbert	*P.* 'Concolor Filbert'		Gypsyweed	*Veronica officinalis*
gooseberry	*P. grossularioides*		Gypsywort	*Lycopus europaeus*
herb-scented	*P. tomentosum*		Hackmatack	*Larix laricina, Populus balsamifera*
lemon	*P. crispum*		Hardhack, golden	*Potentilla fruticosa*

Harebell, southern	*Campanula divaricata*
Harvest-lice	*Agrimonia*
Haw	*Virburnum, V. nudum*
black	*Bumelia lanuginosa, Viburnum lentago*
	V. prunifolium
possum	*Ilex decidua, Viburnum acerifolium,*
	V. nudum
red	*Crataegus*
sweet	*Viburnum prunifolium*
Hawthorn	*Crataegus, C. arkansana*
English	*C. laevigata, C. monogyna*
Paul's scarlet	*C. laevigata 'Paulii'*
Washington	*C. phaenopyrum*
Hazel	*Corylus*
witch	*Hamamelis, H. virginiana,*
	H. vernalis
Hazelnut	*Corylus*
European	*C. avellana*
Heal-all	*Prunella vulgaris*
Healing herb	*Symphytum officinale*
Heartsease	*Viola × wittrockiana, V. tricolor*
Hedge plant	*Ligustrum*
Helenium	*Helenium autumnale*
Heliotrope	*Heliotropium, H. arborescens*
garden	*Valeriana officinalis*
Hellebore	*Helleborus*
Helmet flower	*Aconitum napellus, Sinningia cardinalis*
Hemlock	*Conium maculatum, Tsuga*
Canada	*Tsuga canadensis*
Hemp	*Cannabis sativa*
bowstring	*Calotropis gigantea, Sansevieria*
Cuban	*Furcraea hexapetala*
Deccan	*Hibiscus cannabinus*
Deckaner	*H. cannabinus*
Indian	*H. cannabinus, Apocynum cannabinum*
Manila	*Musa textilis*
sisal	*Agave sisalana*
Hemp plant	*Agave sisalana, Sansevieria*
Hen-and-chickens	*Echeveria, Sempervivum soboliferum*
	S. tectorum
Henequen	*Agave fourcroydes*
Herb Gerard	*Aegopodium podagraria*
Herb-of-grace	*Ruta graveolens*
Herb Robert	*Geranium robertianum*
Herniary	*Herniaria*
Hibiscus	*Hibiscus*
Chinese	*H. rosa-sinensis*
Hawaiian	*H. rosa-sinensis*
Hickory	*Carya*
shagbark	*C. ovata*
shellbark	*C. ovata, C. laciniosa*
Holly	*Ilex*
American	*I. opaca*
box-leaved	*I. crenata*
Burford's	*I. cornuta 'Burfordii'*
Chinese	*I. cornuta*
horned	*I. cornuta*
Japanese	*I. crenata*
sea	*Eryngium maritimum*
Wilson's	*I. wilsonii*
Hollyhock, common	*Alcea rosea*
Holm, sea	*Eryngium maritimum*
Honesty	*Lunaria, L. annua*
Honeyshuck	*Gleditsia triacanthos*
Honeysuckle	*Aquilegia canadensis, Justicia californica,*
	Lonicera, Rhododendron prinophyllum
coral	*Lonicera sempervirens*
trumpet	*Campsis radicans, Lonicera sempervirens*
yellow	*Lonicera flava*

Hop	*Humulus*
common	*H. lupulus*
European	*H. lupulus*
Horehound	*Marrubium*
common	*M. vulgare*
silver	*M. incanum*
water	*Lycopus*
white	*M. vulgare*
Horsefly	*Baptisia tinctoria*
Horseheal	*Inula helenium*
Horsemint	*Monarda, Mentha longifolia, Monarda*
	punctata
Horseradish	*Armoracia rusticana*
Horsetail	*Equisetum arvense, E. hyemale*
Houseleek	*Sempervivum*
common	*S. tectorum*
roof	*S. tectorum*
Huckleberry	*Gaylussacia, Vaccinium*
Hyacinth, grape	*Muscari*
wood	*Endymion*
Hydrangea, oakleaf	*Hydrangea quercifolia*
Hyssop	*Hyssopus, H. officinalis*
anise	*Agastache foeniculum*
blue	*Hyssopus officinalis*
blue giant	*Agastache foeniculum*
fennel giant	*A. foeniculum*
fragrant giant	*A. foeniculum*
giant	*Agastache*
rose	*H. officinalis 'Rosea'*
white	*H. officinalis 'Alba'*
Immortelle	*Helichrysum, Xeranthemum annuum*
Indigo	*Indigofera*
blue false	*Baptisia australis*
false	*Amorpha, A. fruticosa, Baptisia*
plains wild	*Baptisia australis*
wild	*Baptisia, B. tinctoria*
wild blue	*B. australis*
Inkberry	*Ilex glabra*
Insect flower	
Dalmation	*Chrysanthemum cinerariifolium*
Persian	*C. coccineum*
Iris	*Iris*
crested	*Iris cristata*
crested, dwarf	*Iris cristata*
Florentine	*I. × germanica var. florentina*
yellow	*I. pseudacorus*
wild	*I. versicolor*
Irish-lace	*Tagetes filifolia*
Ironbark	*Eucalyptus*
Ivry-leaves	*Gaultheria procumbens*
Ivy	*Cissus, Hedera, Kalmia latifolia*
Baltic	*Hedera helix 'Baltica'*
English	*H. helix*
ground	*Glechoma hederacea*
Ivybush	*Kalmia latifolia*
Jacinth, Spanish	*Endymion hispanicus*
Jack-in-the-pulpit	*Arisaema triphyllum*
Jacob's-ladder	*Pedilanthus tithymaloides* subsp.
	tithymaloides, Polemonium, P. caeru-
	leum, P. reptans, Smilax herbacea
Jasmine	*Jasminum*
Cape	*Gardenia jasminoides*
Carolina	*Gelsemium*
confederate	*Trachelospermum jasminoides, Jasminum*
	nitidum
star	*J. gracillimum, J. multiflorum, J. niti-*
	dum, Trachelospermum jasminoides
Jaundice berry	*Berberis vulgaris*
Jessamine	*Jasminum*

Carolina yellow	*Gelsemium*	African corn	*Ixia*
night	*Cestrum nocturnum*	bugle	*Watsonia, W. rosea*
poet's	*Jasminum officinale*	corn	*Ixia maculata*
yellow	*Gelsemium*	fragrant plantain	*Hosta plantaginea*
Jewelweed	*Impatiens, I. capensis, I. pallida*	garland	*Hedychium*
Job's-tears	*Coix lacryma-jobi*	ginger	*Hedychium*
Johnny-jump-up	*Viola pedunculata, V. tricolor*	lemon	*Hemerocallis lilioasphodelus, Lilium parryi*
Judas tree	*Cercis, C. siliquastrum*	Madonna	*Lilium candidum, Eucharis grandiflora*
Juneberry	*Amelanchier*	midsummer plantain	*Hosta undulata* 'Erromena'
Juniper	*Juniperus, J. chinensis* var. *chinensis*	plantain	*Hosta*
creeping	*J. horizontalis*	scarlet Turk's-cap	*Lilium chalcedonicum*
Jute	*Corchorus capsularis*	Lily-of-the-field	*Anemone, Sternbergia lutea*
bastard	*Hibiscus cannabinus*	Lily-of-the-valley	*Convallaria, C. majalis*
bimli	*H. cannabinus*	Lilyturf	*Liriope, Ophiopogon*
bimlipatum	*H. cannabinus*	big blue	*L. muscari*
China	*Abutilon theophrasti*	Lion's-ear	*Leonotis leonurus*
Kale	*Brassica oleracea,* Acephala Group	Lion's-heart	*Physostegia*
Kenaf	*Hibiscus cannabinus*	Lion's-tail	*Agastache cana*
Khas-khas	*Vetiveria zizanioides*	Live-forever	*Sedum telephium, Sempervivum*
Khus-khus	*V. zizanioides*	Lobelia	*Lobelia*
King's-crown	*Justicia carnea*	great	*L. siphilitica*
Kinnikinick	*Arctostaphylos uva-ursi*	Locust	*Robinia*
Knotweed	*Polygonum, P. hydropiperoides*	honey	*Gleditsia, G. triacanthos*
Kohlrabi	*Brassica oleracea,* Gongylodes Group	sweet	*G. triacanthos*
Labdanum or ladanum	*Cistus ladanifer*	Loquat	*Eriobotrya japonica*
Ladies'-delight	*Viola* × *wittrockiana*	Loosestrife	*Lysimachia, Lythrum, L. virgatum*
Lady's-earrings	*Impatiens capensis*	garden	*Lysimachia vulgaris*
Lady's-mantle	*Alchemilla*	Lousewort	*Pedicularis canadensis*
alpine	*A. alpina*	Lovage	*Levisticum officinale*
Lamb's-ears	*Stachys byzantina, S. olympica*	black	*Smyrnium olusatrum*
Larkspur	*Consolida, C. orientalis, Delphinium*	Love-in-a-mist	*Nigella damascena, Passiflora foetida*
rocket	*Consolida ambigua*	Love-lies-bleeding	*Amaranthus caudatus*
Laurel	*Cordia alliodora, Ficus benjamina, Kalmia, Laurus, L. nobilis*	Lucky plant	*Sansevieria*
		Lungwort	*Mertensia, Pulmonaria*
Lavender	*Lavandula*	blue	*P. officinalis*
English	*L. angustifolia*	Mace, sweet	*Tagetes lucida*
French	*L. dentata, L. dentata* var. *candicans, L. stoechas*	Madder	*Rubia tinctorum*
		Magnolia	*Magnolia*
sea	*Limonium*	southern	*M. grandiflora*
spike	*Lavandula angustifolia* subsp. *angustifolia*	star	*M. stellata*
		Mahonia, holly	*Mahonia aquifolium*
sweet	*L. heterophylla*	Maidenhair	*Adiantum*
Leather flower	*Clematis, C. versicolor, C. viorna, C. virginiana*	American	*A. pedatum*
		Mallow	*Hibiscus, Malva, M. alcea* var. *fastigiata*
Leek	*Allium ampeloprasum,* Porrum Group	giant	*Hibiscus*
lily	*A. moly*	Indian	*Abutilon, A. theophrasti*
wild	*A. ampeloprasum, A. tricoccum*	marsh	*Althaea officinalis*
Lemon	*Citrus limon*	musk	*Abelmoschus moschatus, Malva, M. moschata*
Chinese dwarf	*C. limon*		
dwarf	*C. limon*	rose	*Hibiscus*
Meyer	*C. limon*	white	*Althaea officinalis*
Lemongrass	*Cymbopogon citratus*	Mandrake	*Mandragora, Podophyllum peltatum*
West Indian	*C. citratus*	Manzanita	*Arctostaphylos*
Leopard's-bane	*Doronicum, D. pardalianches, Senecio doronicum*	Maple	*Acer*
		flowering	*Abutilon*
Lettuce	*Lactuca*	parlor	*Abutilon*
garden	*L. sativa*	Marguerite	*Chrysanthemum frutescens, C. leucanthemum*
miner's	*Montia perfoliata*		
Lichen	*Parmelia conspersa*	golden	*Anthemis tinctoria*
Licorice	*Glycyrrhiza glabra*	Marigold	*Tagetes*
false	*Helichrysum petiolatum*	African	*T. erecta*
Licorice plant	*H. petiolatum*	Aztec	*T. erecta*
Lilac	*Syringa, S. patula, S. vulgaris*	big	*T. erecta*
California	*Ceanothus* 'Julia Phelps'	French	*T. patula*
Japanese	*S. reticulata* var. *japonica*	pot	*Calendula officinalis*
Persian	*S. persica, Melia azedarach*	signet	*T. tenuifolia*
Lily	*Lilium*	sweet-scented	*T. lucida*

Marjoram	*Origanum, O. vulgare*	Greek	*Myrtus communis*
annual	*O. majorana*	running	*Vinca minor*
golden	*O. vulgare* 'Aureum'	Swedish	*Myrtus communis*
hop	*O. dictamnus*	wax	*Myrica cerifera*
pot	*O. onites*	Nannyberry	*Viburnum lentago, V. nudum, V.*
sweet	*O. majorana*		*prunifolium*
wild	*O. vulgare*	Nap-at-noon	*Ornithogalum umbellatum*
winter sweet	*O. heracleoticum*	Narcissus	*Narcissus*
Masterwort	*Angelica atropurpurea, Astrantia, A.*	poet's	*N. poeticus*
	major, Heracleum sphondylium subsp.	polyanthus	*N. tazetta*
	montanum	Nasturtium	*Tropaeolum*
Matricary	*Matricaria*	dwarf	*T. minus*
Maypop	*Passiflora incarnata*	garden	*T. majus*
Meadowsweet	*Filipendula, Spiraea alba, S. latifolia*	tall	*T. majus*
Mealberry	*Arctostaphylos uva-ursi*	Navelwort	*Hydrocotyle*
Medlar	*Mespilus, Mimusops elengi*	Nettle	*Urtica*
Japanese	*Eriobotrya japonica*	dead	*Lamium, L. album*
Menthella	*Mentha requienii*	dumb	*L. album*
Mignonette	*Reseda, R. odorata*	false	*Boehmeria*
Milfoil	*Achillea millefolium, Myriophyllum*	hedge	*Stachys*
Milkweed	*Asclepias*	spotted dead	*Lamium maculatum*
Mint	*Mentha*	stinging	*Cnidoscolus texanus, Urtica dioica*
apple	*M. suaveolens*	white dead	*Lamium album*
bergamot	*M. × piperita* var. *citrata*	Nicotiana	*Nicotiana alata*
Corsican	*M. requienii*	Ninebark	*Physocarpus*
curly	*M. spicata*	dwarf	*P. opulifolius* 'Nanus'
dotted	*Monarda punctata*	Nose-bleed	*Achillea millefolium*
eau de Cologne	*Mentha*	Nutmeg flower	*Nigella sativa*
lemon	*M. aquatica* var. *citrata, Monarda*	Oak	*Quercus*
	citriodora	Jerusalem	*Chenopodium botrys*
licorice	*Agastache breviflora*	post	*Quercus stellata*
orange	*Mentha aquatica* var. *citrata*	Obedience	*Physostegia, P. virginiana*
	M. × piperita var. *citrata*	Obedient plant	*Physostegia*
	M. piperita var. *crispii*	Old-maid	*Catharanthus roseus*
pineapple	*M. suaveolens* 'Variegata'	Old-man	*Artemisia abrotanum*
red	*M. × gentilis*	Old-man-and-	*Sempervivum tectorum*
Scotch	*M. × gentilis*	woman	
squaw	*Hedeoma pulegioides*	Old-man's-beard	*Chionanthus virginicus, Vittaria lineata*
water	*Mentha aquatica*	Olive	*Olea europaea*
Mirasol	*Helianthus annuus*	fragrant	*Osmanthus fragrans*
Money plant	*Lunaria*	sweet	*O. fragrans*
Monkey flower	*Mimulus*	tea	*O. fragrans*
Monkshood	*Aconitum, Astrophytum myriostigma*	Onion	*Allium, A. cepa*
Moonflower	*Ipomoea alba*	Egyptian	*A. cepa*, Proliferum Group
Moonwort	*Lunaria*	flowering	*Allium neapolitanum*
Morning-glory	*Ipomoea*	Japanese bunching	*Allium fistulosum*
bush	*Convolvulus cneorum*	sea	*Ornithogalum caudatum, Scilla verna,*
Mosquito plant	*Agastache cana, Azolla caroliniana,*		*Urginea maritima*
	Cynanchum ascyrifolium	Spanish	*Allium fistulosum*
Mother-in-law's-	*Gasteria, Sansevieria trifasciata*	tree	*A. cepa*, Proliferum Group
tongue		two-bladed	*A. fistulosum*
Mother-of-thyme	*Thymus praecox* subsp. *arcticus*	Welsh	*A. fistulosum*
Mountain-lover	*Paxistima canbyi*	Orach	*Atriplex, A. hortensis*
Mourning-bride	*Scabiosa atropurpurea*	garden	*A. hortensis*
Mugwort	*Artemisia, A. vulgaris*	Orange	
white	*A. lactiflora*	hardy	*Poncirus trifoliata*
Mulberry	*Morus*	trifoliate	*P. trifoliata*
American	*M. rubra*	Orchid, bee	*Ophrys apifera*
white	*M. alba*	Oregano	*Origanum, O. vulgare* var. *prismaticum*
Mullein	*Verbascum, V. olympicum, V. thapsus*	de la Sierra	*Monarda fistulosa* var. *menthifolia*
moth	*V. blattaria*	Greek	*Origanum heracleoticum*
Mustard	*Brassica*	Orpine	*Sedum, S. telephium*
Myrrh	*Myrrhis, Myrrhis odorata, Cistus crispus*	Orris	*Iris × germanica* var. *florentina,*
Myrtle	*Cyrilla racemiflora, Myrtus, M.*		*I. pallida*
	communis, Umbellularia californica,	Osier	*Salix*
	Vinca minor	Oxlip	*Primula elatior*
classic	*Myrtus communis*	Paintbrush, Indian	*Asclepias tuberosa, Castilleja californica,*
crape, crepe	*Lagerstroemia indica*		*C. coccinea*

Palm	
needle	*Yucca filamentosa*
petticoat	*Copernicia macroglossa*
umbrella	*Cyperus alternifolius*
Pansy	*Viola × wittrockiana*
garden	*V. × wittrockiana*
Paradise plant	*Justicia carnea*
Parsley	*Petroselinum crispum*
Chinese	*Coriandrum sativum*
curly	*Petroselinum crispum* var. *crispum*
Italian	*P. crispum* var. *neopolitanum*
Parsnip	*Pastinaca, P. sativa*
wild	*Angelica archangelica*
Pasqueflower	*Anemone nuttalliana, A. patens, A. pulsatilla*
Passionflower	*Passiflora*
blue	*P. caerulea*
Patchouli	*Pogostemon cablin*
Peach	*Prunus persica*
Peach-bells	*Campanula persicifolia*
Pear	*Pyrus, Pyrus communis*
Pecan	*Carya illinoinensis*
Pellitory-of-the-wall	*Anacyclus officinarum*
Penny flower	*Lunaria annua*
Pennyroyal	*Mentha pulegium*
American	*Hedeoma pulegioides*
mock	*H. pulegioides*
Pennywort, water	*Hydrocotyle*
Peony	*Paeonia, P. lactiflora*
Chinese	*P. lactiflora*
garden	*P. lactiflora*
white	*P. lactiflora* 'Festiva Maxima'
Pepper	*Capsicum, Piper*
bell	*C. annuum,* Grossum Group
capsicum	*C. annuum,* Longum Group
cayenne	*C. annuum,* Longum Group
chili	*Capsicum, C. annuum,* Longum Group
cone	*C. annuum,* Conoides Group
green	*Capsicum, C. annuum,* Grossum Group
mild water	*Polygonum hydropiperoides*
ornamental	*Capsicum, C. annuum,* Conoides Group
red	*Capsicum, C. annuum,* Longum Group
sweet	*Capsicum, C. annuum,* Grossum Group
Tabasco	*C. frutescens*
Tabasco-sauce	*C. frutescens*
Peppergrass	*Lepidium*
Peppermint	*Mentha × piperita*
Pepperwort	*Lepidium, Marsilea*
Perilla	*Perilla, P. frutescens*
Periwinkle	*Catharanthus, Vinca*
lesser	*V. minor*
Madagascar	*Catharanthus roseus*
rose	*C. roseus*
white	*C. roseus* 'Alba'
Petunia	*Petunia × hybrida*
Phlox	*Phlox*
perennial	*P. paniculata*
white	*P. paniculata*
Pie-marker	*Abutilon theophrasti*
Pie-plant	*Rheum rhabarbarum*
Pigweed	*Amaranthus hybridus, A. retroflexus, Chenopodium, C. album*
Pilewort	*Ranunculus ficaria*
Pincushion flower	*Leucospermum, Scabiosa*

Pincushions	*Scabiosa atropurpurea*
Pine	*Pinus*
Austrian	*P. nigra*
Eastern white	*P. strobus*
frankincense	*P. taeda*
loblolly	*P. taeda*
old-field	*P. taeda*
Prince's	*Chimaphila, C. umbellata* var. *cisatlantica*
white	*Pinus strobus*
Pineapple shrub	*Calycanthus floridus*
Piney	*Paeonia officinalis* subsp. *officinalis*
Pink	*Dianthus*
alpine	*D. alpinus*
cheddar	*D. gratianopolitanus*
clove	*D. caryophyllus*
cottage	*D. plumarius*
grass	*D. plumarius, Calopogon*
Indian	*Lobelia cardinalis, Silene laciniata, Spigelia marilandica*
mullein	*Lychnis coronaria*
sea	*Armeria, Sabatia stellaris*
Piprage	*Berberis vulgaris*
Pipsissewa	*Chimaphila, C. umbellata* var. *cisatlantica*
Plantain	*Musa acuminata, M. × paradisiaca, Plantago*
common	*P. major*
Pleurisy root	*Asclepias tuberosa*
Plum	
American	*Prunus americana*
beach	*P. maritima*
chickasaw	*P. angustifolia*
Japanese	*Eriobotrya japonica, Prunus japonica, P. salicina*
sand	*P. angustifolia, P. angustifolia* var. *watsonii*
shore	*P. maritima*
wild	*P. americana*
Plume flower	*Justicia carnea*
Plume plant	*J. carnea*
Poke	*Phytolacca americana*
Virginian	*P. americana*
Pokeberry	*Phytolacca*
Pokeweed	*Phytolacca*
Pomegranate	*Punica granatum*
Poor-man's-weatherglass	*Anagallis arvensis*
Poplar	*Populus, Liriodendron tulipifera*
balsam	*P. balsamifera*
rough-barked	*P. balsamifera*
Poppy	*Papaver*
California	*Eschscholzia, E. californica*
corn	*Papaver rhoeas*
field	*P. rhoeas*
Flanders	*P. rhoeas*
opium	*P. somniferum*
plume	*Macleaya cordata*
Potato vine	*Solanum jasminoides, S. wendlandii*
Prim	*Ligustrum vulgare*
Primrose	*Primula, P. vulgaris*
English	*P. vulgaris*
evening	*Oenothera, O. biennis*
white	*P. sieboldii* 'Alba'
Privet	*Ligustrum*
common	*L. vulgare*
Puccoon	*Lithospermum, L. canescens*
red	*Sanguinaria canadensis*
yellow	*Hydrastis*

Pulmonaria	*Pulmonaria officinalis*
Pumpkin	*Cucurbita*
autumn	*C. pepo*
summer	*C. pepo*
Purslane	*Portulaca, P. oleracea*
winter	*Montia perfoliata*
Pussy-toes	*Antennaria*
Pyrethrum	*Chrysanthemum cinerariifolium, C. coccineum*
Dalmatia	*C. cinerariifolium*
Queen-of-the-meadow	*Filipendula ulmaria*
Quince	*Cydonia oblonga*
Ragged-robin	*Lychnis flos-cuculi*
Ramie	*Boehmeria nivea*
Rampion	*Campanula rapunculus*
German	*Oenothera biennis*
Rattletop	*Cimicifuga*
Rattleweed	*Baptisia tinctoria*
Redbud	*Cercis, C. canadensis*
white eastern	*C. canadensis*
Red Robin	*Geranium robertianum*
Redroot	*Ceanothus*
Rhubarb	*Rheum, R. rhabarbarum*
garden	*R. rhabarbarum*
Ribwort	*Plantago*
Roanoke-bells	*Mertensia virginica*
Rocambole	*Allium sativum, A. sativum* var. *ophioscorodon*
Rocket	*Barbarea vulgaris, Diplotaxis, Hesperis*
dame's	*Hesperis matronalis*
dyer's	*Reseda luteola*
sweet	*Hesperis matronalis*
wall	*Brassica eruca*
yellow	*Barbarea vulgaris*
Rocket-salad	*Eruca vesicaria* subsp. *sativa*
Romona	*Salvia*
Romero	*Trichostema lanatum*
Roquette	*Eruca vesicaria* subsp. *sativa*
Rose	*Rosa*
apothecary's	*R. gallica* 'Officinalis'
autumn damask	*R. damascena* 'Bifera'
Banksia	*R. banksiae*
Bourbon	*R. × borboniana*
briar, brier	*R. canina, Rubus coronarius*
burnet	*R. spinosissima*
cabbage	*R. centifolia*
Cherokee	*R. laevigata*
chestnut	*R. roxburghii*
China	*Hibiscus rosa-sinensis, Rosa chinensis*
Chinquapin	*R. roxburghii*
Christmas	*Helleborus niger*
climbing	*Rosa setigera*
damask	*R. damascena*
dog	*R. canina*
fairy	*R. chinensis* 'Minima'
French	*R. gallica*
Harison's yellow	*R. × harisonii*
hybrid Bourbon	*R. × borboniana*
hybrid perpetual	*R. × borboniana*
Japanese	*Kerria, Rosa rugosa*
Lenten	*Helleborus orientalis*
memorial	*Rosa wichuraiana*
moss	*Portulaca, R. centifolia* 'Muscosa'
musk	*R. moschata*
polyantha	*R. × rehderana*
prairie	*R. setigera*
pygmy	*R. chinensis* 'Minima'
rock	*Cistus, Helianthemum*

Scotch	*Rosa spinosissima*
Turkestan	*R. rugosa*
York-and-Lancaster	*R. damascena* 'Versicolor'
Roselle	*Hibiscus sabdariffa*
Rosemary	*Ceratiola ericoides, Rosmarinus, R. officinalis*
marsh	*Limonium*
pine-scented	*R. angustissimus*
prostrate	*R. officinalis* 'Prostratus'
Rose-of-China	*Hibiscus rosa-sinensis*
Rue	*Ruta graveolens*
Rugula	*Eruca vesicaria* subsp. *sativa*
Runaway Robin	*Glechoma hederacea*
Rupturewort	*Herniaria glabra*
Rush, scouring	*Equisetum hyemale*
Safflower	*Carthamus tinctorius*
Saffron	
bastard	*Carthamus tinctorius*
false	*C. tinctorius*
meadow	*Colchicum autumnale*
Sage	*Salvia*
autumn	*S. greggii*
anise	*S. guaranitica*
baby	*S. microphylla*
blue	*S. azurea* subsp. *pitcheri S. caerula, S. clevelandii*
clary	*S. sclarea*
garden	*S. officinalis*
gray	*S. leucophylla*
Jerusalem	*Pulmonaria officinalis, Salvia hierosolymitana*
Mexican bush	*S. leucantha*
nutmeg	*S. guaranitica*
pineapple-scented	*S. elegans*
purple	*S. leucophylla*
rosy leaf	*S. involucrata*
Russian	*Perovskia abrotanoides, P. atriplicifolia*
silver	*Salvia argentea*
white	*Artemisia ludoviciana, Salvia apiana*
wood	*Teucrium canadense, T. scorodonia*
Sagebrush	*Artemisia*
Saltbush	*Atriplex, A. halimus*
Samphire	*Crithmum maritimum, Salicornia, S. europaea*
Sandberry	*Arctostaphylos uva-ursi*
Sanguinary	*Achillea millefolium*
Santolina	*Santolina, S. neapolitana*
dwarf gray	*S. chamaecyparissus*
gray	*S. chamaecyparissus*
green	*S. virens, S. viridis*
pinnately-leaved	*S. pinnata*
Sassafras	*Sassafras albidum*
Satin flower	*Lunaria*
Savory	*Satureja*
alpine	*Acinos alpinus*
summer	*Satureja hortensis*
winter	*S. montana*
Scabious	*Scabiosa*
sweet	*S. atropurpurea*
Schnittlauch	*Allium schoenoprasum*
Sea eryngo	*Eryngium maritimum*
Sea holly	*E. maritimum*
Sea holm	*E. maritimum*
Self-heal	*Prunella vulgaris*
Senna	*Cassia*
wild	*C. hebecarpa, C. marilandica*
Serviceberry	*Amelanchier*
Shad	*Amelanchier*
Shadbush	*Amelanchier, A. canadensis*

Shallot	*Allium cepa*, Aggregatum Group
Sheepberry	*Viburnum lentago, V. prunifolium*
Shower tree	*Cassia*
Shrimp plant	*Justicia brandegeana*
Silk plant, Chinese	*Boehmeria nivea*
Silkweed	*Asclepias*
Silverbush	*Convolvulus cneorum, Sophora tomentosa*
Silver-dollar	*Lunaria annua*
Skirret	*Sium sisarum*
Sloe	*Prunus alleghaniensis, P. americana, P. spinosa*
Smallage	*Apium graveolens*
Smartweed	*Polygonum*
Smilax	*Smilax, Asparagus asparagoides*
Smokebush	*Cotinus, C. coggygria*
Smoke plant	*C. coggygria*
Smoke tree	*Cotinus, C. coggygria, Dalea spinosa*
Snake plant	*Sansevieria trifasciata*
Snakehead	*Chelone*
Snakeroot	*Asarum canadense, Sanicula*
black	*Cimicifuga racemosa, Sanicula*
white	*Eupatorium rugosum*
Snapweed	*Impatiens*
Sneezeweed	*Helenium, Achillea ptarmica*
Sneezewort	*Achillea ptarmica*
Snowdrop	*Galanthus, G. nivalis*
Snowflake	*Lamium album, Leucojum*
giant	*Leucojum aestivum*
summer	*Leucojum aestivum, Ornithogalum umbellatum*
Soapwort	*Saponaria*
Solomon's-seal	*Polygonatum*
small	*P. biflorum*
Sorrel	*Rumex*
dock	*Rumex*
French	*R. scutatus*
garden	*R. acetosa, R. scutatus*
Indian	*Hibiscus sabdariffa*
Jamaican	*H. sabdariffa*
lady	*Oxalis crassipes*
white or pink	*O. crassipes*
wood	*O. crassipes*
Southernwood	*Artemisia abrotanum*
Spearmint	*Mentha spicata*
curly	*M. spicata* 'Crispata'
Speedwell	*Vernonica, V. officinalis*
thyme-leaved	*V. serpyllifolia*
Spicebush	*Lindera benzoin*
Spike bush	*Eleocharis*
Spinach, Cuban	*Montia perfoliata*
mountain	*Atriplex hortensis*
Spindle tree	*Euonymus, E. japonica*
Spiraea, false	*Sorbaria, S. sorbifolia*
Spruce	*Picea*
hemlock	*Tsuga*
Spurge	*Euphorbia*
cypress	*Euphorbia cyparissias*
Squill	*Scilla, Urginea maritima*
bell-flowered	*Endymion hispanicus*
red	*Urginea maritima*
St.-John's-wort	*Hypericum, H. patulum, H. perforatum*
Stagbush	*Viburnum prunifolium*
Star-of-Bethlehem	*Campanula isophylla, Ornithogalum arabicum, O. pyrenaicum, O. umbellatum*
Stars-of-Persia	*Allium christophii*
Statice	*Limonium, L. latifolium*
Stepmother's flower	*Viola × wittrockiana*

Stock	*Matthiola, M. incana*
Brampton	*M. incana*
imperial	*M. incana*
Stonecrop	*Sedum*
Storksbill	*Pelargonium*
Strawberry	*Fragaria*
alpine	*F. vesca*
beach	*F. chiloensis*
sow-teat	*F. vesca*
woodland	*F. vesca*
Strawberry shrub	*Calycanthus floridus*
Stringybark	*Eucalyptus*
Succory	*Cichorium intybus*
Sugarplum	*Amelanchier*
Sumac	*Rhus*
staghorn	*R. typhina*
Venetian	*Cotinus coggygria*
Sundrops	*Oenothera fruticosa, O. perennis, O. pilosella*
Sweet Betsy	*Calycanthus floridus*
Sweet Betty	*Saponaria officinalis*
Sweetbriar	*Rosa eglanteria*
Sweet maudlin	*Achillea ageratum*
Sweet shrub	*Calycanthus, C. floridus*
Syringa	*Philadelphus*
Tacamahac	*Populus balsamifera*
Talewort	*Borago officinalis*
Tansy	*Tanacetum, T. vulgare*
curly	*T. vulgare* var. *crispum*
fern-leaf	*T. vulgare* var. *crispum*
Tarragon	*Artemisia dracunculus*
French	*A. dracunculus* var. *sativa*
Tassel flower	*Amaranthus caudatus, Brickellia*
Tea, Mexican	*Chenopodium ambrosioides, Ephedra viridis*
mountain	*Gaultheria procumbens*
Oswego	*Monarda didyma*
Spanish	*Chenopodium ambrosioides*
Teaberry	*Gaultheria procumbens, Viburnum cassinoides*
Teasel	*Dipsacus*
common	*D. sylvestris*
fuller's	*D. sativus*
Thistle	*Cirsium*
blessed	*Cnicus, C. benedictus, Silybum marianum*
holy	*S. marianum*
milk	*S. marianum*
St. Mary's	*S. marianum*
Thorn	*Crataegus*
quick-set	*Crataegus laevigata*
Washington	*C. phaenopyrum*
white	*C. laevigata*
Thoroughwort	*Eupatorium, E. perfoliatum*
Thousand-seal	*Achillea millefolium*
Thrift	*Armeria, A. maritima*
Thyme	*Thymus, T. doerfleri*
cat	*Teucrium marum*
caraway	*Thymus herba-barona*
creeping	*T. praecox*
English	*T.* 'Broad-leaf English'
French	*T. vulgaris* 'Narrow-leaf French'
golden	*T.* 'Clear Gold'
golden lemon	*T. × citriodorus* 'Aureus'
lemon, culinary	*T. × citriodorus*
mother-of-thyme	*T. praecox* subsp. *arcticus*
odorous	*T. pallasianus*
silver	*T.* 'Argenteus'
wild	*T. serpyllum*

woolly	*T. praecox* subsp. *arcticus* 'Lanuginosus'
Tickseed	*Bidens, Coreopsis*
Toadflax	*Linaria, Spergula arvensis*
Tobacco, flowering	*Nicotiana alata*
jasmine	*N. alata*
Tomato	*Lycopersicon, L. lycopersicum*
cherry	*L. lycopersicum* var. *cerasiforme, Physalis peruviana*
pear	*L. lycopersicum* var. *pyriforme*
husk	*Physalis*
strawberry	*Physalis alkekengi, P. peruviana P. pruinosa, P. pubescens*
Tonguegrass	*Lepidium*
Touch-me-not	*Impatiens, I. noli-tangere, Mimosa pudica*
spotted	*Impatiens capensis*
Trumpet creeper	*Campsis, C. radicans*
Trumpet flower	*Bignonia capreolata, Campsis*
evening	*Gelsemium sempervirens*
Trumpet vine	*Campsis radicans*
Tuberose	*Polianthes tuberosa*
Tuberroot	*Asclepias tuberosa*
Tulasi	*Ocimum sanctum*
Tulsi, krishna	*O. sanctum*
sri	*O. sanctum*
Tulip	*Tulipa*
lady	*T. clusiana*
water-lily	*T. kaufmanniana*
Turnip, Indian	*Arisaema triphyllum, Psoralea esculenta*
Turnsole	*Heliotropium*
Turtlehead	*Chelone*
Valerian	*Valeriana, V. officinalis*
Greek	*Polemonium, P. caeruleum*
Vase vine	*Clematis, C. viorna*
Velvetleaf	*Abutilon theophrasti, Kalanchoe beharensis*
Velvet plant	*Gynura aurantiaca, Verbascum thapsus*
Verbena, lemon	*Aloysia triphylla*
Vetiver	*Vetiveria zizanioides*
Viburnum, maple-leaved	*Viburnum acerifolium*
Viola	*Viola cornuta*
blue	*V. cornuta* 'Blue Perfection'
white	*V. cornuta* 'Alba'
yellow	*V. lutea* 'Splendens'
Violet	*Viola*
dame's	*Hesperis matronalis*
dog	*V. canina, V. riviniana*
English	*Viola odorata*
florist's	*V. odorata*
garden	*V. odorata*
horned	*V. cornuta*
sweet	*V. odorata*
Virgilia	*Cladrastis lutea*
Virgin's-bower	*Clematis, C. virginiana*
Waldmeister	*Galium odoratum*
Wattle	*Acacia*
Sydney golden	*A. longifolia*
Waxflower	*Chamaelaucium, Chimaphila, Stephanotis floribunda*

Weld	*Reseda luteola*
White-man's-foot	*Plantago major*
Whiteweed	*Chrysanthemum leucanthemum*
Widdy	*Potentilla fruticosa*
Wig tree	*Cotinus coggygria*
Willow	*Salix*
goat	*S. caprea*
pussy	*S. caprea, S. discolor*
water	*Justicia*
Windflower	*Anemone*
Wine plant	*Rheum rhabarbarum*
Winterberry	*Ilex glabra, I. verticillata*
Wintergreen	*Chimaphila, Gaultheria procumbens, Pyrola*
spotted	*Chimaphila maculata*
Wishbone flower	*Torenia*
Wishbone plant	*Torenia*
Wistaria, wisteria	*Wisteria, W. frutescens*
Withe-rod	*Viburnum cassinoides, V. nudum*
Woad	*Isatis*
dyer's	*I. tinctoria*
Woadwaxen	*Genista tinctoria*
Woodbine	*Clematis virginiana, Lonicera periclymenum*
Woodroof	*Galium odoratum*
Woodruff	*Asperula, Galium odoratum*
sweet	*Galium odoratum*
Woodwaxen	*Genista tinctoria*
Woolflower	*Celosia*
Woolly blue-curls	*Trichostema lanatum*
Wormseed	*Artemisia maritima, Chenopodium ambrosioides*
American	*C. ambrosioides*
Wormwood	*Artemisia, Vanilla barbellata*
camphor-scented	*A. camphorata*
common	*A. absinthium*
fringed	*A. frigida*
Roman	*A. pontica, Corydalis sempervirens*
Russian	*A. gmelinii*
sweet	*A. annua*
tree	*A. arborescens*
Woundwort	*Anthyllis vulneraria, Stachys*
Yarrow	*Achillea*
common	*A. millefolium*
fern-leaf	*A. filipendulina*
pale-yellow	*A. taygetea*
sweet	*A. ageratum*
woolly	*A. tomentosa*
Yaupon	*Ilex cassine, I. vomitoria*
dwarf	*I. vomitoria* 'Nana'
Yellowroot, shrub	*Xanthorhiza, X. simplicissima*
Yellowwood	*Cladrastis, C. lutea, Rhodosphaera rhodanthema*
Yew	*Taxus*
columnar	*T. × media* 'Hicksii'
conical	*T. × media* 'Hatfieldii'
Japanese	*T. cuspidata*
upright	*T. × media* 'Kelseyi'

BOTANICAL NAME TO COMMON NAME INDEX

Abutilon — flowering maple, parlor m., Indian mallow

A. theophrasti — China jute, butter-print, Indian mallow, pie-marker

Acacia — wattle

A. longifolia — Sidney golden wattle

Achillea — yarrow

A. ageratum — sweet maudlin, sweet yarrow

A. filipendulina — fern-leaf yarrow

'Coronation Gold' — fern-leaf yarrow

'Moonshine' — fern-leaf yarrow

A. millefolium — milfoil, nose-bleed, sanguinary, thousand-seal, yarrow

A. ptarmica 'The Pearl' — sneezeweed, sneezewort

A. taygetea — pale-yellow yarrow

A. tomentosa — woolly yarrow

'King Edward' — woolly yarrow

Acinos

A. alpinus — alpine savory

Aconitum — aconite, monkshood

A. napellus — helmut flower, monkshood

Acorus

A. calamus — sweet flag, calamus

Adiantum — maidenhair fern, maidenhair

A. pedatum — American maidenhair, maidenhair fern, five-finger f., northern maidenhair

Agastache — giant hyssop

A. breviflora — licorice mint

A. cana — mosquito plant, lion's tail

A. foeniculum — anise hyssop, blue giant hyssop, fennel g. h., fragrant g. h.

Agave — century plant

A. fourcroydes — henequen

A. sisalana — sisal hemp, hemp plant

Agrimonia — agrimony, cocklebur, harvest-lice

A. eupatoria — agrimony

Agrostemma — corn cockle

A. githago — corn cockle, purple c.

Ajuga — bugleweed

A. reptans — carpet bugleweed

Alcea — hollyhock

A. rosea — hollyhock

Alchemilla — lady's-mantle

A. alpina — alpine lady's-mantle

A. vulgaris — lady's-mantle

Allium — onion

A. ampeloprasum — wild leek

Porrum Group — leek

'American Flag' — leek

A. cepa — onion

Aggregatum Group — shallot

Proliferum Group — Egyptian o., tree o.

A. christophii — stars-of-Persia

A. fistulosum — Welsh o., ciboule, Japanese bunching o., Spanish o., two-bladed o.

A. flavum

A. giganteum

A. karataviense

A. moly — lily leek

A. neapolitanum — daffodil garlic, flowering o.

A. ostrowskianum

A. pulchellum

A. rosenbachianum

A. sativum — garlic

A. sativum var. *ophioscorodon* — rocambole, serpent garlic

A. schoenoprasum — chive, cive, schnittlauch

A. scorodoprasum — giant garlic

A. senescens var. *glaucum*

A. sphaerocephalum — round-headed garlic

A. tuberosum — Chinese chive, garlic c., Oriental garlic

Aloe

A. barbadensis — aloe, Barbados a., Curaçao a., medicinal a.

Aloysia

A. triphylla — lemon verbena

Althaea

A. officinalis — marsh mallow, white m.

Amaranthus — amaranth

A. caudatus — love-lies-bleeding, tassel flower

Amelanchier

A. canadensis — serviceberry, juneberry, shadbush, shad, sugarplum

Amsonia — bluestar

A. tabernaemontana — amsonia

Anacyclus

A. officinarum — pellitory-of-the-wall

Anchusa — alkanet, bugloss

A. officinalis — alkanet, bugloss

Anemone — windflower, lily-of-the-field

A. blanda

A. hupehensis var. *japonica* — Japanese anemone

A. pulsatilla — pasqueflower

Anethum — dill

A. graveolens — dill

'Bouquet' — dill

Angelica

A. archangelica — angelica, archangel, wild parsnip

Antennaria — pussy-toes

Anthemis — dog fennel, chamomile

A. marschalliana — chamomile

A. tinctoria — golden marguerite

Anthriscus

A. cerefolium — chervil

Apium

A. graveolens — wild celery

A. graveolens var. *dulce* — celery

'French Dinant'

'Golden Self-Blanching'

'Giant Pascal'

'Summer Pascal'

'Utah 52–70'

Aquilegia — columbine

A. alpina 'Alba' — white columbine

A. chrysantha — yellow columbine

A. vulgaris — garden columbine, European crowfoot

Arctostaphylos — bearberry, manzanita

A. uva-ursi	bearberry, mealberry, hog cranberry, kinnikinick, sandberry, mountain box, bear's grape, creashak	**Borago**	borage
		B. officinalis	borage, talewort, cool-tankard
Arisaema		**Brassica**	cole, mustard
A. dracontium	green-dragon, dragonroot	*B. eruca*	wall rocket
A. triphyllum	jack-in-the-pulpit	*B. oleracea*	wild cabbage
A. triphyllum subsp. *stewardsonii*		Acephala Group	red-flowered kale, white-flowered k.
Armeria	thrift, sea pink	Capitata Group	cabbage
A. maritima	thrift, pink or white	'Golden Acre'	
Armoracia		'Green Parade Hybrid'	
A. rusticana	horseradish, red cole	'Mammoth Red Rock'	
Artemisia	sagebrush, mugwort, wormwood	'Red Acre'	
A. abrotanum	southernwood, old man	'Red Drumhead'	
'Tangerine'	southernwood	'Ruby Ball'	
A. absinthium	absinthe, common wormwood	Gemmifera Group	brussels sprouts
'Lambrook Silver'	absinthe	'Jade Cross'	
A. annua	sweet wormwood	Gongylodes Group	kohlrabi
A. arborescens	tree wormwood, tree artemisia	'Early Purple Vienna'	
A. camphorata	camphor-scented wormwood	'Early White Vienna'	
A. dracunculus var. *sativa*	French tarragon	'Prima'	
A. frigida	fringed wormwood	**Buxus**	box, boxwood
A. gmelinii	Russian wormwood	*B. microphylla*	
A. lactiflora	white mugwort	'Green Pillow'	dwarf box
A. ludoviciana var. *albula*	silver-king artemisia	*B. microphylla* 'Nana'	dwarf box
A. pontica	Roman wormwood	*B. microphylla* var. *koreana*	Korean box
A. schmidtiana	wormwood	*B. sempervirens*	box
'Nana'	silver mound artemisia	*B. sempervirens* 'Suffruticosa'	dwarf edging box
Asarum	wild ginger, asarabacca	'Myrtifolia'	box
A. canadense	wild ginger, snakeroot	**Calamintha**	calamint
A. europaeum	European ginger	*C. grandiflora*	calamint
A. virginicum	wild ginger	**Calendula**	
Asclepias	milkweed, silkweed, butterfly flower	*C. officinalis*	pot marigold
A. tuberosa	butterfly weed, pleurisy root, tuberroot, Indian paintbrush	**Calycanthus**	sweet shrub
		C. floridus	Carolina allspice, pineapple s., strawberry s., sweet Betsy
Asparagus		**Campanula**	bellflower
A. officinalis	garden asparagus	*C. carpatica*	tussock bellflower
Astrantia	masterwort	*C. divaricata*	southern harebell
A. major	masterwort	*C. persicifolia*	peach-bells
Atriplex	saltbush, orach	*C. rapunculus*	rampion
A. halimus	sea orach, saltbush	**Campsis**	trumpet creeper, trumpet flower, crown plant
A. hortensis	orach, garden o., mountain spinach		
Baptisia	false indigo, wild indigo	*C. radicans*	trumpet creeper, trumpet vine, cow-itch, trumpet honeysuckle
B. australis	blue false indigo, plains f. i., wild blue i.		
		Capsicum	pepper, green p., red p., chili p.
B. tinctoria	wild indigo, rattleweed	*C. annuum*	
Barbarea	winter cress, upland cress	Conoides Group	cone pepper
B. vulgaris	winter cress, rocket, yellow r.	'Black Prince'	ornamental pepper
Bellis	daisy	'Fiesta'	o. p.
B. perennis	English daisy	'Fips'	o. p.
Berberis	barberry	'Floral Gem'	o. p.
B. thunbergii	Japanese barberry	'Mosaic'	o. p.
'Crimson Pygmy'	Japanese barberry	'Nosegay'	o. p.
B. vulgaris	common barberry, jaundice berry, piprage	'Pinocchio'	o. p.
		'Red Boy'	o. p.
Beta	beet	'Teno'	o. p.
B. vulgaris, Cicla Group	swiss chard, ruby s. c.	'Variegata'	o. p.
'Rhubarb'	s. c.	Grossum Group	sweet pepper, bell p., green p., pimento
'Ruby Red'	ruby s. c.		
'White Fordhook Giant'	s. c.	'Golden Bell'	sweet pepper
		'Whopper'	s. p.
Betula		'Sweet Chocolate'	s. p.
B. papyrifera	white birch	'Sweet Cream'	s. p.
Boehmeria	false nettle	'Wisconsin Lakes'	s. p.
B. nivea	ramie, Chinese silk plant, China grass		

Longum Group	cayenne p., capsicum p., chili p., red p.
C. frutescens	Tabasco p., Tabasco-sauce p.
Carthamus	
C. tinctorius	false saffron, bastard s., safflower
Carum	
C. carvi	caraway
Carya	hickory
C. illinoinensis	pecan
C. ovata	shagbark hickory, shellbark h.
Cassia	senna, shower tree
C. marilandica	wild senna
Catharanthus	periwinkle
C. roseus 'Albus'	white periwinkle, Madagascar periwinkle, old-maid
Ceanothus	redroot
C. 'Julia Phelps'	California lilac
Cedronella	
C. canariensis	balm-of-Gilead
Cedrus	cedar
C. deodara	deodar
Celosia	woolflower
C. cristata	cockscomb
Cercis	redbud, Judas tree
C. canadensis	redbud
'Alba'	white eastern redbud
Cestrum	
C. nocturnum	night jessamine
Chamaemelum	
C. nobile	chamomile, garden c., Russian c.
Chelidonium	celandine
C. majus	celandine
Chelone	turtlehead, snakehead
C. glabra	balmony
Chenopodium	goosefoot, pigweed
C. ambrosioides	Mexican tea, Spanish t., wormseed, American w.
C. bonus-henricus	fat hen
C. botrys	ambrosia, feather geranium, Jerusualem oak
Chimaphila	pipsissewa, wintergreen, wax flower, prince's pine
C. umbellata	pipsissewa
Chionanthus	fringe tree
C. virginicus	fringe tree, old-man's-beard
Chrysanthemum	
C. balsamita	costmary, mint geranium, alecost
C. cinerariifolium	pyrethrum, Dalmatia p., Dalmatian insect flower
C. coccineum	painted daisy, pyrethum, Persian insect flower
C. frutescens	marguerite
C. leucanthemum	oxeye daisy
C. parthenium	feverfew
C. × *superbum*	Shasta daisy
Cichorium	chicory
C. intybus	chicory, barbe-de-capuchin, red-leaved chicory
Cimicifuga	bugbane, rattletop
C. racemosa	black cohosh, black snakeroot
Cistus	rock rose
C. crispus	myrrh
C. ladanifer	labdanum or ladanum
Citrus	
C. limon	lemon, Chinese dwarf l., dwarf l.,
'Meyer'	Meyer l.
'Ponderosa'	lemon
Cladrastis	yellowwood
C. lutea	yellowwood, virgilia

Clematis	virgin's bower, leather flower, vase vine
C. lanuginosa 'Alba'	white clematis
C. × *jouiniana* 'Mrs. Robert Brydon'	clematis
C. virginiana	woodbine, virgin's bower, leather flower, devil's-darning-needle
Cnicus	blessed thistle
C. benedictus	blessed thistle
Coix	
C. lacryma-jobi	Job's-tears
Colchicum	
C. autumnale	autumn crocus
Comptonia	
C. peregrina	sweet fern
Consolida	larkspur
C. ambigua	rocket larkspur
C. orientalis	larkspur
Convallaria	lily-of-the-valley
C. majalis	lily-of-the-valley
Convolvulus	bindweed
C. cneorum	silverbush
Coptis	goldthread
C. trifolia	goldthread
Coreopsis	tickseed
C. tinctoria	calliopsis
Coriandrum	
C. sativum	coriander, Chinese parsley
Cornus	dogwood, cornel
C. florida	flowering dogwood
Corylus	hazelnut
C. avellana	European hazelnut
Cotinus	smoke tree, smokebush
C. coggygria	smoke tree, smokebush, smoke plant, Venetian sumac, wig tree
Cotoneaster	
C. apiculatus	cranberry cotoneaster
Crataegus	hawthorn, thorn, thorn apple, red haw
C. arkansana	hawthorn
C. laevigata	English h., quick-set, white thorn
C. laevigata 'Paulii'	Paul's scarlet hawthorn
C. phaenopyrum	Washington h., Washington thorn
Crithmum	
C. maritimum	samphire
Crocus	
C. angustifolius	
C. kotschyanus	
C. sativus	saffron crocus
C. sieberi	
C. speciosus	
C. speciosus 'Albus'	
C. tomasinianus	
Cupressus	cypress
C. sempervirens	Italian cypress
Cydonia	quince
C. oblonga	quince
Cymbopogon	oil grass
C. citratus	lemongrass, West Indian l., fever grass
Cytisus	broom
C. scoparius	Scotch broom
C. supinus	broom
Delphinium	larkspur. See **Consolida**
Deutzia	
D. gracilis	deutzia
Dianthus	pink
D. × *allwoodii*	
D. alpinus 'Petite'	alpine pink

D. caryophyllus 'Snowflake'	clove pink, carnation, divine flower
D. gratianopolitanus 'Nanus Compactus' 'Tiny Rubies'	cheddar pink
D. plumarius 'Essex Witch' 'Her Majesty' 'Mrs. Simkins' 'Nanus'	cottage pink, grass pink
D. 'White Lace'	pink
Dicentra	
D. spectabilis	bleeding heart
Dictamnus	
D. albus	fraxinella, gas plant, burning bush, dittany
'Rubra'	fraxinella
Digitalis	foxglove
D. grandiflora	yellow foxglove
D. lanata	Grecian foxglove
D. purpurea 'Alba'	foxglove
Dipsacus	teasel
D. sativus	fuller's teasel
D. sylvestris	teasel
Doronicum	leopard's-bane
D. pardalianches	leopard's-bane
Echeveria	hen-and-chickens
E. × imbricata	
Echium	viper's bugloss
E. vulgare	v. b., blueweed, blue-devil
Elaeagnus	
E. pungens	thorny elaeagnus
Eleocharis	spike bush
E. dulcis	Chinese water chestnut
Endymion	wood hyacinth
E. hispanicus	Spanish bluebell, S. jacinth, bell-flowered squill
'Alba'	Spanish bluebell
Ephedra	joint fir
E. viridis	Mexican tea
Epimedium	barrenwort, epimedium
E. × versicolor 'Sulphureum'	barrenwort, bishop's hat
E. × youngianum 'Niveum'	barrenwort
Equisetum	horsetail, scouring rush
E. arvense	horsetail
E. hyemale	scouring rush, horsetail
Eranthis	winter aconite
E. hyemalis	winter aconite
Erigeron	fleabane
Eriobotrya	
E. japonica	loquat, Japanese medlar, J. plum
Eryngium	eryngo
E. maritimum	sea holly, sea holm, sea eryngo
Eschscholzia	California poppy
E. californica	C. poppy
Eucalyptus	eucalypt, Australian gum, gum tree, ironbark, stringybark
E. torquata	coral gum
Euonymus	spindle tree
E. fortunei 'Colorata' 'Erecta'	
Eupatorium	boneset, thoroughwort
E. perfoliatum	boneset
E. rugosum	white snakeroot
Euphorbia	spurge

E. cyparissias	cypress spurge
Ferula	
F. assafoetida	asafetida
Ficus	fig
F. carica 'Brown Turkey'	fig, fig tree
Filipendula	meadowsweet
F. ulmaria	queen-of-the-meadow
F. vulgaris	dropwort
Foeniculum	
F. vulgare	fennel
F. vulgare	bronze fennel
F. vulgare subsp. *vulgare* var. *azoricum*	Florence fennel, finocchio, anise
Forsythia	forsythia
Fothergilla	
F. major	
Fragaria	strawberry
F. chiloensis	beach strawberry
F. vesca	woodland strawberry, sow-teat s.
'Alpine'	alpine s.
'Fraises des Bois'	a.s.
'Baron von Solemacher'	a.s.
'Rugens'	a.s.
Fritillaria	fritillary
F. imperialis	crown-imperial
Fumaria	fumitory
F. officinalis	earth-smoke
Furcraea	
F. hexapetala	Cuban hemp
Galanthus	snowdrop
G. nivalis	snowdrop
Galium	bedstraw, cleavers
G. mollugo	white bedstraw, false baby's-breath
G. odoratum	woodruff, sweet w., woodroof
G. verum	yellow bedstraw, our-lady's-b.
Gardenia	
G. jasminoides	gardenia, Cape jasmine
Gaultheria	
G. procumbens	wintergreen, checkerberry, teaberry, mountain tea, ivry-leaves
Gelsemium	yellow jessamine, Carolina yellow j., Carolina jasmine
G. sempervirens	evening trumpet flower, Carolina jessamine
Genista	broom
G. germanica	broom
G. tinctoria	dyer's broom, dyer's greenweed, woodwaxen, woadwaxen
Geranium	cranesbill
G. maculatum	wild geranium, wild c., spotted c., alumroot
G. robertianum	herb Robert, red Robin
Glechoma	
G. hederacea	gill-over-the-ground, ground ivy, runaway robin, field balm, alehoof
Gleditsia	honey locust
G. triacanthos	honeyshuck, honey locust, sweet locust
Gossypium	cotton
G. hirsutum	upland cotton
Hamamelis	witch hazel
H. vernalis	witch hazel
H. virginiana	witch hazel
Hedeoma	
H. pulegioides	American pennyroyal, mock p., pudding grass

Hedera	ivy	'Nana'	dwarf yaupon
H. helix	English ivy	*I. wilsonii*	Wilson's holly
'Baltica'	Baltic ivy	**Impatiens**	balsam, jewelweed, snapweed, touch-me-not
Hedychium	ginger lily, garland l.		
H. flavescens	yellow ginger	*I. capensis*	jewelweed, spotted t., lady's-earrings
Helenium	sneezeweed	**Indigofera**	indigo
H. autumnale	helenium	*I. tinctoria*	indigo
'Riverton Gem'		**Inula**	
Helichrysum	everlasting, immortelle	*I. helenium*	elecampane
H. angustifolium	white-leaf everlasting, curry plant	**Ipomoea**	morning-glory
H. petiolatum	false licorice, licorice plant	*I. alba*	moonflower
Heliotropium	heliotrope, turnsole	**Iris**	flag, fleur-de-lis
H. arborescens	heliotrope, cherry-pie	*I. cristata*	dwarf crested i., crested i., crested dwarf i.
Helleborus	hellebore		
H. atrorubens		*I. × germanica* var. *florentina*	orris, Florentine iris
H. foetidus		*I.* 'Great Lakes'	iris
H. lividus subsp. *corsicus*		*I. pallida*	orris
H. niger	Christmas rose	'Dalmatica'	
H. orientalis	Lenten rose	*I. pseudacorus*	yellow iris, yellow flag, water f.
Hemerocallis	daylily	**Isatis**	woad
H. lilioasphodelus	yellow daylily, lemon d., lemon lily	*I. tinctoria*	dyer's woad, asp-of-Jerusalem
H. × luteola	yellow daylily	**Ixia**	corn lily, African corn lily
Herniaria	herniary	*I. maculata*	corn lily
H. glabra	rupturewort	**Jasminum**	jasmine, jessamine
Hesperis	rocket	*J. officinale*	poet's jessamine
H. matronalis	dame's rocket, sweet r.	**Juniperus**	juniper
Hibiscus	mallow, rose m., giant m., hibiscus	*J. chinensis* var. *chinensis*	
H. cannabinus	kenaf, Indian hemp, Deckaner h., Deccan h., bastard jute, bimli j., bimlipatum j.	'Pyramidalis'	juniper
		J. horizontalis	creeping j.
		J. virginiana	red cedar
H. rosa-sinensis	Chinese hibiscus, Hawaiian h., China rose, rose-of-China, blacking plant	**Justicia**	water willow
		J. brandegeana	shrimp plant
Hosta	plantain lily, daylily	*J. carnea*	Brazilian-plume, plume flower, plume plant, flamingo p., paradise p., king's-crown
H. plantaginea	fragrant plantain lily		
'Royal Standard'			
H. undulata	midsummer plantain lily	**Lactuca**	lettuce
'Erromena'		*L. sativa*	garden lettuce
Humulus	hop	'Bibb'	
H. lupulus	hop, European h., bine	'Oak Leaf'	
Hydrangea	hydrangea	'Ruby'	
H. quercifolia	oak-leaf h.	**Lagerstroemia**	
Hydrastis	orangeroot, yellow puccoon	*L. indica*	crape myrtle
H. canadensis	goldenseal	**Lamium**	dead nettle
Hydrocotyle	water pennywort, navelwort	*L. album*	snowflake, d. n., white d. n., dumb nettle, archangel
H. asiatica	gotu kola		
Hypericum	St.-John's-wort	*L. maculatum*	spotted dead nettle
H. patulum	St.-John's-wort	*L. maculatum* 'Album'	white spotted dead nettle
'Sungold'			
H. perforatum	St.-John's-wort	**Laurus**	laurel, sweet bay
Hyssopus	hyssop	*L. nobilis*	laurel, bay, sweet bay
H. officinalis	blue h.	**Lavandula**	lavender
'Alba'	white h.	*L. angustifolia*	English lavender
'Rosea'	rose h.	*L. angustifolia* subsp. *angustifolia*	lavender
Iberis	candytuft		
I. sempervirens	candytuft	'Alba'	
'Little Gem'		'Atropurpurea'	
Ilex	holly	'Gray Lady'	
I. cornuta	Chinese holly, horned h.	'Mitchum Blue'	
'Burfordii'	Burford's holly	'Hidcote'	
I. crenata	Japanese holly, box-leaved h.	'Munstead'	
I. crenata var. *paludosa*		'Nana'	
'Bullata'	Japanese holly, box-leaved h.	'Rosea'	
'Hetzii'		*L. dentata*	French lavender
'Rotunda'		*L. dentata* var. *candicans*	French lavender
'Stokesii'			
I. glabra		*L. heterophylla*	sweet lavender
I. opaca	American holly	**Lemna**	duckweed
I. vomitoria	yaupon		

Leonotis	lion's-ear	*M. aquifolium*	Oregon g., mountain g., holly mahonia, holly barberry, blue barberry
L. leonurus	lion's-ear	**Malus**	apple, crab apple
Leontopodium		'Red Spy'	dwarf apple
L. alpinum	edelweiss	*M. angustifolia*	southern wild crab apple, American crab, wild crab
Leonurus	motherwort	*M.* 'Guiding Star'	crab apple
Lepidium	peppergrass, pepperwort, tonguegrass	*M. hupehensis*	crab
		Malva	mallow, musk m.
L. sativum	garden cress	*M. alcea* var. *fastigiata*	mallow
Leucojum	snowflake	**Marrubium**	horehound
L. aestivum	giant s., summer s.	*M. incanum*	silver horehound
Levisticum		*M. vulgare*	horehound, white h.
L. officinale	lovage	**Matthiola**	stock
Ligustrum	privet, hedge plant	*M. incana*	stock, gillyflower, Brampton stock, imperial stock
L. vulgare	privet, prim	**Melissa**	balm
'Lodense'	dwarf privet	*M. officinalis*	lemon b., bee b., sweet b., b.
'Nanum'	dwarf privet	**Mentha**	mint
Lilium	lily	*M. aquatica*	water mint
L. candidum	Madonna lily	*M.* 'Eau de Cologne'	eau de Cologne mint
L. chalcedonicum	scarlet Turk's-cap lily	*M.* × *gentilis*	red mint, Scotch m.
Limonium	sea lavender, marsh rosemary, statice	*M. longifolia*	horsemint
		M. × *piperita*	peppermint
L. latifolium	statice	*M.* × *piperita* var. *citrata*	orange mint, bergamot m., lemon m.
Linaria	toadflax	*M. pulegium*	pennyroyal
Lindera		*M. requienii*	Corsican m., menthella, creme-de-menthe plant
L. benzoin	spicebush, Benjamin bush		
Linum	flax	*M. spicata*	spearmint
L. perenne	perennial flax	'Crispata'	curly m.
L. usitatissimum	flax	'Crispii'	curly m.
Liriope	lilyturf	*M. suaveolens*	apple m.
L. muscari	big blue lilyturf	'Variegata'	pineapple m.
Lobelia		**Mertensia**	bluebells, lungwort
L. siphilitica	great lobelia, blue cardinal flower	*M. virginica*	bluebells, Virginia b., cowslip, Virginia c., Roanoke-bells
Lobularia			
L. maritima	sweet alyssum, purple sweet alyssum	**Mimulus**	monkey flower
L. maritima		**Monarda**	wild bergamot, horsemint
'Carpet of Snow'	dwarf sweet alyssum	*M. citriodora*	lemon mint
'Purple Carpet'		*M. didyma*	bee balm, Oswego tea, white bee balm
Lonicera	honeysuckle	'Alba'	
L. flava	yellow honeysuckle	'Croftway Pink'	pink b. b.
L. sempervirens	trumpet h., coral h.	'Rosea'	pink b. b.
Lunaria	honesty, money plant, moonwort, satin flower	'Snow White'	white b. b.
		M. fistulosa	wild bergamot
L. annua	honesty, silver-dollar, penny f.	*M. fistulosa* var. *menthifolia*	oregano de la Sierra
Lychnis	campion, catchfly	*M. punctata*	horsemint, dotted mint
L. coronaria	mullein pink, rose campion	**Montia**	miner's lettuce
L. coronaria 'Alba'	white campion	*M. perfoliata*	miner's lettuce, winter purslane, Cuban spinach
L. flos-cuculi	cuckoo flower, ragged-robin	**Morus**	mulberry
Lycopersicon	tomato	'Alba'	white m.
L. lycopersicum var. *cerasiforme*	cherry tomato	'Rubra'	red m., American m.
'Tiny Tim'		**Musa**	banana
L. lycopersicum var. *pyriforme*	pear tomato	*M. textilis*	abaca, Manila hemp
		Myosotis	forget-me-not, scorpion grass
'Yellow Pear'		*M. sylvatica*	garden forget-me-not
L. pimpinellifolium	currant tomato	**Myrica**	
Lycopus	bugle, gypsywort, water horehound	*M. pensylvanica*	bayberry, candleberry, swamp c.
L. europaeus	gypsywort	**Myrrhis**	
Lysimachia	loosestrife	*M. odorata*	sweet cicely, anise, myrrh, sweet chervil
L. vulgaris	garden loosestrife		
Lythrum	loosestrife	**Myrtus**	myrtle
L. virgatum	loosestrife	*M. communis*	classic myrtle, Greek myrtle, Swedish m.
'Dropmore Purple'			
Macleaya		'Microphylla'	dwarf myrtle
M. cordata	plume poppy, tree celandine		
Magnolia	magnolia		
M. grandiflora	southern magnolia, bull bay		
M. stellata	star magnolia		
M. virginiana	sweet bay		
Mahonia	Oregon grape, holly g.		

Nandina		**Paxistima**	
N. domestica	heavenly bamboo, sacred b.	*P. canbyi*	cliff-green, mountain-lover
Narcissus	daffodil	**Pedicularis**	
N. asturiensis	miniature daffodil	*P. canadensis*	lousewort
N. poeticus	poet's narcissus	**Pelargonium**	geranium of florists, storksbill
N. pseudonarcissus	daffodil, trumpet narcissus	*P. abrotanifolium*	southernwood geranium
'Cassata'	daffodil	*P. acerifolium*	maple-leaved g.
'Mount Hood'	daffodil	*P.* × *blandfordianum*	
N. tazetta	polyanthus narcissus	*P. capitatum*	rose-scented geranium
N. triandrus	angel's tears	'Attar of Roses'	
Nepeta	catmint	'Logee's Snowflake'	
N. cataria	catnip, catmint	'Skelton's Unique'	
N. × *faassenii*	catmint	*P.* × *citrosum*	orange g.
N. mussinii	catmint	'Prince of Orange'	
Nicotiana		*P.* 'Concolor Filbert'	filbert g.
N. alata	jasmine tobacco, flowering tobacco, nicotiana	*P. crispum*	lemon g.
		'French Lace'	l. g.
'Affinis'	white nicotiana	'Minor'	
'Grandiflora'		'Prince Rupert'	
'Green Sherbet'	green nicotiana	*P. denticulatum*	pine g.
Nigella	fennel flower, wild fennel	'Filicifolium'	fern-leaf g.
N. damascena	love-in-a-mist, wild fennel	*P.* × *domesticum*	
N. sativa	black cumin, nutmeg flower, Roman coriander	'Clorinda'	eucalyptus-scented g.
		P. × *fragrans*	nutmeg g.
Ocimum	basil	'Variegatum'	nutmeg g.
O. basilicum	sweet basil	*P. frutetorum*	zonal g.
'Citriodorum'	lemon basil	*P. fulgidum*	
'Minimum'	bush basil	'Scarlet Unique'	pungent-scented g.
'Purpurascens'	purple basil	*P. glutinosum*	pheasant's-foot g.
O. sanctum	sacred basil, tulasi, Krishna tulsi, Sri tulsi	*P. graveolens*	rose g., sweet-scented g.
		'Camphor Rose'	camphor-scented g.
Oenothera	evening primrose, sundrops	'Lady Plymouth'	rose g.
O. biennis	evening primrose	'Rober's Lemon Rose'	lemon-rose g.
Origanum	marjoram		
O. dictamnus	dittany-of-Crete, Crete dittany, hop m.	*P. grossularioides*	gooseberry g.
		P. × *hortorum*	zonal g.
O. heracleoticum	Greek oregano, pot marjoram, winter sweet m.	*P.* × *jatrophifolium*	pheasant's-foot g.
		P. × *limoneum*	English finger-bowl g.
O. majorana	sweet marjoram, annual m.	'Lady Mary'	English finger-bowl g.
O. onites	pot marjoram	*P.* × *nervosum*	lime g.
O. vulgare	wild marjoram	'Toronto'	ginger-scented g.
'Aureum'	golden marjoram	*P. odoratissimum*	apple g.
O. vulgare var. *prismaticum*	oregano	*P. quercifolium*	oak-leaved g., almond g., village-oak g.
Ophrys		'Giganteum'	musty oak-scented g.
O. apifera	bee orchid	'Village Hill Oak'	
Ornithogalum		*P. radens*	crowfoot g.
O. umbellatum	star-of-Bethlehem, nap-at-noon, summer snowflake, dove's-dung	'Dr. Livingston'	lemon g.
		P. scabrum	apricot g., strawberry g.
Osmanthus	devilweed	*P. tomentosum*	peppermint g., herb-scented g.
O. fragrans	sweet olive, fragrant o., tea o.	**Perilla**	
Osmunda	flowering fern	*P. frutescens*	perilla
O. cinnamomea	cinnamon fern, fiddleheads, buckhorn	**Perovskia**	
		P. abrotanoides	Russian sage
Oxalis	wood sorrel, lady's sorrel	*P. atriplicifolia*	Russian sage
O. crassipes	pink sorrel	**Petroselinum**	parsley
Paeonia	peony	*P. crispum*	parsley
P. lactiflora	peony, garden p., Chinese p.	*P. crispum* var. *crispum*	curly parsley
'Festiva Maxima'	white peony	'Banquet'	
P. officinalis subsp. *officinalis*	piney	'Bravour'	
		'Paramount'	
Papaver	poppy	*P. crispum* var. *neapolitanum*	Italian parsley
P. rhoeas	corn p., field p., Flanders p.		
P. somniferum	opium poppy	**Petunia**	
Parmelia		*P.* × *hybrida*	petunia
P. conspersa	lichen	'White Cascade'	
Passiflora	passionflower	**Phlox**	phlox
P. caerulea	blue p.	*P. paniculata*	perennial phlox
P. incarnata	maypop	'Mary Louise'	white phlox

Physalis	ground cherry, husk tomato
P. heterophylla	g. c., clammy g. c.
Physocarpus	ninebark
P. opulifolius	
'Nanus'	dwarf ninebark
Physostegia	false dragonhead, lion's-heart, obedience, obedient plant
P. virginiana	obedience
Phytolacca	pokeweed, pokeberry
P. americana	poke, Virginian p.
Pinckneya	
P. pubens	fever tree
Pinus	pine
P. nigra	Austrian p.
P. strobus	white p., Eastern w. p.
'Nana'	dwarf white pine
P. taeda	loblolly p., old-field p., frankincense p.
Plantago	plantain, ribwort
P. major	p., white-man's foot, cart-track plant
Platycodon	balloon flower
P. grandiflorus	balloon flower
'Mariesii'	
Pogostemon	
P. cablin	patchouli
Polemonium	Jacob's-ladder, Greek valerian
P. reptans	Jacob's-ladder
Polianthes	
P. tuberosa	tuberose
Polygonum	knotweed, smartweed, fleece flower
P. hydropiperoides	knotweed, mild water pepper
Polystichum	shield fern
P. acrostichoides	Christmas fern, dagger f., canker brake
Poncirus	
P. trifoliata	trifoliate orange, hardy orange
Populus	poplar, aspen, cottonwood
P. balsamifera	balm-of-Gilead, balsam p. hackmatack, tacamahac
Potentilla	cinquefoil, five-finger
P. fruticosa	shrubby c., golden hardhack, widdy
'Katherine Dykes'	shrubby c.
P. nepalensis	Nepal cinquefoil
P. tridentata	three-toothed cinquefoil
Poterium	
P. sanguisorba	salad burnet, garden burnet
Primula	primrose
P. elatior	oxlip
P. sieboldii	
'Alba'	white p.
P. veris	cowslip
Prunella	self-heal
P. vulgaris	self-heal, heal-all, all-heal
Prunus	
P. Americana	American plum
P. angustifolia	chickasaw plum, sand p.
P. domestica	plum
P. maritima	beach plum
P. pensylvanica	pin cherry
P. persica	peach
Pteridium	bracken, brake
P. aquilinum	bracken, brake, pasture b., hog-pasture b.
Pulmonaria	lungwort
P. officinalis	blue l., Jerusalem sage, Jerusalem cowslip
Punica	
P. granatum	pomegranate
Pyrus	pear

P. communis	pear
Quercus	oak
Q. stellata	post oak
Ranunculus	buttercup, crowfoot
R. ficaria	lesser celandine, small c., pilewort
Reseda	mignonette
R. luteola	weld, dyer's rocket
Rhamnus	
R. purshiana	bearberry
Rheum	rhubarb
R. rhabarbarum	rhubarb, garden r., pie plant, wine plant
Rhododendron	
'Marie's Choice'	white evergreen azalea
Rhus	
R. typhina	sumac
Ribes	currant, gooseberry
R. alpinum	alpine c., mountain c.
R. sativum	red currant, garden c.
Rosa	rose, brier
R. banksiae	Banksia r.
R. × *borboniana*	Bourbon r.
R. canina	dog r., brier r., dog b.
R. centifolia	cabbage r.
'Cristata'	moss r.
'Muscosa'	moss r.
R. chinensis	China r.
'Minima'	fairy r., pygmy r.
R. 'Cinderella'	
R. damascena	damask r.
'Bifera'	autumn damask r.
'Versicolor'	York-and-Lancaster r.
R. eglanteria	eglantine, sweetbrier
R. gallica	French r.
'Officinalis'	apothecary's r.
R. × *harisonii*	Harison's yellow r.
R. laevigata	Cherokee r.
R. moschata	musk r.
R. × *rehderana*	polyantha r.
R. roxburghii	chestnut r., chinquapin r.
R. rugosa	Turkestan r., Japanese r.
R. setigera	prairie r., climbing r.
R. spinosissima	Scotch r., burnet r.
R. 'Schneezwerg'	snowdwarf
R. wichuraiana	memorial r.
R. wichuraiana × *laevigata*	climbing r.
'Silver Moon'	
Rosmarinus	rosemary
R. angustissimus	pine-scented r.
R. officinalis	rosemary
'Albus'	white r.
'Benedin Blue'	
'Blue Spears'	
'Lockwood de Forest'	
'Prostratus'	prostrate rosemary, golden p. r.
'Tuscan Blue'	
Rubia	
R. tinctorum	madder
Rubus	bramble
R. allegheniensis	blackberry, sow-teat blackberry
Rudbeckia	coneflower
R. hirta	black-eyed Susan
Rumex	dock, sorrel, dock s.
R. acetosa	garden sorrel
R. obtusifolius	broad dock, bitter d.
R. scutatus	French sorrel
Ruta	rue

R. graveolens	rue
'Blue Beauty'	
Salix	willow, osier
S. caprea	goat willow, pussy willow
Salvia	sage, ramona
S. argentea	silver sage
S. caerula	blue sage
S. clevelandii	blue sage
S. elegans	pineapple-scented sage
S. greggii	autumn sage
S. guaranitica	anise sage
S. involucrata	rosy leaf s.
S. leucantha	Mexican bush s.
S. leucophylla	gray sage, purple sage
S. microphylla	baby sage
S. officinalis	garden sage, including dwarf form
'Albiflora'	white-flowered garden s.
'Aurea'	golden g. s.
'Holt's Mammoth'	garden s.
'Purpurascens'	purple g. s.
'Purpurea'	purple variegated garden s.
'Tricolor'	variegated garden s.
S. sclarea	clary
S. viridis	annual clary
Sambucus	elder, elderberry
S. canadensis	American e.
'Acutiloba'	American e.
Sanguinaria	bloodroot
S. canadensis	red puccoon, bloodroot
Sanguisorba	burnet
S. canadensis	Canadian burnet
Sansevieria	bowstring hemp, devil's tongue, good-luck plant, lucky plant, hemp plant
S. trifasciata	snake plant, mother-in-law's tongue
Santolina	
S. chamaecyparissus	gray santolina, lavender cotton
'Nana'	dwarf gray santolina
S. neapolitana	
S. pinnata	
S. virens	green santolina
Saponaria	soapwort
S. officinalis	bouncing Bet
Sassafras	
S. albidum	sassafras
Satureja	savory, calamint
S. hortensis	summer savory
S. montana	winter savory
'Nana'	dwarf winter savory
Scabiosa	scabious, pincushion flower
S. atropurpurea	pincushions, sweet s., mourning-bride
Sedum	stonecrop, orpine
S. morganianum	donkey's tail
S. telephium	orpine, live-forever
Sempervivum	houseleek, live-forever
S. tectorum	houseleek, roof h., hen-and-chickens, old-man-and-woman
Silybum	
S. marianum	holy thistle, St. Mary's t., blessed t., milk t.
Sium	
S. sisarum	skirret
Solanum	
S. jasminoides	potato vine
S. melongena var. *esculentum*	eggplant, mad apple
'Black Beauty'	
'Long Black'	melongene, aubergine

'Chinese Long Sword'	
S. pseudocapsicum	Jerusalem cherry
Solidago	goldenrod
S. californica	California g.
Sorbaria	false spiraea
S. sorbifolia	false spiraea
Sorbus	mountain ash
S. americana	American mountain ash
Stachys	betony, hedge nettle, woundwort
S. byzantina	lamb's-ears, woolly betony
S. grandiflora	
S. officinalis	betony
Stellaria	chickweed
Sternbergia	
S. lutea	winter daffodil, lily-of-the-field
Stokesia	Stokes' aster
S. laevis	Stokes' a.
Symphytum	comfrey
S. officinale	comfrey
S. officinale	white comfrey
Syringa	lilac
S. patula	lilac
S. × *persica* var. *laciniata*	Persian lilac
S. reticulata var. *Japonica*	Japanese tree lilac
S. vulgaris	lilac
'Addie V. Hallock'	
'Ellen Willmott'	
'Monge'	
'President Poincare'	
Tagetes	marigold
T. erecta	African m., big m., Aztec m.
T. filifolia	Irish-lace
T. lucida	sweet-scented m., sweet mace
T. patula	French m.
'Petite Yellow'	
T. tenuifolia	signet m.
'Lulu'	dwarf m.
Tanacetum	tansy
T. vulgare	tansy, golden-buttons
T. vulgare var. *crispum*	fern-leaf tansy
Taraxacum	dandelion
T. officinale	dandelion
Taxus	yew
T. cuspidata	Japanese yew
'Columnaris'	Japanese yew
'Densa'	low, dense y.
T. × *media*	yew
'Hatfieldii'	conical y.
'Hicksii'	columnar y.
'Kelseyi'	upright y.
Teucrium	germander
T. canadense	American g., wood sage
T. chamaedrys	germander
'Prostratum'	dwarf, procumbent g.
T. fruticans	tree germander
T. marum	cat thyme
Thuja	arborvitae
T. occidentalis	American arborvitae
Thymus	thyme
T. 'Argenteus'	silver thyme
T. 'Broad-leaf English'	English t.
T. × *citriodorus*	lemon t., culinary
'Aureus'	golden lemon t.
T. carnosus	
T. 'Clear Gold'	

T. doerfleri	
T. glabrescens	
T. herba-barona	caraway t.
T. leucotrichus	
T. 'Long-leaf Gray'	
T. nummularius	
T. pallasianus	odorus t.
T. praecox	creeping t.
T. praecox subsp. *arcticus*	mother-of-thyme
'Albus'	white creeping t.
'Coccineus'	crimson c. t.
'Lanuginosus'	woolly thyme
'Rosea'	creeping t.
'Splendens'	red c. t.
T. richardii subsp. *nitidus*	
T. serpyllum	wild t., lemon t., not culinary
T. vulgaris	French t.
'Narrow-leaf French'	
T. 'Woolly-stemmed Sharp'	
T. 'Woolly-stemmed Sweet'	
T. zygis	
Torenia	wishbone flower, wishbone plant
T. fournieri	white wishbone flower
'Alba'	
Trachelospermum	
T. jasminoides	star jasmine, confederate j.
Tragopogon	
T. pratensis	goatsbeard
Trichostema	blue-curls
T. lanatum	woolly blue-curls, romero
Trifolium	clover
T. pratense	red clover
Tropaeolum	nasturtium, bitter Indian
T. majus	garden n., tall n., Indian cress
T. minus	dwarf n.
Tsuga	hemlock
T. canadensis	Canada hemlock
Tulipa	tulip
T. 'Blizzard'	tulip
T. clusiana	lady t.
T. 'General de Wet'	early, tawny orange t.
T. kaufmanniana	water-lily t.
T. 'Sweet Harmony'	pale yellow Darwin t.
T. tarda	species t.
T. 'Triumphator'	tulip
Tussilago	coltsfoot
T. farfara	coltsfoot
Urginea	

U. maritima	sea onion, squill, red s.
Urtica	nettle
U. dioica	stinging n.
Vaccinium	blueberry, huckleberry, cranberry, bilberry
V. angustifolium var. *laevifolium*	blueberry
Valeriana	valerian
V. officinalis	valerian, garden heliotrope
Verbascum	mullein
V. blattaria	moth m.
V. olympicum	mullein
V. thapsus	mullein, flannel plant, velvet p.
Veronica	speedwell, brooklime
V. officinalis	speedwell
V. serpyllifolia	thyme-leaved s.
Vetiveria	
V. zizanioides	vetiver, khus-khus, khas-khas
Viburnum	arrowwood
V. acerifolium	dockmackie, maple-leaved viburnum, arrowwood, possum haw
V. carlesii	
V. cassinoides	teaberry, withe-rod
V. plicatum 'Mariesii'	
V. prunifolium	black haw, sweet h., sheepberry, nannyberry, stagbush
Vinca	periwinkle
V. minor	periwinkle, lesser p., myrtle, running m.
Viola	violet
V. canina	dog violet
V. cornuta	horned v., viola
'Alba'	white viola
'Blue Perfection'	blue viola
'Scottish Yellow'	
V. lutea 'Splendens'	yellow viola
V. odorata	sweet violet
V. tricolor	Johnny-jump-up, heartsease
V. × *wittrockiana*	pansy, ladies-delight, heartsease, stepmother's flower
Vitis	grape
V. aestivalis 'Fredonia'	grape
Watsonia	bugle lily
W. rosea	bugle lily
Wisteria	wistaria, wisteria
W. frutescens	wisteria
Xanthorhiza	shrub yellow-root
X. simplicissima	yellow-root
Yucca	
Y. filamentosa	Adam's-needle, needle palm
Zingiber	ginger
Z. officinale	true ginger, ginger, Canton g.